SICILY &
THE ÆOLIAN
ISLANDS

REGIONS OF ITALY

Florence and Tuscany
Naples and Campania
Umbria, the Marches, and San Marino
Venice & North East Italy

REGIONS OF FRANCE

Auvergne and the Massif Central
Brittany
Champagne-Ardennes and Burgundy
The Dordogne and Lot
Languedoc and Roussillon
The Loire Valley
Normandy, Picardy, and Pas de Calais
Paris
Provence and the Côte d'Azur
The Rhône Valley and Savoy
South West France

Also:
Alsace: the complete guide

REGIONS OF PORTUGAL

Algarve and Southern Portugal
Lisbon and Central Portugal
Northern Portugal

SICILY &
THE ÆOLIAN
ISLANDS

Paul Blanchard

A&C Black • London

Published by A&C Black (Publishers) Ltd,
35 Bedford Row, London WC1R 4JH

© Paul Blanchard, 1998

Photographs © Paul Blanchard

Maps and plans drawn by John Flower and Robert Smith
© A&C Black (Publishers) Ltd

ISBN 0–7136–4376–5

A CIP catalogue record for this book is
available from the British Library

Typeset in 9 on 11pt Optima.
Printed in Hong Kong through Colorcraft Ltd

To Isabella and Melissa

Acknowledgments

I wish to thank the many friends without whose generous gifts of time, energy and
expertise this book would not have been possible – particularly Stefania Raffadali,
Tino Vittorio, Salvo Raeli and Rosa Anna Musumeci in Sicily, and Gillian Arthur and
Jane Zaloga in Florence. My deepest gratitude also goes to the Italian State Tourist
Board (ENIT), London and Rome, and to the regional, provincial and local tourist
offices for their invaluable assistance.

CONTENTS

1	**Introduction**	**1**
2	**History and Art**	**4**
	Sicily in Antiquity 4; Sicily in the Middle Ages 5;	
	The Renaissance in Sicily 7;	
	Sicily and the Baroque 7; the Modern Age in Sicily, 7	
3	**Touring the Region**	**9**
	Before You Leave 9; Getting There 11;	
	On Arrival 14; Accommodation 15; Getting Around 15;	
	Helpful Hints 20	
4	**Food and Wine**	**25**
	Sicilian Cuisine 26; Wine 29	
5	**Western Sicily**	**34**
	Palermo 34; The Conca d'Oro 58; Ustica 69; Erice 71;	
	Segesta 76; Trapani and the Egadi Islands 78; Pantelleria 87;	
	Motya and Marsala 88; Selinunte 92;	
	Sciacca and Eraclea Minoa 97; Agrigento 99;	
	The Isole Pelagie 111; Practical Information 112	
6	**Southeastern Sicily**	**121**
	Ragusa and the Ragusano 121; Syracuse and Its Territory 129;	
	Enna and the Interior 152; Practical Information 167	
7.	**Northeastern Sicily**	**173**
	Catania and Mt Ætna 173; Taormina 188;	
	The Peloritan Peninsula 192; The Æolian Islands 199;	
	Cefalù 207; The Nebrodi and Madonie Mountains 210;	
	Practical Information 217	
	Glossary	**227**
	Index	**231**

Maps and plans

Sicily and the Æolian Islands 32-33

Agrigento 104-105
Catania 176-177
Enna 153
Erice 71
Lipari 198
Marsala 90
Messina 196
Noto 148
Palermo 38-39
Ragusa 123
Syracuse, the north and Neapolis 132
Syracuse, Ortygia 142
Taormina 189
Trapani 80

Grid references for the maps are given in the text where appropriate, eg, **Palazzo Reale** (Map 14).

1.INTRODUCTION

Knowst though the land where the lemon-trees bloom,
Where the gold orange glows in the deep thicket's gloom,
Where a wind ever soft from the blue heaven blows,
And the groves are of laurel and myrtle and rose?
J.W. von Goethe, Wilhelm Meister, 1821,
translated by Thomas Carlyle, 1824

The Mediterranean has fascinated visitors for centuries. Far more than just a land of fine beaches and transparent waters, it is a crossroads of civilisations – a place where Eastern and Western, European, African and Asian influences meet and mingle. In the words of the 18th-century English writer Samuel Johnson, 'the grand object of travelling is to see the shores of the Mediterranean'; one who has not done so 'is always conscious of an inferiority, from his not having seen what it is expected a man should see'.

For the luminaries of Old Europe, the Mediterranean was ideally suited to the rediscovery of oneself and one's place in the world. And we, today, can hardly blame them for thinking so. Certainly, the arctic wilderness, the equatorial rainforest or the vast deserts, plains and woodlands in between, are more primeval, more 'natural': but this is precisely the point. More than a cradle of civilisation in the West, the Mediterranean is its womb; for in the many thousands of years that separate us from the first inhabitants of this extraordinary region, the relations between man and nature have developed so continuously and so intensely that to isolate a natural object from its human context is impossible. The Mediterranean is a mirror in which we ourselves are reflected – *mare nostrum*, 'our sea' in the sense of the 'sea of our being' – and we are an infinitude of mirrors that gleam in the light reflected from its waters. Whatever our ethnic origin may be, we are also Mediterranean; for our deepest human essence is here deposited in every stone, plant, and animal, and returns, periodically and forcefully, to make its presence felt.

Goethe and his fellow Romantics knew this well. But sensitive observers from our own time seem to have noticed it, too. The land has been humanised, through and through: and we in our own tissued consciousness bear the results of this humanisation.' To go to the Mediterranean and to *pene-*

1

trate the Mediterranean, therefore, is a fascinating act of self-discovery.

And what place could be more suitable to such an adventure than Sicily, the quintessentially Mediterranean island. 'Many parts of this region are surely the most heavenly spots upon earth,' wrote one of Europe's earliest travel writers, Patrick Brydone. 'If Ætna resembles hell within, it may with equal justice be said to resemble paradise without. It is indeed a curious consideration, that this mountain should reunite every beauty and every horrour; and, in short, all the most opposite and dissimilar objects in nature.' (*A Tour Through Sicily and Malta, 1773*.) That the island possesses some of the most dramatic landscape in Europe is well known – and equally famous are the singular monuments of art and architecture with which its Greek and Roman, Norman and Arabic, French, Spanish and Italian inhabitants have bejewelled it.

Naturally, to know Sicily is to know the Sicilians, whose character has charmed and appalled visitors for centuries – charmed by virtue of its warmth and sensuality, appalled because of its apparent disregard for reason, moderation, or even rule by law. 'The habits of thought and living are so entirely different', wrote Lord Byron in 1820, 'and the difference becomes so much more striking the more you live intimately with them – that I know not how to make you comprehend a people who are at once temperate and profligate – serious in their character and buffoons in their amusements, capable of impressions and passions which are at once sudden and durable.' His observations may well be applied, more than a century and a half later, to many Sicilians: nevertheless it must be borne in mind that Sicilian society is as sophisticated as it is ancient, and that in matters of civic virtue, or even just social etiquette, Northerners of even the best background have a great deal to learn from their Mediterranean counterparts.

This guide offers a selection of some 30 Sicilian cities, towns and nature reserves, which together provide a fitting introduction to the region. Places are arranged in geographic 'constellations', leaving you the freedom to choose the route best suited to your personal tastes. Each constellation forms a chapter, at the end of which you'll find suggestions on how to get there and back, what to do and when, where to stay and where to eat. A lot of care has gone into the preparation of these chapters, in the conviction that pleasant accommodation, delicious food and good wine can go a long way to determining the success or failure of a holiday.

You might find yourself leafing through the guide rather more than you expect: for although its general organisation is loose and open, the specific places are dealt with much more 'intensely', offering historic walking tours that take you round the major sights (or through the finest countryside) step by step. In most cases these walks are designed to last about two hours, after which you'll be more than ready for some form of refreshment, or – in the case of larger towns like Palermo or Syracuse (where you'll be ambling about for three to four hours) – even for a cat-nap.

Finally, a word of warning: Italy possesses some two-thirds of the world's artistic heritage, and it's an old heritage, in constant need of conservation and restoration. If during your visit some of the works of art and architecture described in the guide are covered (in the case of buildings or public sculpture) or away for cleaning (paintings), don't let it spoil your day: just move on. The more memorable moments of a foreign journey are often those one least expects – and Sicily is indeed a land of the unexpected.

2. HISTORY AND ART

by Jane Zaloga

Introduction

Like a vividly coloured tapestry, the artistic heritage of the island of Sicily has been woven of rare and exotic threads garnered from diverse civilisations. Its eclectic art and architecture are a testament to the island's volatile history and to the myriad cultures that have occupied its shores. The island's auspicious position at the centre of the Mediterranean Sea virtually guaranteed an incessant barrage of foreign invasion – Greeks, Arabs, French and Spanish, to name but a few – with each group promoting its own cultural ideals. Likewise, the island's propensity to natural disaster, such as earthquakes and volcanic eruptions, has periodically and selectively changed the face of the land. Further devastation of the artistic legacy can be attributed more recently to bombings and neglect. Nevertheless, despite a history of unrelenting tumult, one thing has been relatively constant in the experience of Sicily – the ability to adapt to changing circumstances. With this, Sicily has been able to create and re-create, absorbing the traditions of its most recent invaders and transforming them into something uniquely Sicilian – a magnificent fusion of the greatest of the cultures of the East, West, North and South.

Sicily in Antiquity

The first invaders to reach the shores of Sicily were expansionist Greeks who arrived in the 8th century BC, establishing what would become **Magna Graecia**, or Greater Greece. The founding of Catania and Syracuse on the eastern shores of the island heralded the first flowering of culture and commerce in Sicily. The relatively peaceful period following the Greeks' defeat of their Carthaginian rivals (who had established their own colonial city of Palermo on the western coast of Sicily), in 480BC, enabled Sicily to participate fully in the Golden Age of Classical Greece.

The **Greek influence** on Sicily was profound. The cities of Magna Graecia reflected the sophisticated urbanity of their mainland counterparts, featuring markets, theatres, and a plethora of temples dedicated to various deities. The colonial cities of Sicily, in fact, boast some of the most important examples of **Greek temple architecture** anywhere. Agrigento's haunting Valley of the Temples bears witness to the ancient architect's quest for perfection and immense scale, particularly in the awesome remains of the largest known Doric temple, the unfinished Temple of Olympian Zeus (or Olympieion). In Selinunte, a treasure trove of Doric temples (now known simply as Temples A to G) attests to the extent of the ancients' penchant for monumental construction. The sculpted metopes that once decorated the friezes of these temples (now in the Archaeological Museum in Palermo) showcase the development of realistic depiction in **sculpture**. Dramatic arts also were promoted in Greek Sicily, as may be seen in the remains of the spectacular **theatres** of Segesta, Syracuse and Taormina

If the arts flourished under Greek occupation, the ascendancy of the Republic of **Rome** signalled a change of fortune for Sicily. Rome captured Syracuse in 212BC and quickly took control of the prosperous island. Sicily became a playground for rich Romans, who built luxurious villas, such as the one still visible at Piazza Armerina, lavishly decorated with coloured marbles and extravagant mosaics. While holidaying Roman patricians frolicked, the sophisticated and prosperous urban life of Magna Graecia faded away. Tributes, taxes, and absentee landholders were the heavy toll of Roman domination. Subservience to and exploitation by northerners had only just begun for Sicily.

Sicily in the Middle Ages

Because the Romans left little of their own and destroyed much of what they had found, subsequent invasions by Goths and Vandals in the early 5th century AD were relatively harmless for the island. Likewise, few traces remain of the Byzantine invaders of the following century, though their rule of what had become the provincial island of Sicily lasted for some 300 years.

At the dawn of the 9th century, a glimmer of light passed over the neglected island with the **Saracen invasions**. The Arabs brought with them sophisticated agricultural techniques and new crops which reinvigorated the economy of the depressed island. Renewed interest in the Western Classical learning of the Greeks, Romans and Jews went hand in hand with Arab advances in science and philosophy during this relatively peaceful period noted for its religious tolerance. Under Arab domination, Sicily was destined to become an important place in the Muslim world; however, there remains no visual evidence of the island's revived cultural life, except to the extent that it was borrowed by the next invaders, **the Normans**.

In 1061, the Norman Roger de Hauteville (made Count of Sicily by Pope Nicholas II, but often called Roger I; ruled 1031–1101) conquered Messina, eventually taking all of Sicily and introducing yet another element into its artistic culture. During the reigns of Roger I and his son, who was crowned king and ruled as Roger II (1112–54), the court at **Palermo** was renowned for its wealth and erudition, and the capital was transformed into one of the most splendid cities in Europe. Taking advantage of the multi-cultural influences of their kingdom, the Normans embellished Palermo with a fusion of the rich mosaic tradition of the Byzantines, the elaborate woodwork legacy of Islamic North Africa, and their own use of poly-chromed marble decoration. These elements may be seen together in Palermo's sumptuous Palatine Chapel. The mosaic-encrusted church at Monreale and the mosque-inspired domes of San Giovanni degli Eremitani in Palermo are likewise testament to the far-flung influences of the Norman period.

The magnificent court of the Normans eventually yielded to that of their successors, **the Hohenstaufens**, who came from Swabia in Central Europe. The 13th-century court of the Swabian Frederick II (nicknamed *Stupor Mundi*, or Wonder of the World) surpassed even that of the Normans and was considered one of the most brilliant of Europe. At court, an attitude of religious tolerance that nurtured Jewish, Muslim and Christian cultures stimulated a wide-ranging patronage of learning and literature.

Outside the circle of this enlightened court, however, were the stirrings of religious persecutions and feudal rebellions. Frederick's major architec-tural patronage consisted, significantly, of a string of Byzantine- and Muslim-influenced **fortified castles**, such as the Castello Maniace in Syracuse and the Castello di Lombardia at Enna, which spanned the island as defensive measures against unruly nobles.

In 1268 Swabian rule ended and the crown of Sicily passed to the French **Charles of Anjou**. The Sicilian nobility violently rebelled against the Angevins and invited the Spanish to enter Sicilian politics in the person of Peter III of Aragon.

During the four centuries of **Spanish domination**, the island once again reverted to its provincial position, serving absentee landholders. However, the Spanish did leave behind several reminders of their presence, particu-larly during the 13th–15th centuries. Their influence can be seen in the florid **Catalan-Gothic architectural style** of Palermo Cathedral and of the church of San Giorgio Vecchio in Ragusa.

The Renaissance in Sicily

In the 15th and 16th centuries, when much of the rest of Italy was reawakening to the ideals of the Classical past in the age of the Renaissance, Sicily remained decidedly behind. One of the few lights to shine in the region during the Renaissance period was the painter **Antonello da Messina**, whose masterpiece, the *Virgin Annunciate* (now in the Galleria Regionale in Palermo) shows the influence of his training in Naples, probably under Flemish masters, and of his exposure to both Venetian and Central Italian painting. Antonello's innovative experiments with the oil technique may have revolutionised much of Northern Italian painting, especially in Venice.

Both sculpture and architecture during the Renaissance were likewise poorly represented and generally dominated by foreign influences. A Dalmatian, Francesco Laurana, and two Lombards, Domenico Gagini and his son, Antonello, were the main proponents of what might be called a Renaissance style in sculpture and architecture. For the most part, however, a curious mix of Gothic and Renaissance forms prevailed on the island.

Sicily and the Baroque

Perhaps the most noteworthy of later artistic developments in Sicily is the flourishing of an exuberant, highly dramatic Baroque style in architecture in the 17th century. Beginning in the early 1600s with the Quattro Canti in Palermo and culminating with the vivaciously sculpted façades of the churches of San Giorgio and San Giuseppe in Ragusa Ibla and Modica's San Giorgio in the 18th century, Sicilian Baroque was marked by theatricality and extravagance, which focused quite strongly on the emotional qualities of fantasy and dynamism.

The interiors of these Baroque marvels extend the drama of the exteriors with the use of lavish coloured marble inlays and fanciful stucco sculptural decoration. Best known of these fantastic interiors are Palermo's oratories of Santa Cita and San Domenico, in which a profusion of saints, allegorical figures, and putti swirl and billow in the ebullient spirit of the period.

The Modern Age in Sicily

With Sicilian ties to Naples, Rome and France in the 18th century, the spirited, full-bodied Sicilian Baroque architectural style gave way to a much more austere, planar **Neoclassical style**. This movement, however, was relatively short lived, as the approach of the 20th century brought with it a return to rich detailing in the flowering **Art Nouveau** (or Liberty Style, as it is known in Italian). An awareness of Sicily's rich architectural heritage offered a range of motifs from which architects and designers could draw, spanning from the ancient ruins of the Greek period to Catalan-Gothic details.

Today the tapestry which is the art and architecture of Sicily is becoming threadbare in places with neglect and mishap, badly in need of attention and restoration. Still, its splendour impresses, dazzling the visitor with Greek temples and Byzantine mosaics, Catalan-Gothic and Baroque churches – in short, parading the treasures of many epochs and multiple cultures, a spectacular and eclectic testament to the diverse civilisations that have shaped this incredible island.

3. TOURING THE REGION

Before You Leave

Climate

Sicily has one of the most pleasant climates in Europe. Especially on the coast, cloudless skies are the norm and temperatures are mild throughout the year (the average varies between 11°C/52°F in winter and 25°C/77°F in summer). November and December are the rainiest months, July and August the sunniest. As you move into the mountainous interior, where the temperate influence of the Mediterranean fades, the temperature range becomes considerably greater and precipitation more frequent. Winter in these regions can be quite severe (even snowy), and summer blazing hot. Typical of all seasons is the warm African wind known as *scirocco*, which can blow for three or four days in a row and often carries fine grains of Sahara sand. Other common winds are the chill northerly *tramontana* and the mild easterly *grecale*. The best months for visiting Sicily are March (when the almond trees brighten the landscape with their delicate white blossoms), April (when the orange groves fill the air with their sweet scent), May (when the mantle of wild flowers is at its peak), September (when the figs, grapes and prickly pears come in) and October (the month for walnuts, chestnuts and the very first oranges). In July and August, and during Easter week, the island can be crowded.

An important thing to bear in mind, if you're not used to the southern sun, is the general lack of shade in Sicily. The evergreen Mediterranean scrub (*macchia mediterranea*) that once covered much of the coast has all but vanished before the inexorable advance of civilisation; and the tall forests have retreated to the tops of the higher mountains and to the more remote slopes of Ætna. The plants that characterise Sicily today are not native to the island, but were imported at various times in the past: vines and olives, almonds, pistachios, pomegranates and other fruit trees in antiquity, by the Greeks from the Near East; carobs, palms, mulberries, cotton, sugar cane and bitter oranges in the 10th and 11th centuries, by the Arabs, from North Africa; sweet oranges in the 16th century, by the Portuguese, from China; prickly pears and *agavi* in the 17th century, by the Spanish, from Central America. Like the great fields of wheat (first culti-vated extensively in Sicily by the Romans), they are unlikely to protect you from heat stroke, though they will certainly make your stay enjoyable in other ways.

Formalities

Passports or ID cards are necessary for EU travellers entering Italy; American travellers must carry passports. No visa is required for a EU, US, or Canadian citizen holding a valid passport for a visit of less than 90 days. Citizens of other countries should check current visa requirements with the nearest Italian consulate before departure. Italian law requires travellers to carry some form of identification at all times. Also, all foreign visitors to Italy must register with the police within three days of arrival. If you are staying at a hotel, this formality is attended to by the management. If staying with friends or in a private home, you must register in person at the nearest police station. For information or help (including an interpreter), call the visitors' assistance numbers in Rome: 06 461950 or 06 486609.

Information

Brochures and other material can be obtained from:

UK
Italian State Tourist Board, 1 Princes Street, London W1R 8AY (tel. 0171 408 1254, fax 0171 493 6695).

USA
Italian Government Tourist Board, c/o Italian Trade Commission, 499 Park Avenue, New York, NY 10022 (tel. 212 843 6885, fax 212 843 6886); Italian Government Travel Office, 401 North Michigan Avenue, Suite 3030, Chicago 1, IL 60611 (tel. 312 644 0996, fax 312 644 30197); Italian Government Travel Office, 12400 Wilshire Blvd, Suite 550, Los Angeles, CA 90025 (tel. 310 820 0098, fax 310 820 6357).

Canada
Italian Government Travel Office, 1 Place Ville Marie, Suite 1914, Montreal, Québec H3B 3M9 (tel. 514 866 7667, fax 514 866 0975).

The London office issues free an invaluable *Traveller's Handbook* (in the USA, *General Information for Travelers to Italy*), usually revised every year.

Disabled Travellers

All new public buildings are now obliged by law to provide easy access and specially designed facilities for the disabled. Unfortunately the conversion of historical buildings, including many museums and monuments, is made problematic by structural impediments such as narrow pavements (which make mobility difficult for everyone). In many towns, the presence of stepped walkways makes it impossible to get around in a wheelchair – or even to push a baby in a pram. Hotels that are able to give hospitality to the disabled are indicated in the annual list of hotels published by the local tourist boards. Airports and train stations provide assistance and certain trains are equipped to transport wheelchairs. Access is allowed to the centre of towns (normally closed to traffic) for cars with disabled drivers or passengers, and special parking places are reserved for them. For further information, contact the tourist board in the city of interest.

Getting There

By Air

There are no direct scheduled flights from the United Kingdom or North America to Sicily, though there are flights from several British and North American cities to Milan and Rome, from which connections may be made with internal lines to Palermo and Catania. The carriers offering non-stop service between the UK and Italy are *British Airways* (tel. 0181 897 4000), *Alitalia* (tel. 0171 602 7111) and *Meridiana* (tel. 0171 839 2222). *Air France*, *Lufthansa* and *Sabena* offer flights connecting through Paris, Frankfurt and Brussels, respectively (with Lufthansa you can fly direct from Frankfurt to Catania). These may cost less than the direct flights.

Alitalia (tel. 1 800 223 5730) flies non-stop from New York (JFK or Newark) to Rome or Milan, from Boston and Chicago to Rome, and from Los Angeles to Rome or Milan; *American* from Chicago to Milan; *Canadian* from Toronto and Montreal to Rome; *Continental* (tel. 1 800 231 0856) from New York to Rome; *Delta* (1 800 241 4141) from New York to Milan and Rome; *TWA* (tel. 1 800 892 4141) from New York to Rome and Milan and from Los Angeles to Rome; and *United* (tel. 1 800 5382 929) from Washington DC to Rome. *British Airways*, *Air France*, *KLM* and *Sabena* offer flights connecting through London, Paris, Amsterdam and Brussels. These are often more economical than the direct flights.

Many agencies specialise in discount tickets from North America. These include *Access International*, 101 West 3 St, Suite 104, New York, NY 10001 (tel. 1 800 TAKE OFF), *Nouvelles Frontières*, 800 Boulevard de Maisonneuve Est, Montreal, PQ H2L 4L8 (tel. 1 514 288 9942), *Stand Buys*,

311 West Superior St, Chicago, IL 60610 (tel. 1 800 331 0257) and *Travel Brokers*, 50 Broad St, New York, NY 10004 (tel. 1 800 999 8748). Students may find special bargains through youth-travel agencies such as *Council Travel*, 205 East 42 St, New York, NY 10017 (tel. 212 661 1450), STA, 48 East 11 St, New York, NY 10003 (tel. 212 477 7166) and *Travel Cuts*, 187 College St, Toronto, ON M5T 1P7 (tel. 1 416 979 2406).

Last but not least, direct charter flights offer a quick, convenient way to reach Sicily from the UK. Prices are usually a bit lower than those of scheduled flights, and there are no connections to be made – or missed. Contact *Sky Shuttle* (tel. 0181 748 1333) or LAI (tel. 0171 837 8492) for details, or see your travel agent.

By Rail

To travel from London to Palermo by train is certainly an adventure, but it takes nearly two full days and is not significantly cheaper than flying. It only makes sense if you're thinking of stopping at other destinations along the way.

The principal Italian cities are linked with the UK by a variety of rail routes, the most direct being from London via Paris and Turin, or via Paris and Milan. These services have sleeping cars (first class: single or double compartment; second class: three-berth compartments) and couchettes (seats converted into couches at night: first class: four; second class: six) and connect with trains directed to Sicily. Couchettes and sleeping compartments should be booked well in advance, although those that are not occupied at the time of departure can be hired directly from the conductor without paying a supplement. Reciprocal booking arrangements exist with Austria, Belgium, Denmark, France, the UK, Hungary, Luxembourg, the Netherlands, Portugal, Spain and Switzerland.

Information and tickets on the *Italian State Railways* (but not seat reservations) can be obtained in the UK from Citalia, Marco Polo House, 3-5 Lansdowne Road, Croydon, Surrey CR9 1LL (tel. 0181 686 0677) and Wasteels Travel, 121 Wilton Road, London SW1V 1J2 (tel. 0171 834 7066).

In North America obtain information from CIT, 342 Madison Avenue, Suite 207, New York, NY 10173 (tel. 212 697 1482 for schedules, 212 697 2100 for rail pass information, 1 800 223 7987 to order tickets only, or 1 800 CIT TOUR for general information, fax 212 697 1394); Los Angeles Office, 6033 West Century Blvd, Los Angeles, CA 90045 (tel. 310 338 8616, fax 310 670 4269); Montreal Office, 1450 City Councillors Street, Suite 750, Montreal H3A 2E6 (tel. 514 845 9101, fax 514 845 9137); Toronto Office, 111 Avenue Road, Suite 808, Toronto M5R 3JH (tel. 416 927 7712, fax 416 927 7206).

By Bus

A bus service operates, taking two days between London (Victoria Coach Station) and Rome (Piazza della Repubblica) via Dover, Paris, Mont Blanc, Aosta, Turin, Genoa, Milan, Bologna and Florence, daily from June to September and once or twice a week for the rest of the year. Reductions are available for students. Information in London from the National Express office at Victoria Coach Station (tel. 0171 730 0202), from local National Express Agents and in Italy from SITA offices.

By Car

The easiest approaches to Italy by road are the motorways through the Mont Blanc, San Bernard, Frejus, or Mont Cenis tunnels, or over the Brenner pass. British drivers taking their own cars by any of the routes across France, Belgium, Luxembourg, Switzerland, Germany and Austria need the vehicle registration book, a valid national driving licence, an international insurance certificate (the 'green card', valid for 45 days), and a nationality plate (attached to the rear of the vehicle so as to be illuminated by the tail lamps). A Swiss Motorway Pass is needed for Switzerland and can be obtained from the Royal Automobile Club (tel. 01345 333 1133), the Automobile Association (tel. 01256 20123), or at the Swiss border. If you don't own the vehicle you are driving you must possess the owner's written permission for its use abroad. Foreign drivers hiring a car in Italy need only a valid national driver's licence.

By Sea

Sicily has excellent maritime connections, and if you are arriving from the north you should seriously consider travelling by ferry from Genoa, Livorno or Naples to Palermo. Overnight cabins are comfortable and reasonably priced, and the approach to Palermo by sea is unforgettable. Professional seafarers consider it one of the most beautiful ports in the world. If you are travelling with your car, be sure to book several weeks ahead of time – especially in summer. Service from Genoa and Livorno (daily except Sun, in 19hr) is operated by *Grandi Traghetti* (information and tickets in the UK from Viamare Travel, Graphic House, 2 Sumatra Rd, London NW6 1PU, tel. 0171 431 4560); and from Naples (daily, in 10hr) by *Tirrenia Navigazione* (represented in the UK by Serena Holidays, 40-42 Kenway Rd, London SW5, tel. 0171 373 6548; in Naples, tel. 081 720 111, fax 720 1441). There is also a catamaran that makes the run between Naples and Palermo in 4hr (daily, Mar–Oct); for details, contact *Navitalia* in Palermo (tel. 091 584 535).

Most travellers going to Sicily drive or take the train to Villa San Giovanni (Calabria), then cross the Strait of Messina by ferry. The crossing lasts 20–35 minutes, and ferries come and go continuously. Rail tickets include passage on ferries of the Italian State Railways (Piazzale Don Blasco, Messina, tel. 090 675 201 ext. 552); a service is also run by *Società Caronte Shipping* (Viale della Libertà, Messina, tel. 090 44982). If you happen to be in Reggio Calabria there are hydrofoils to Messina (daily, 15 minutes) operated by *Aliscafi SNAV* (Via San Raineri 22, Messina, tel. 090 7775, fax 090 717 358). SNAV also provides hydrofoil service to the Æolian Islands from Messina/Reggio Calabria (daily, 2 hours) and from Naples (daily, Jun–Sep; in Naples, tel. 081 720 1595).

On Arrival

Information

The Italian State Tourist Board (in Italian, *ENIT, Ente Nazionale Italiano per il Turismo*) has information offices at the border crossings with Austria (Valico Autostradale Lupo di Brennero) and France (Casello Roverino di Ventimiglia), as well as at Milano Linate and Rome Leonardo da Vinci airports. Within Italy each *regione* has information services; where possible, these have been indicated in the text.

Money Matters

In Italy the monetary unit is the Italian *lira* (plural, *lire*, abbreviated to L). Travellers' cheques and Eurocheques are the safest way of carrying money while travelling and most credit cards are now generally accepted in hotels, shops and restaurants (and increasingly at petrol stations). The commission on cashing travellers' cheques can be quite high. For banking hours, see under 'Helpful Hints' below. Money can be changed at banks, post offices, travel agencies and some hotels, restaurants and shops, though the rate of exchange can vary considerably from place to place. Exchange offices are usually open seven days a week at airports and most main railway stations. A limited sum in lire can be obtained from conductors on international trains and at certain stations. For small amounts of money, the difference between hotel and bank rates may be negligible, as banks tend to take a fixed commission on transactions.

If you are a non-EU resident, remember that you can claim **sales tax rebates** on purchases made in Italy provided the total expenditure is more than L300,000. Ask the vendor for a receipt describing the goods acquired and send it back to him when you get home (but no later than 90 days after the date of the receipt). The receipt must be checked and stamped by Italian Customs upon leaving Italy. On receipt of the bill, the vendor will forward the sales tax rebate (the present tax rate is 19 per cent on most goods) to your home address.

Accommodation

Hotels

In this guide a selection of hotels has been given at the end of each chapter. The hotels listed, regardless of their cost, have been chosen on the basis of their personality or character: all have something special about them (beautiful surroundings, distinctive atmosphere) and even the humblest are quite comfortable. The local tourist offices will help you find accommodation on the spot; nevertheless you should try to book well in advance, especially if you're planning to travel between May and October. Hotels equipped to offer hospitality to the disabled are indicated in the tourist boards' hotel lists.

Campsites

Camping is well organised throughout Italy. Full details of the sites in Italy are published annually by the Touring Club Italiano, Corso Italia 10, 20122 Milano (tel. 02 85261, fax 02 852 6362) in *Campeggi e Villaggi Turistici in Italia*. The national headquarters of the Federazione Italiana del Campeggio, at 11 Via Vittorio Emanuele, 50041 Calenzano (Firenze), tel. 055 882 391, fax 055 882 5918, also publishes an annual guide (*Guida Camping d'Italia*) and maintains an information office and booking service.

Getting Around

By Rail

The Italian State Railways (*FS – Ferrovie dello Stato*) now run nine categories of trains: (1) *ES* (*Eurostar*), high-speed trains running between major Italian cities; (2) *EC* (*Eurocity*), international express trains running between the main Italian and European cities; (3) *EN* (*Euronotte*), overnight international express trains with sleeping car or couchette service; (4) *IC* (*Intercity*), express trains running between major Italian cities; (5) *E* (*Espressi*), long-distance trains not as fast as the Intercity trains; (6) *D* (*Diretti*), intermediate-distance trains making more stops than the Espressi; (7) *IR* (*Interregionali*), the new name for Diretti; (8) *R* (*Regionali*), local trains stopping at all stations; and (9) *M* (*Metropolitani*), surface or underground commuter trains. Service in all categories is improving rapidly as the State Railways proceed in their ambitious modernisation programme.

Seats can be booked in advance, as early as two months and as late as three hours before departure, from the main cities at the station booking office (open daily 7.00–22.00), or at travel agencies representing the Italian State Railways. Seats on a Eurostar can be reserved up to 30 minutes before departure at the Eurostar booking counter in the station. The timetable of the train services changes in late September and late May every year. Excellent timetables are published twice a year by the Italian State Railways (*In Treno*; one volume for the whole of Italy; trains with facilities for the disabled are marked) and by several private publishers. These can be purchased at news-stands and train stations.

Tickets must be bought at the station (or from travel agents representing the Italian State Railways) before starting a journey, otherwise a fairly large supplement has to be paid to the ticket-collector on the train. Time should be allowed for buying a ticket, as there are often long queues at the station ticket counters. Some trains charge a special supplement; and on others seats must be booked in advance. It is therefore always necessary to specify which train you are intending to take, as well as the destination, when buying tickets. And don't forget: you must stamp the date of your journey on the ticket using one of the meters located on or near the station platforms *before you get on the train*. If you buy a return ticket, you must stamp your ticket before beginning the outbound and the return journey. In the main stations the better known credit cards are now generally accepted (although a special ticket window must be used when buying a ticket with a credit card). There are limitations on travelling short distances on some trains.

Fares in Italy are still much lower than in the UK or the USA. Children under four travel free and between four and twelve pay half price. There are also reductions for families and for groups of as few as three persons. For travellers over the age of 60 (with Senior Citizen Railcards), the *Rail Europ Senior* card offers a 30 per cent reduction on Italian rail fares. The *Inter-rail* card (valid one month), which can be purchased in Britain or North America by young people up to the age of 26, is valid in Italy. In Italy the *Carta d'Argento* and the *Carta Verde* (both valid one year) allow a 20 per cent reduction on rail fares respectively for those over 60 and between the ages of 12 and 26. A *Biglietto chilometrico* (Cumulative Ticket) is valid for 3000km over a two-month period and can be used by up to five people at the same time. The *Euro Domino* and *Euro Domino Junior* cards, available to those resident outside Italy, gives freedom of the Italian railways for three, five or ten days. These cards can be purchased in the UK or at main stations in Italy. The *Carta Blu* is available for the disabled. Other forms of discounted travel are *Rail Inclusive Tours*, which offer transport, accommodation, excursions, etc., in a single package; the *Tessera di Autorizzazione* (Special Concession Card), which provides a 20 per cent discount for frequent travel in first class, second class or both; *Carta Primaclasse* (First Class Card), which permits the bearer to purchase up to eight first-class tickets at a 50 per cent discount.

Restaurant cars are attached to most international and internal long-distance trains. Some trains now also have self-service restaurants. Also, snacks, hot coffee and drinks are sold throughout the journey from a trolley wheeled down the train. At every large station snacks are on sale from trolleys on the platform and you can buy them from the train window. These include carrier-bags with sandwiches, drink and fruit (*cestini da viaggio*) or individual sandwiches (*panini*).

Additional services available at main stations include assistance for the disabled; special car-hire offers; automatic ticketing; porterage; and left luggage offices (open 24 hours at the main stations; often closed at night at smaller stations). Porters are entitled to a fixed amount, shown on notice boards at all stations, for each piece of baggage.

By Bus

Sicily's extensive local bus system takes you to out-of-the-way places not reached by rail, and even where bus and rail routes do coincide, the bus usually costs a bit less and offers the added convenience of dropping you in the centre of town, and not at a sleepy station out in the country. Although service is diminishing as increasing numbers of residents become independently mobile (most buses now carry schoolchildren from the villages to the towns in the early morning and from the towns to the villages in the afternoon), buses still serve most towns at least once a day; generally speaking, they leave major cities from a depot at or near the train station. Accurate area timetables can be obtained from the local tourist boards; tickets can be purchased at the bus depot (where there is one) or on board.

City buses are an excellent means of getting about in most towns. Almost everywhere tickets must be purchased before boarding (at tobacconists, bars, news-stands, information offices, etc.) and stamped on board.

By Car

Regardless of whether you are driving your own car or a hired vehicle, Italian law requires that you carry a valid driving licence accompanied by an Italian translation or by a declaration issued by the *Automobile Club d'Italia (ACI)* at its frontier or provincial offices. You must also keep a red triangle in the car in case of accident or breakdown. This serves as a warning to other traffic when placed on the road at a distance of 50m from the stationary car. It can be hired from ACI for a minimal charge and returned at the frontier.

It is now compulsory to wear seat-belts in the front seat of cars in Italy, and crash helmets are compulsory when driving or riding a motorcycle. Traffic is generally faster (and more aggressive) than in Britain or America, and the degree of congestion in even the smallest towns defies the imagination. In urban areas, the speed limit is 50km/h (31mph); on main roads, 90km/h 56mph); on superhighways, 130km/h (80mph). Pedestrians have the right of way at zebra crossings (although you're taking your life in your hands if you step into the street without looking). Unless otherwise indicated, cars entering a road or roundabout from the right are given precedence. Trams and trains always have the right of way from either left or right. If an oncoming driver flashes his headlights, it means he is proceeding and not giving you precedence. In towns Sicilian drivers frequently change lanes without warning; they tend to ignore pedestrian crossings; and they view red lights with a certain cynicism. Everywhere the drivers of motorcycles, mopeds and Vespas weave in and out of traffic, snapping up the right of way. The concept of the safe following distance is unknown, and if you leave a gap between your car and the vehicle in front of you, it will be filled immediately. As a rule, you should not try to use your car in the historic centres of Sicilian towns. Even if you *do* find your way in (and many towns have closed their centres to motor traffic; see below), the labyrinth of one-way streets is such that you may never find your way out.

Roads in Italy

Italy probably has the finest motorways in Europe. They are called *autostrade* and they are indicated by green signs or, near the entrance ramps, by large overhead light boards. Tolls are charged according to the rating of the vehicle and the distance covered. All *autostrade* have service areas open 24 hours and most have SOS points every 2km (1¼ miles). At the entrance to motorways, the two directions are indicated by the name of the most important town (and not by the nearest town), which can be momentarily confusing. Similar to *autostrade*, but not provided with service stations, SOS points or emergency lanes, are the dual-carriageway fast roads called *superstrade* (also indicated by green signs).

You'll also find an excellent network of secondary highways (*strade statali or provinciali*, indicated by blue signs), which are usually well engineered and provide fine views of the countryside. Local traffic, however, can be extremely heavy, especially around major cities. Throughout Italy buildings of historic interest are often indicated by yellow signs (although there are long-term plans to change the colour to brown), townships (*comuni*) and their component villages (*frazioni*), by white signs. The territory of a *comune* is often much larger than the town of the same name that is its administrative centre – another source of confusion.

Fuel and Service

Petrol stations are open 24 hours on motorways, elsewhere 7.00-12.00, 15.00-20.00; winter 7.30-12.30, 14.30-19.30. Twenty-four-hour self-service stations can also be found in or near the larger towns. Pumps are operated by L10,000 or L50,000 banknotes. All varieties of petrol (including diesel and unleaded) are now readily available in Italy, although they cost more than in the UK and considerably more than in America. Most stations offer basic maintenance service.

Parking

Many cities in Sicily have taken the wise step of closing their historic centres to traffic (except for residents), which makes them much more pleasant to visit on foot. Access is allowed to hotels and for the disabled. It is advisable to leave your car in a supervised car park, although with a bit of effort it is almost always possible to find a place to park free of charge, away from the town centre. Always lock your car when parked and never leave anything of value inside it.

Car Hire

You can arrange to hire a car before departure through the airlines (at specially advantageous rates in conjunction with their flights) or in Italy through any of the principal car-hire firms (the best known include *Maggiore*, *Avis* and *Hertz*), which offer daily, five-day, weekly and weekend rates. Special leasing rates are available for periods of 30 days and over. The State Railways also offer special rail-car combinations.

Maps

The *Touring Club Italiano* (TCI) publishes several sets of excellent maps, including *Carta Stradale d'Europa: Italia* on a scale of 1:1,000,000; the *Atlante Stradale Touring* (1:800,000); and the *Carta Stradale d'Italia* (1:200,000). The last is divided into 15 sheets covering the regions of Italy. These are also published as an atlas (with a comprehensive index) called the *Atlante Stradale d'Italia*, in three volumes. The one entitled Sud covers our area. These maps can be purchased from the TCI offices and at many booksellers; in London they are obtainable at Stanfords, 12-14 Long Acre, WC2 9LP. *The Istituto Geografico Militare*, Via Cesare Battisti 10, Florence, publishes a map of Italy on a scale of 1:100,000 in 277 sheets and a field survey, partly 1:50,000, partly 1:25,000, which are invaluable for the detailed exploration of the country, especially its more mountainous regions; the coverage is, however, still far from complete at the larger scales and some of the maps are out of date. For the computer literate, *Route 66 Geographic Information Systems BV* of Veenendaal, The Netherlands, distributes software that calculates and displays routes from any origin to any destination in Italy.

By Air

There are direct flights from Palermo to Pantelleria and Lampedusa, and from Catania to Lampedusa. These are the only internal air connections offered in Sicily and certainly the quickest, easiest way to reach these islands.

Cycling and Walking

Cycling and walking holidays have become more popular in Italy in recent years and more information is now available locally. The local offices of the *Club Alpino Italiano* (*CAI*) and the World Wild Fund for Nature provide all the information necessary. Maps are published by the *Istituto Geografico Militare* (see above) and by CAI at a scale of 1:50,000.

Taxis

Taxis are hired from ranks or by telephone; there are no cruising cabs. Fares vary from city to city but are generally cheaper than London taxis, though considerably more expensive than New York taxis. No tip is expected, but 1000 lire or so can be given. A supplement is charged for night service and for luggage. There is a heavy surcharge when the destination is outside the town limits (ask roughly how much the fare is likely to be).

Helpful Hints

Opening Times

The opening times of museums, sites, and monuments have been given at the end of each chapter, but they often change without warning. The tourist boards in major cities keep updated timetables of most **museums** in their area of competence. Entrance fees to Italian museums vary (from free to L12,000) by age and nationality; British citizens under 18 and over 60 are entitled to free admission to national museums and monuments thanks to reciprocal arrangements in Britain. During the *Settimana per i Beni Culturali e Ambientali* (Cultural and Environmental Heritage Week), usually held early in December, entrance to national museums is free for all.

Churches in Italy open quite early in the morning (often for 6.00 Mass). They normally close for a couple of hours during the middle of the day, although cathedrals and some of the large churches may be open without a break during daylight hours. The sacristan will show closed chapels, crypts, etc. and a small tip should be given. Some churches now ask that sightseers do not enter during a service, but normally visitors may do so, provided they are silent and do not approach the altar in use. At all times they are expected to cover their legs and arms and generally dress with decorum. In Holy Week most of the pictures are covered and are on no account shown.

Shops generally open Monday–Saturday 8.30/9.00–13.00 and 15.30/16.00–19.30/20.00. Shops selling clothes, etc., are usually closed on Monday morning; food shops on Wednesday afternoon, except from mid-June to mid-September, when all shops instead close on Saturday afternoon. In resorts, during July and August, many shops remain open from early morning until late at night. **Banks** are open Monday to Friday, 8.30–13.30, 14.30–15.45. They are closed on Saturday and holidays and close early (about 11.00) on days preceding national holidays.

Public Holidays

The Italian National Holidays, when offices, shops and schools are closed, are 1 January, 25 April (Liberation Day), Easter Sunday and Easter Monday, 1 May (Labour Day), 15 August (Assumption), 1 November (All Saints' Day), 8 December (Immaculate Conception), Christmas Day and 26 December (St Stephen). Each town keeps its patron saint's day as a holiday.

Health

British citizens, as members of the EU, have the right to claim health services in Italy if they have the E111 form (available from post offices). There are also a number of private holiday health insurance policies. Italy has no medical programme covering US citizens, who are advised to take out an insurance policy before travelling. First aid services (*pronto soccorso*) are available at all hospitals, train stations and airports. Chemist shops (*farmacie*) are usually open Monday–Friday 9.00–13.00, 16.00–19.30 or 20.00. A few are open on Saturdays, Sundays and holidays (listed on the door of every chemist). In all towns there is at least one chemist shop open at night (shown on the door of every chemist). For emergencies, dial 113 (State Police) or 112 (Carabinieri).

Embassies and Consulates

Help is given to British, US and Canadian travellers who are in difficulty by the British and US consulates in Naples and by the British, US and Canadian Embassies in Rome. They will replace lost or stolen passports and will give advice in emergencies. The **British Consulate** in Naples is located at Via Crispi 122 (tel. 081 663 511); the **US Consulate** is in Piazza della Repubblica (tel. 081 583 8111, fax 081 761 1869); the **Canadian Embassy** in Rome is at Via G.B. de Rossi 27 (tel. 06 445 981, fax 06 4459 8750). There are also **British Honorary Consuls** in Messina (Mr Richard Brown, tel.

090 672924) and in Palermo (Mr Luigi Tagliavia, tel. 091 326412), and a **United States Consular Agency** in Palermo (tel. 091 611 0020, fax 091 611 0434).

Crime

Pickpocketing is a widespread problem in towns all over Italy: it is always advisable not to carry valuables in handbags and to be particularly careful on public transport. Never wear conspicuous jewellery, including neck-laces and watches; women, when walking, should keep their handbags on the side of their bodies nearest the wall (never on the street side). Crime should be reported at once to the police, or the local Carabinieri office (found in every town and small village). A detailed statement has to be given in order to get an official document confirming loss or damage (essential for insurance claims). Interpreters are provided. For all emergencies, dial 113.

Telephone and Postal Services

Stamps are sold at tobacconists and post offices. Correspondence can be addressed c/o the post office by adding *fermo posta* to the name of the locality. There are numerous **public telephones** all over Italy and card-operated phones are becoming increasingly common in major cities and resort areas. Local calls cost L 200. Cards offering L 5000 of L 10,000 in prepaid calls are available at post offices, tobacconists and certain news-stands. They are particularly convenient for phoning abroad. Long-distance calls in Italy are made by dialling the city code (for instance, 091 for Palermo), then the phone number; international and intercontinental calls, by dialling 00 plus the country code, then the city code (for numbers in Britain, without the initial zero) and the phone number (for instance, the central London number 855 2000 would be 0044 171 855 2000). You can reach an AT&T operator at 172 1011, MCI at 172 1022, or Sprint at 172 1877.

Suggestions on Tipping

A service charge of 15 to 18 per cent is added to **hotel** bills. The service charge is already included when all-inclusive prices are quoted, but it is customary to leave an additional tip in any case. As a guideline and depending on the category of your hotel, the following tips are suggested: chambermaid, L 1000/day; concierge, L 3000/day (additional tip for extra services); bellhop or porter, L 1500/bag; doorman (for calling a cab), L 1000; room-service waiter, L 1000 and up (depending on amount of bill); valet service, at least L 1000; hotel bar, 15 per cent.

A service charge of approximately 10-15 per cent is added to most **restaurant** bills (it will be marked: *servizio*. It is customary, however, to leave a small additional tip (L 1000-2000) for good service. In cafés and bars, leave 15 if you were served at a table and if a bill does not already include service; and L 100-500 while standing at a counter or bar drinking coffee, cocktails, etc.

At **opera, concerts and the theatre**, tip ushers L 1000 and up, depending on the price of your seat.

Language

Even a few words of Italian are a great advantage in Sicily, where English is not so widely spoken as in the rest of Italy. Local dialects vary greatly and are usually unintelligible to the foreigner; but even where dialect is universally used nearly everybody can speak and understand standard Italian.

Words should be pronounced well forward in the mouth, and no nasal intonation exists in Italian. Double consonants call for special care as each must be sounded. Consonants are pronounced roughly as in English with the following exceptions; *c* and *cc* before e and i have the sound of *ch* in chess; *sc* before e and i is pronounced like *sh* in ship; *ch* before e and i has the sound of *k*; *g* and *gg* before e and i are always soft, like *j* in jelly; *gh* is always hard, like *g* in get; *gl* is nearly always like *lli* in million (there are a few exceptions, e.g. *negligere*, where it is pronounced as in English); *gn* is like *ny* in lanyard; *gu* and *qu* are always like *gw* and *kw*. *S* is hard like *s* in six except when it occurs between two vowels, when it is soft, like the English *z* or the *s* in rose; *ss* is always hard. *Z* and *zz* are usually pronounced like *ts*, but occasionally have the sound of *dz* before a long vowel. Vowels are pronounced much more openly than in Southern English and are given their full value; there are no true diphthongs in Italian and every vowel should be articulated separately. The stress normally falls on the last syllable but one; in modern practice an accent-sign is written regularly only when the stress is on the last syllable, e.g. *città*, or to differentiate between two words similarly spelt but with different meaning: e.g. *e* (and); *è* (is).

Manners and Customs

Throughout Italy it is customary to open conversation in shops, etc., with the courtesy of *buon giorno* ('good day') or *buona sera* ('good afternoon/evening'). The expression *prego* ('don't mention it') is everywhere the obligatory and automatic response to *grazie* ('thank you'). The phrases *per piacere* or *per favore* ('please'), *permesso* ('excuse me'), used when pushing past someone (essential on public vehicles), *scusi* ('sorry'; also, 'I beg your pardon', when something is not heard), should not be forgotten. You'll be wished *Buon appetito!* before beginning a meal, to which you should reply *Grazie, altrettanto*. This pleasant custom may be extended to fellow passengers taking a picnic meal on a train. Shaking hands is an

23

essential part of greeting and leave-taking. In shops and offices a certain amount of self-assertion is taken for granted, since queues are not the general rule and it is incumbent on the enquirer or customer to get himself a hearing.

There are few restrictions on photography in Italy, but permission is necessary to photograph the interiors of churches and museums and may sometimes be withheld. Care should be taken before photographing individuals, notably members of the armed forces and the police. Photography is forbidden on train stations and airports as well as in frontier zones and near military installations.

The metric system of weights and measures is used in Italy: the *metro* is the unit of length, the *grammo* of weight, the *ara* of land-measurement, the *litro* of capacity. Greek-derived prefixes (deca-, etto-, chilo-) are used with those names to express multiples; Latin prefixes (deci-, centi-, milli-) to express fractions (*kilometro* – 1000 metri, *millimetro* – 1000th part of a *metro*). For approximate calculations the metro may be taken as 39 inches and the *chilometro* as 0.6 mile, the *litro* as 1.75 pint, an *etto* as 3.5 oz and the *chilo* as 2.2 lbs.

4.FOOD AND WINE

Italian food is usually good and inexpensive. Generally speaking, the least pretentious **ristorante** or **trattoria** (there is very little difference between the two) provides the best value. In this guide you'll find a selection of restaurants at the end of each chapter. The places listed have been chosen on the basis of the quality and distinction of their menu, and even the simplest are quite good.

A full **Italian meal** usually consists of an appetiser, a first course of soup or pasta, an entrée of meat or fish accompanied by a vegetable, then salad, fruit and/or dessert. Odd as it may seem, this combination is not fattening, as the various food groups are all present in carefully established proportion. If you want to be on the safe side, though, try having pasta and a salad at lunch (you'll burn off the calories in the afternoon), and your meat and vegetables in the evening. Or just go with a **pizza**, which is made to order in a *pizzeria* but can be bought on the run in **cafés**, bakeries, and any number of other places. Excellent refreshments, including sandwiches and salads, can be found in cafés, many of which have outside tables. As a rule, if you eat at the bar you must pay the cashier first, then present your receipt to the barman in order to get served. If you sit at a table the charge is usually higher, and you will be given waiter service (so you should not pay first).

Remember always that **pasta** is *the* essential ingredient of Italian cuisine – and the one where the Italian culinary fantasy is at its best. An ordinary Italian supermarket usually stocks about 50 different shapes, but some experts estimate that there are more that 600 shapes in all. *Pasta corta* ('short pasta') is much more varied than *pasta lunga* ('long pasta'). The latter may be tubular (like macaroni), or threadlike (*spaghetti, vermicelli, capellini*); smooth (*fettucce, tagliatelle, linguine*), ruffled (*lasagne ricce*), or twisted (*fusilli*). *Pasta corta* comes in the shape of shells (*conchiglie*), stars (*stelle*), butterflies (*farfalle*), etc., and may be smooth (*penne*) or fluted (*rigatoni*). The differences of shape translate into differences of flavour, even when the pasta is made from the same dough, or by the same manufacturer. The reason for this is that the relation between the surface area and the weight of the pasta varies from one shape to another, causing the sauce to adhere in different ways and to different degrees. But even when pasta is served without a sauce, experts claim to perceive considerable differences in flavour due to the fact that different shapes cook in different ways.

Bear in mind that Italy is considered to have the best **coffee** in Europe. *Caffè* (or *espresso*, black coffee) can be ordered *alto* or *lungo* (diluted), *corretto* (with a liqueur, or *macchiato* (with hot milk). A *cappuccino* is an espresso with more hot milk than a *caffè macchiato* and is generally considered a breakfast drink. A glass of hot milk with a dash of coffee in it, called *latte macchiato*, is another early-morning favourite. In summer, many customers take *caffè freddo* (iced coffee). **Ice cream** (*gelato*) is another widely famed Italian speciality. It is always best in a *gelateria*, where it is made on the spot.

Sicilian Cuisine

by Gillian Arthur

Many people say that the food in Sicily is hotter, spicier and more diverse than that found on the mainland. It is certainly true that Sicily has one of the richest and most exotic cuisines in Italy. The variety in Sicilian food is due to the abundance and freshness of raw ingredients found on the island and equally as a result of the successive waves of conquerers who have all left their culinary mark on Sicily. Sitting at the crossroads of the Mediterranean, Sicily was invaded by the Greeks, Romans, Arabs, Normans, Spanish and countless other wayfarers. The influences of all these diverse civilisations can be seen in modern Sicilian cuisine.

In a culinary sense the relationship between the land and the kitchen can never be underestimated. Sicily is blessed with a mild climate, a long growing season and hence a plentiful supply of raw ingredients. It is a land of sun and sea, and Sicilian cuisine is based on these two elements. The sun provides tomatoes, chillies, olives, citrus fruit, wheat and aubergines among other things, while the seas are brimming with tuna, sardines, anchovies and swordfish. These basic ingredients are combined in exotic ways to produce a spicy and flavourful style of cooking, quite distinct from the styles found elsewhere in Italy.

Starters

Sicilians are famous for their *antipasti*. On entering a restaurant there is often a table, strategically placed to attract the diner's eye, laden with a wide variety of dishes that are consumed before the pasta course. Antipasti vary widely from region to region and from season to season and tend to be mainly vegetable based. Their function is to excite the palate and get the gastric juices flowing in preparation for the serious business ahead. They include such dishes as *arancini*, rice balls filled with meat or cheese dipped in egg and breadcrumbs, deep-fried and generally eaten hot; *caponata*, a mixture of vegetables such as spinach, cauliflower, endive and celery fried separately in olive oil and then sprinkled with vinegar before adding capers (this is also often served as a separate side dish); green and black olives stuffed with capers or anchovy fillets, and olives coated in breadcrumbs and deep fried; *pomodori ripieni*, which are tomatoes halved and filled with a mixture of breadcrumbs, olives, currants and dried tuna eggs; and an infinite variety of vegetables marinated in olive oil.

Pasta

Sicilians are very attached to pasta in all shapes and sizes, and it forms an important part of daily life. Sicilians believe that pasta was invented in Sicily in the 10th century BC as a means of preserving wheat; the recipe was then handed on to the Greeks. They are very particular about their pasta and like to eat it more *al dente* than in the north of Italy. They say that it is impossible to get two Sicilians to agree about how well done the pasta should be; however, they all agree that the cooking of the pasta is a matter of crucial importance. Pasta is served with an infinite variety of sauces depending on the region and the season, but among the most typical are the following.

Pasta alla Norma is found all over Sicily but is particularly good around Catania. It is commonly believed that the name is taken from Bellini's famous opera, but it is more likely that it derives from the dialect word *norma*, meaning 'normal'. A rich tomato-based sauce with fried aubergine and basil, it is traditionally served with salted or baked ricotta rather than parmesan cheese. Another dish that combines all the classic ingredients is *pasta con le sarde*: spaghetti with sardines, capers, wild fennel, anchovies, pine nuts, currants, tomatoes, onions and saffron, usually served in the spring when there is an abundance of wild fennel and sardines are at their best. Another simpler pasta dish is *past 'cca muddica*, served with oil, anchovies and breadcrumbs. Other pasta dishes include *crispeddi*, stuffed pasta filled with anchovies and ricotta before being fried, and *maccarruni*, which is thought to be the prototype of all pasta dishes, being made from semolina and water, served with rich sauces and salted ricotta cheese. Other choices for a first course include *cuscusu*, which is equivalent to couscous, imported by the Arabs in AD800. Found most commonly on the west coast of Sicily, it is served boiled with a variety of seafood.

Breadcrumbs play a large part in Sicilian cooking, they are often used as garnish for pasta and fish. They are also used extensively for frying – almost all fried food is breaded – and for stuffing vegetables. Parmesan is very rarely served with pasta, being replaced by breadcrumbs or grated salted ricotta cheese.

Main Courses

Seafood features extensively in main courses. Sardines in particular play a key role, and the most typical way of preparing them is *sarde a beccafico*, so called as the stuffed sardines resemble little birds. The cleaned sardines are covered in a mixture of breadcrumbs, anchovies, pine nuts and currants, covered in orange juice and baked in the oven. Another typical dish is *involtini di pesce spada* or swordfish rolls, which use the same filling as in the previous dish to stuff the slices of swordfish. This type of filling, based on a mixture of currants and pine nuts, is called *passoli e pinoli* and is typically Sicilian. Further inland main courses tend to be meat or cheese based and include dishes such as goat cooked over an open fire or stuffed with tomatoes, artichokes and asparagus. Rabbit, both wild and domesticated, is also common and is cooked with garlic, onion and parsley.

Vegetables

Typical vegetable dishes include boiled dried broad beans cooked with oil and wild fennel to a pureé, known locally as *maccu*. This dish is first eaten on 19 March to celebrate the feast of San Giuseppe. Broad beans are also eaten raw, with pecorino cheese, when fresh and young. An unusual dish is *insalata di arance* – oranges sliced and dressed with olive oil, salt and pepper.

Peppers are an essential ingredient of many dishes. In their smaller version, *peperoncino*, they are used either whole or powdered to add heat to such dishes as *spaghetti aglio olio e peperoncino*, one of the easiest dishes in the world. In their larger incarnation, as capsicums or bell peppers, they feature either roasted or stuffed as side dishes. Tomatoes are another key ingredient in modern Sicilian cooking. It took a long time for them to enter the kitchen after their introduction by the Spanish, as originally they were used for medicinal and ornamental purposes. These days tomatoes are used in an endless variety of ways, including fresh in salads, cooked in sauces, sun dried and marinated in olive oil and herbs, and made into *estratto* or concentrated tomato paste. Aubergine, or eggplant, is another ubiquitous vegetable, often grilled or fried and then dressed with olive oil and served as part of the antipasto table, or combined with other ingredients as a sauce for pasta.

Cheese

The centre of the island is also the centre of cheese production. The tradition of cheesemaking is a legacy of the Greeks, and styles and methods of cheesemaking are similar to those found in modern-day Greece. The majority of cheese produced in Sicily is made from sheep's milk and is called *pecorino*. It comes in all shapes and sizes, including fresh, aged and salted cheeses with or without the addition of whole peppercorns. Fresh ricotta is an essential ingredient in Sicilian dishes. It features in desserts and pasta sauces and is eaten as a topping for bread and honey. The cheese produced around Enna is especially prized for the addition of saffron. Cheese is also served as a main course, cut into thin slices fried in olive oil and oregano and then sprinkled with vinegar, which is similar to the Greek method of preparation.

Desserts

The Sicilian kitchen is best known for its traditional desserts and sweet-meats. The most famous of these is *cannoli*, a sweet pastry roll filled with sweetened ricotta, pistachio nuts and candied fruits. Equally famous is *cassata*, brought to Sicily by the Arabs. This dish is what is known as a *semi-freddo*, literally meaning 'half frozen', and is rather different from the versions found in other parts of the world. Classic *cassata* is a sponge cake covered in ricotta that has been enriched with vanilla, cinnamon and chocolate and then covered in a sugar glaze and refrigerated. The *frutti alla martorana*, found in sweetshops all over Sicily, are marzipan sweets made into a wide variety of shapes, particularly fruit. These traditional Sicilian sweets were originally made by the nuns of the convent of La Martorana in Palermo. They hung the marzipan fruits in the trees, in an attempt to fool a visiting bishop into thinking that fruit bloomed in Sicily in the winter. Excellent *granita* (water ices) and *gelato* (ice cream) are also available. Ice-based desserts developed in Sicily as a result of the year-round availability of snow on Mt Ætna. Other traditional sweets are generally based on almond or pistachio nuts and include *torrone*, nougat made from honey and almonds and traditionally eaten at Christmas.

Wine

Wine has been made in Sicily since 1400BC, and modern winemaking dates from the occupation by the Normans. Historically, the Sicilian wine industry has been plagued by the problem of huge surpluses, with large amounts of mediocre wine being produced. However, dramatic technological developments have led to improvements in quality. There are now nine *DOC* wines, including light fruity whites, elegant reds and famous dessert wines such as *Marsala* (*DOC* stands for *denominazione di origine controllata* and is a system of classification based on the region where the wine is made). Wine is produced all over Sicily, from the slopes of Mt Ætna to the Æolian Islands, although the bulk of the wine comes from the western province of Trapani, which produces three DOC wines, *Alcamo*, *Marsala* and *Moscato di Pantelleria*. There are also many blended and table wines produced, destined for the export market as Sicilians drink less wine per head than other Italians. Wines are made from indigenous Sicilian grape varieties such as *Inzolia, Cataratto, Nero d'Avola* and *Perricone*, as well as from better-known varieties such as *Pinot Noir, Chardonnay and Cabernet Sauvignon*. Some of the wines more widely available are listed below.

Alcamo is a white wine, soft and fruity and produced from *Catarratto Bianco* grapes in western Sicily. The best-known producer is **Rapitalà**. **Corvo** makes several wines using grapes from all over Sicily. They include good, consistent, medium-bodied whites, smooth reds and a fortified wine, *Corvo Stravecchio*, which is barrel aged to an amber gold colour. They also make one of the best reds on the island, *Duca Enrico*, which is aged in small oak barrels and shows a perfect balance between fruit and wood. Another label to look out for is **Donnafugata**, producing excellent red, white and rosé wines in central Sicily. Wines are also produced on the volcanic slopes of Ætna, which benefit from a cool climate and lots of sunshine; the red is full bodied and ages well, while the white is dry and delicate. *Faro* is another DOC region around the Straits of Messina producing an intense red wine in very small quantities. One of the best-known Sicilian producers is **Regaleali**, which makes some of the best wines in Italy. The Tasca family, which owns the vineyard, has been making wine since 1580 and produces an excellent white *Nozze d'Oro* created to celebrate a 50th wedding anniversary, as well as a delicious rosé and the outstanding red, *Rosso del Conte*. *Cerasuolo di Vittoria* is a fragrant red wine, aged in oak and produced in southeast Sicily. It is elegant, well balanced, cherry-red in colour and strong, with an alcohol content of 13 per cent.

Sicily has a long tradition of making good **dessert wine**. On the Æolian Islands *Malvasia* grapes are grown to make strong white wines in a sweet or semi-sweet version. The best *Malvasia* comes from the island of Salina. One of the best known-wines from Sicily is the fortified *Marsala*, created by John Woodhouse in 1773 for the British market. Unfashionable until it was recently revived, it is grown in western Sicily from *Cataratto, Grillo* and *Inzolia* grapes. Around 20 to 35 million litres are produced annually of widely varying types and qualities. *Marsala* is aged for up to five years in wooden barrels to produce a wine of around 17 per cent alcohol. The driest type is called *vergine* or *solera* and can be drunk as an aperitif; the sweeter variety is called *fine* and is usually used as an addition to desserts. A good sparkling dessert wine is *Moscato*, grown in southeast Sicily and on the island of Pantelleria.

Buying vegetables at Gangi

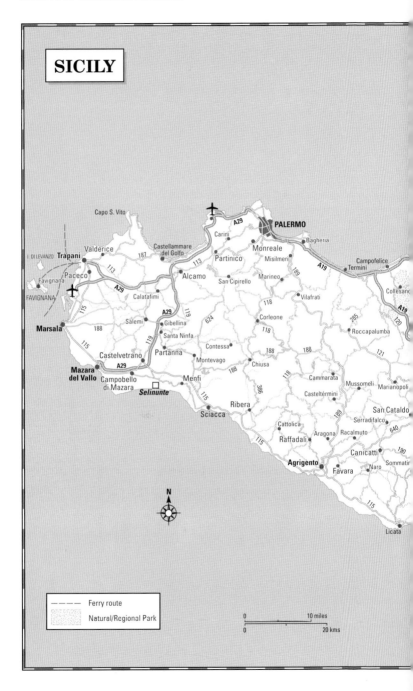

SICILY

Capo S. Vito

I. DI LEVANZO   **Trapani**   Valderice   Castellammare
del Golfo

Favignana   Paceco

FAVIGNANA

Calatafimi

Marsala   188   Sàlemi   Gibellina

Santa Ninfa

Castelvetrano   Partanna

**Mazara
del Vallo**   Campobello
di Mazara   *Selinunte*   Menfi

Carini   Monreale   Bagheria

PALERMO

A29

Partinico   Misilmeri   Campofelice
Termini

Alcamo   San Cipirello   Marineo   A19

Vilafrati   Collesano

A19

118   Corleone   285   120

118   Roccapalumba

Contessa   188   188   121

Montevago   Chiusa

386   Cammarata   Mussomeli   Marianopoli

Casteltèrmini

Ribera   San Cataldo

Sciacca   Cattolica   Serradifalco   640

Raffadali   Aragona   Racalmuto

Canicatti   190

Agrigento   Naro   Sommatir

Favara

115   Licata

N

Ferry route

Natural/Regional Park

0   10 miles
0   20 kms

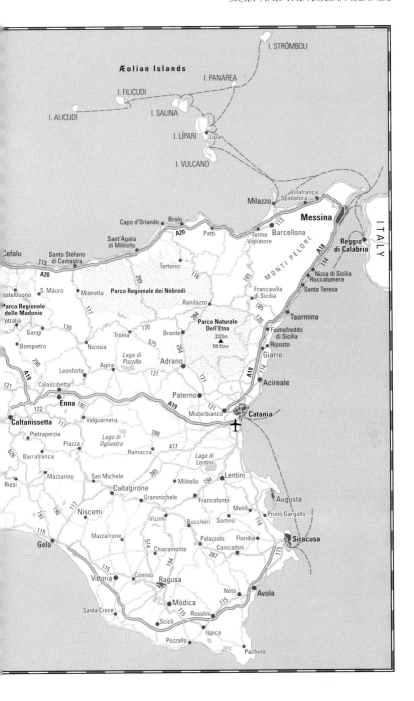

5. WESTERN SICILY

Sicilians know that there are at least two Sicilys: one in the west and one in the east. The former is largely Arabic and Norman in feeling, the latter, predominantly Greek. Western Sicily, with its capital at Palermo, is more traditional in character; eastern Sicily, which revolves around the bustling industrial hub of Catania, is more dynamic. To view Sicily in these terms alone, of course, is to oversimplify the island's rich and fascinating history. Nevertheless, advocates of the east-west theory will tell you there is more than a grain of truth in their interpretation – and that this truth is rooted in historical events. If the Greeks elected not to push their colonies further westward than Selinunte, it is because the Carthaginians, their arch-rivals, had already settled this part of the island. If the Arabs established a firmer foothold in the west, it is because the Classical tradition here was weaker. And if the Normans made Palermo their capital, it was so that all should know that they had firmly and permanently supplanted their predecessors.

Today western Sicily is a land of deep contrasts: round Palermo development has been fast and furious; but away from the capital the character of the region is still very agrarian. The sun-drenched hills along the coast carry some of Sicily's finest vineyards (around Trapani, in particular, Sicily's best wines are grown); and further inland, the windswept landscape is planted with an endless sea of grain. There is something distinctly African about the west: the air is drier and crisper, the earth more arid, the sunlight stronger than elsewhere on the island. Arabic words survive in the dialects and place names; even the towns, with their flat roofs and maze-like streets, have an Arabic feel. And yet, as though by some strange miracle, these North African roots have borne European fruit – especially (but not exclusively) in Norman-Saracenic monuments such as the cathedral of Monreale, or the Cappella Palatina in Palermo, shining examples of what the medieval alchemists called *conjunctio oppositorum*, the meeting of opposites.

Palermo

The hill on which Palermo stands was originally a promontory, surrounded on three sides by the sea. At the innermost and highest point of the headland, Phoenician merchants established a trading post, in the 8th century

BC, from which they did business with the region's Sikel, Elymian and Greek populations. Over time the town developed two distinct centres: *Palæapolis*, the 'old town', was the focus of political and religious power; *Neapolis*, the 'new town', was the business and residential district. The first stood atop the promontory; the second on lower ground, around the harbour. The abundance of safe anchorages won the settlement the name of *Pánormos*, 'all-haven'. This Greek word, applied to a city never dominated by the Greeks, reveals not only the intensity of the Phoenicians' commercial ties with the nearby Greek colonies, but also their desire to assimilate traits of the Greeks' more mature and refined culture. Allied with Carthage after the battle of Himera (480BC), *Pánormos* later became the principal Carthaginian centre in Sicily. Its decline began with the Roman conquest in 254BC, after which the political and economic interests of Sicily shifted to the east-west axis linking Syracuse, the Roman provincial capital, to Lilybæum, seat of the *prætor*, or judicial authority. The harbour, however, retained its ancient importance, and the Roman *Panormus* was made the seat of a *quæstor*, or financial authority.

Occupied by the Vandals and then by Odoacer, conquered by the Ostrogoth Theodoric and the Byzantine Belisarius, Palermo fell to the Arabs in 831, during the first phase of their occupation of Sicily. These new lords made the city the capital of an independent emirate and one of the most successful emporiums in the Mediterranean. Arab chroniclers of the time describe Palermo as a city of magnificent mosques, sumptuous palaces and crowded markets, comparable in size and splendour to Cordova and Cairo. In the 11th century, while Muslim power declined elsewhere in the Mediterranean, Palermo continued to flourish. Taken by the Norman Roger de Hauteville in 1072, it reached new heights of prosperity under his son King Roger (reigned 1130-54), becoming a living testimony to the benefits of political and religious tolerance. Muslim, Jew and Christian lived side by side, in perfect or near-perfect harmony, their rights to life and property guaranteed by one of the most enlightened authoritarian governments of the Middle Ages.

Following the marriage of the Norman princess Constance to Holy Roman Emperor Henry VI, their son Frederick of Hohenstaufen ascended the throne of Sicily in 1208. Frederick, who was one of the more judicious and beneficent sovereigns of medieval Europe as well as a brilliant poet and architect, subsequently made Palermo the capital of the Holy Roman Empire. The presence of his court assured the city's continued splendour. Unfortunately Hohenstaufen rule came to an abrupt end in 1266 when the French Angevins battled their way to the throne; but their despotic rule ended in the famous Rebellion of the Vespers (or 'Sicilian Vespers') of 1282 (the subject of Verdi's opera, *I Vespri Siciliani*), in the aftermath of which the Spanish Aragonese were named their successors.

The Angevins' decision to move the capital of the kingdom to Naples – a decision seconded by the Aragonese – created a lull in Palermitan life that was soon filled by the great feudal families and the mendicant religious orders. The ambitious building programmes of these two groups profoundly altered the character of the city after the 14th century, as the imposing fortress-palaces of the aristocracy and the huge monasteries of the Dominicans, Franciscans and other orders became the focal points of the new town. In the 16th century the tensions between the Spanish and Turkish empires, in which Palermo played a double role as stronghold and capital of a Spanish viceregency, led to another flurry of rebuilding which included intensive fortification and the creation of a ceremonial avenue – the *Kalsa* or *Cassaro* – along which the city's principal civic institutions and most prestigious residential and religious buildings were aligned. The construction, in the early 17th century, of Via Maqueda, at right angles to the Kalsa, and the creation of Piazza Viglieda (the 'Quattro Canti') at the intersection of the two thoroughfares, kicked off the Baroque experience in Palermo – an extraordinary flourishing of palaces, churches, monasteries and oratories that gradually melted into the sober Classicism of the late 18th and early 19th centuries. The creation of Viale della Libertà around the middle of the 19th century opened up a grand new residential district for the affluent middle class who, in later decades, financed the Art Nouveau designs of architect Ernesto Basile, and caused the focus of city life to shift away from the historic centre and into the new quarters to the north. Twentieth-century development has continued along the same axis, and spread into the foothills to the west and south as well. Today the city virtually fills the broad basin around its bay.

Old Palermo

In 1768 Johann Wolfgang Goethe, the German Romantic poet, travelled to Italy to improve his already extensive knowledge of Classical culture. His travel diary, the *Italian Journey*, makes wonderful reading, and his first impression of Palermo is particularly memorable. Goethe arrived by sea, as did most foreign travellers of his century, so he had the now unusual experience of seeing the entire city spread out before him.

'The city faces north with high mountains rising behind it,' he wrote. 'The rays of the afternoon sun were shining across it, so that all the buildings facing us were in shadow but lit by reflected light. The delicate contours of Monte Pellegrino to the right were in full sunshine, and a shore with bays, headlands and promontories stretched far away to the left. In front of the dark buildings, graceful trees of a tender green, their tops illuminated from behind, swayed like vegetal glow-worms. A faint haze tinted all the shadows blue. Instead of hurrying impatiently ashore, we remained on deck until we were driven off. It might be long before we could again enjoy such a treat for the eyes from such a vantage point.'

Thrilled by this vision, Goethe set out to take a closer look at the city, but soon discovered, as we all do, that 'it is easy to grasp in its overall plan, but difficult to get to know in detail'. The old city centre, especially, appeared as 'a confusing labyrinth, where a stranger can find his way about only with the help of a guide'.

This labyrinth is the subject of our first walk, which begins on the high ground where the Phoenicians established their original fortified settlement. This sea-rimmed hill was the heart of the city not only in Phoenician times, but also under the Romans, Byzantines, Arabs, Normans, French and Spanish. First stop will be the great Royal Palace which stands on the ancient acropolis. It includes one of the island's most splendid Norman-Saracenic chapels, the Cappella Palatina, adorned with dazzling mosaics. The route then loops around to the south and east, touching upon the charming little church of San Giovanni degli Eremiti and several of the city's fine patrician palaces. A visit to the cathedral is followed by a stroll through a fascinating street market to the Museo Archeologico, one of Palermo's three great museums (the other two are the Galleria Regionale and Museo Etnografico), where the walk ends. There is a lot to see, and you should be prepared to be on your feet for at least three hours. The walk actually makes a very pleasant morning, especially if you break for coffee, a pastry or ice cream in Via Mariano Stabile, the pedestrian-only promenade just north of the Museo Archeologico. Many of Palermo's better restaurants are also in this neighbourhood.

Easily reached on foot or by taxi, **Palazzo dei Normanni**, also called **Palazzo Reale** (Map 14), stands among cool, green gardens at the very top of the ancient Cassaro, today Corso Vittorio Emanuele. Once the seat of Sicily's medieval rulers, it is now home to the Sicilian Regional Assembly. The original Phoenician fortress was rebuilt by the Romans and Arabs, enlarged by the Normans and rebuilt again by Frederick II. In the 13th century, following the Angevins' decision to make Naples, rather than Palermo, the capital of the kingdom, the building lost its vocation, and by the 16th century all but the Cappella Palatina had been abandoned. There would be little to see here had the Spanish not decided to salvage the palace in 1555 and to make it again a sumptuous residence. The Bourbons added the rooftop observatory in the late 18th century; gazing through its telescope, Giuseppe Piazzi discovered the first asteroid (which he called Ceres, after Sicily's ancient patroness) in 1801.

Inside the palazzo is the **Cappella Palatina**, or Royal Chapel. To reach the entrance you have to go around the back of the building, through the porticoed courtyard, and up the stairs to the first-floor loggia. You enter through the original narthex, now a baptistery (notice the fine Art Nouveau doors, fruit of an early-20th-century restoration). From here ancient bronze doors in beautifully carved surrounds admit to the stunning interior.

The chapel was built c 1132–40 by King Roger II, who in a spirit of political correctness *ante litteram* made certain that each of the chief religions and peoples of his kingdom would be represented within. The **interior** is one of the finest examples of the integration of architecture and decorative

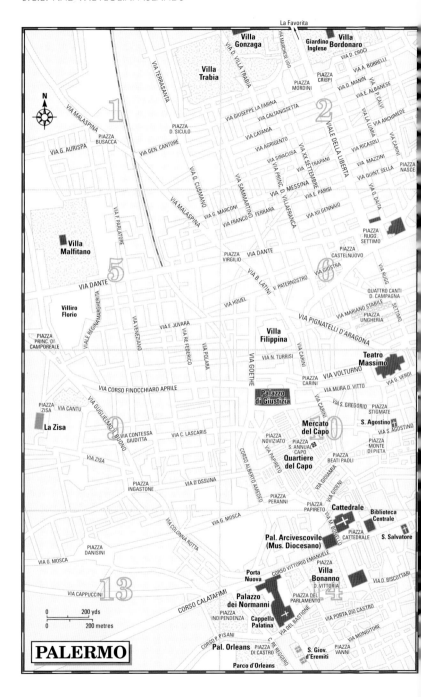

La Favorita

Villa
Gonzaga

Giardino
Inglese

Villa
Bordonaro

VIA MARCHESE UGO

VIA D. VILLA TRABIA

VIA D. CROCI

VIA A. BORRELLI

PIAZZA
CRISPI

PIAZZA
MORDINI

VIA D. MANIN

VIA E. ALBANESE

VIA P. CAVI

Villa
Trabia

VIA TERRASANTA

PIAZZA
D. SICULO

PIAZZA
BUSACCA

VIA G. AURISPA

VIA MALASPINA

N

VIA GEN. CANTORE

VIA GIUSEPPE LA FARINA

VIA CALTANISSETTA

VIA CATANIA

VIA AGRIGENTO

VIA SIRACUSA

VIA PRINC. DI

VIA XX SETTEMBRE

VIALE DELLA LIBERTA

VIA LA LUMIA

VIA ARCHIMEDE

VIA RICASOLI

VIA CARINI

VIA MAZZINI

VIA QUINT. SELLA

PIAZZA
NASCE

VIA G. CUSMANO

VIA G. MARCONI

VIA SAMMARTINO

VIA D. MESSINA

VIA D. VILLAFRANCA

VIA E. PARISI

VIA G. DAITA

VIA MALASPINA

VIA FRANCO FERRARA

VIA XII GENNAIO

PIAZZA
RUGG.
SETTIMO

Villa
Malfitano

VIA F. PARLATORE

VIA DANTE

PIAZZA
VIRGILIO

VIA DANTE

VIA B. LATINI

V. PATERNOSTRO

PIAZZA
CASTELNUOVO

VIA GIOSTRA

VIA RUGG

QUATTRO CANTI
D. CAMPAGNA

PIAZZA
SETTIMO

VIALE REGINA MARGHERITA

Villiro
Florio

VIA HOUEL

VIA MARIANO STABILE

PIAZZA
UNGHERIA

VIA PIGNATELLI D'ARAGONA

PIAZZA
PRINC. DI
CAMPOREALE

VIA VENEZIANO

VIA F. JUVARA

VIA RE FEDERICO

Villa
Filippina

VIA N. TURRISI

VIA CARINI

Teatro
Massimo

VIA CORSO FINOCCHIARO APRILE

VIA POLARA

VIA GOETHE

PIAZZA
CARINI

VIA VOLTURNO

VIA G. VERDI

PIAZZA
ZISA

VIA CANTU

VIA GUGLIELMO IL BUONO

Palazzo
di Giustizia

VIA MURA D. VITTO

VIA S. GREGORIO

PIAZZA
STIGMATE

VIA CARINI

La Zisa

VIA CONTESSA
GIUDITTA

VIA C. LASCARIS

Mercato
del Capo

S. Agostino

VIA S. AGOSTINO

PIAZZA
NOVIZIATO

PIAZZA
S. ANNUA
CAPO

PIAZZA
MONTE
DI PIETA

VIA ZISA

VIA PAPIRETO

Quartiere
del Capo

PIAZZA
BEATI PAOLI

PIAZZA
INGASTONE

VIA D'OSSUNA

CORSO ALBERTO AMEDEO

VIA GIOIAMIA

VIA GIOENI

PIAZZA
PERANNI

PIAZZA
PAPIRETO

Cattedrale

Biblioteca
Centrale

VIA G. MOSCA

VIA COLONNA ROTTA

PIAZZA
CATTEDRALE

S. Salvatore

Pal. Arcivescovile
(Mus. Diocesano)

PIAZZA
DANISINI

Porta
Nuova

CORSO VITTORIO EMANUELE

PIAZZA

Villa
Bonanno

VIA G. MOSCA

VIA CAPPUCCINI

CORSO CALATAFIMI

Palazzo
dei Normanni

D. VITTORIA

PIAZZA DEL
PARLAMENTO

VIA D. BISCOTTARI

VIA PORTA DIO CASTRO

0   200 yds

0   200 metres

PIAZZA
INDIPENDENZA

Cappella
Palatina

VIA DEL BASTIONE

VIA MONGITORE

CORSO P PISANI

Pal. Orleans

PIAZZA
DI CASTRO

C. RE REGGERO

S. Giov.
d'Eremiti

PIAZZA
VANNI

PALERMO

Parco d'Orleans

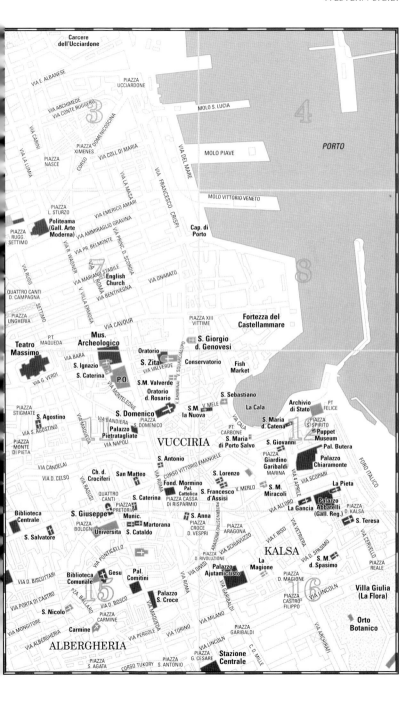

Carcere
dell'Ucciardone

VIA E. ALBANESE

PIAZZA
UCCIARDONE

VIA ARCHIMEDE
VIA CONTE RUGGERO

3

MOLO S. LUCIA

4

PORTO

VIA CARINI

CORSO DOMENICOSCINA

PIAZZA
XIMENES

VIA COLL DI MARIA

PIAZZA
NASCE

MOLO PIAVE

VIA LA LUMIA

VIA DEL MARE

VIA FRANCESCO CRISPI

MOLO VITTORIO VENETO

PIAZZA
L. STURZO

VIA EMERICO AMARI

Politeama
(Gall. Arte
Moderna)

Cap. di
Porto

PIAZZA
RUGG
SETTIMO

VIA R. WAGNER

VIA PR. BELMONTE

VIA AMMIRAGLIO GRAVINA

VIA PRINC. D. SCORDIA

VIA RUGG

VIA MARIANO STABILE

English
Church

VIA ONARATO

7

VIA MARIANO

V. VILLA ERMOSA

VIA BENTIVEGNA

QUATTRO CANTI
D. CAMPAGNA

VIA ROMA

8

P.T.
MAQUEDA

PIAZZA
UNGHERIA

VIA CAVOUR

PIAZZA XIII
VITTIME

Fortezza del
Castellammare

Mus.
Archeologico

Teatro
Massimo

VIA BARA

S. Giorgio
d. Genovesi

Oratorio

S. Ignazio

S. Zita

Conservatorio

Fish
Market

VIA G. VERDI

S. Caterina

VIA VALVERDE

P.O.

S.M. Valverde

S. Sebastiano

PIAZZA
STIGMATE

Oratorio
d. Rosario

VIA S. BAMBINAI

Archivio
di Stato

S. Agostino

S. Domenico

S.M.
la Nuova

V. MELE

La Cala

PT
FELICE

VIA S. AGOSTINO

VIA MARQUEDA

VIA BANDIERA

Palazzo
Pietratagliate

PIAZZA
S. DOMENICO

PT.
CARBONE

S. Maria
d. Catena

PIAZZA
S. SPIRITO

Puppet
Museum

PIAZZA
MONTE
DI PIETA

VIA NAPOLI

VUCCIRIA

S. Maria
di Porto Salvo

S. Giovanni

Pal. Butera

VIA CANDELAI

S. Antonio

Palazzo
Giardino
Garibaldi

Palazzo
Chiaramonte

VIA D. CELSO

Ch. d.
Crociferi

San Matteo

Fond. Mormino

CORSO VITTORIO EMANUELE

S. Lorenzo

MARINA

VIA 4 APRILE

VIA SCOPARI

La Pieta

VIA RAGUSI

QUATTRO
CANTI

S. Caterina

Pal.
Cattolica

VIA ROMA

PIAZZA CASSA
DI RISPARMIO

S. Francesco
d'Assisi

V. MERLO

S. M.
Miracoli

VIA ALLORO

La Gancia

Palazzo
Abbatelli
(Gall. Reg.)

PIAZZA
D. KALSA

Biblioteca
Centrale

S. Giuseppe

PIAZZA
PRETORIA

Munic.

S. Anna

S. Teresa

S. Salvatore

PIAZZA
BOLOGNI

Universita

Martorana

S. Cataldo

PIAZZA
CROCE
D. VESPRI

PIAZZA
ARAGONA

VIA F. RISO

VIA SCHIAVUZZO

KALSA

VIA VETRARIA

VIA PONTICELLO

VIA D. SPASIMO

S. M.
d. Spasimo

PIAZZA
REALE

Biblioteca
Comunale

Gesu

Pal.
Comitini

P.ZA BALLARO

Palazzo
Ajutamicristo

La
Magione

PIAZZA
D. MAGIONE

VIA LINCOLN

Villa Giulia
(La Flora)

VIA D. BISCOTTARI

15

VIA D. BOSCO

Palazzo
S. Croce

VIA ROMA

PIAZZA
CASTRO
FILIPPO

16

VIA PORTA DI CASTRO

S. Nicolo

PIAZZA
CARMINE

VIA MAQUEDA

Orto
Botanico

VIA MONGITORE

Carmine

VIA ALBERGHERIA

ALBERGHERIA

PIAZZA
S. AGATA

CORSO TUKORY

PIAZZA
S. ANTONIO

VIA PERGOLE

VIA TORINO

VIA LINCOLN

PIAZZA
G. CESARE

Stazione
Centrale

PIAZZA
GARIBALDI

C. D. MILLE

VIA ARCHIRAFI

arts to be seen anywhere. Basilican in form, it has three aisles divided by slightly pointed arches and a raised, apsidal sanctuary, the central bay of which is set off from the rest of the church by mosaic-encrusted transennae and crowned by a hemispherical dome. The upper walls of the aisles and sanctuary are decorated with magnificent gold-ground **mosaics** of Jewish and Muslim, as well as Christian inspiration; their overall theme is the Holy Spirit and the theology of light. Rivalled in beauty only by those of Ravenna and Istanbul, the mosaics are made of obliquely set tesserae that shimmer and shine as you move around the room. The earliest, in the east part of the chapel, date from 1140–50 and are thought to have been made by Byzantine Greeks. Their centrepiece is the huge *Christ in Benediction* in the dome of the sanctuary, surrounded by angels and archangels, prophets, saints, and evangelists. There are also a pleasing *Nativity* in the south apse, and a *Madonna with St John the Baptist* in the north apse. *Christ Pantocrator* (The Omnipotent) looks down from the semi-dome behind the altar, above an 18th-century composition of the *Virgin.*

The mosaics of the nave are somewhat later in date (c 1150–70) and are Italian rather than Greek in style. They represent the book of Genesis. The cycle begins in the upper tier of the south wall, next to the sanctuary, with the *Creation*; it ends in the lower tier of the north wall, with *Jacob Wrestling with the Angel.* In the aisles are scenes of unknown date from the lives of St Peter and St Paul, probably executed by local artists. The sequence begins at the east end of the south aisle with *Saul Leaving Jerusalem for Damascus* and ends at the east end of the north aisle, with the *Fall of Simon Magus.* A 15th-century mosaic of *Christ Enthroned between St Peter and St Paul* overlooks the recomposed Norman throne at the west end of the chapel.

Don't leave the Cappella Palatina without looking at the magnificent wooden **ceiling**, which features Arabic stalactite vaults painted with fanciful human figures, scenes of daily life, and Cufic inscriptions. Executed in 1143, this is one of the largest Muslim pictorial cycles in existence. Also noteworthy are the 10 antique granite and cippolino columns of the nave; the ambo, with its striped columns and delicate marble inlays; and the tall paschal candlestick, carved with figures and animals in an acanthus-leaf pattern. The pavement and lower part of the walls are made of white marble inlaid with red, green and gold patterns inspired by Muslim numerology. The wooden choir stalls are modern.

On the floor above are the Royal Apartments, which are usually (but not always) closed to the public. These include the Sala del Parlamento, where the Regional Assembly meets; the Sala dei Viceré, with portraits of Spanish viceroys and their deputies; and the magnificent **Sala di Re Ruggero**, with delightful 12th-century mosaics of plants and animals on the walls, arches and ceiling.

From the Palazzo dei Normanni, Via dei Benedettini leads southwards to

San Giovanni degli Eremiti (Map 14), a charming little church, now deconsecrated, set amid lush gardens. This is all that remains of what was once
the wealthiest monastery in Sicily. It is one of the earliest monuments of
Norman Palermo. Built by Roger II in 1132–48, it incorporates parts of an
earlier Arabic building, probably a mosque. Its distinctive red domes in
their frame of luxuriant palm trees, rose arbours and flowering jasmine, are
among the prettiest sights in Palermo.

A path leads up to the church, skirting the remains of the 13th-century
Benedictine cloister with small arches on twin columns. The aisleless **interior** is divided into two square bays surmounted by domes. The sanctuary,
with its semicircular apse, is flanked by two more apsidal rooms; the
campanile rises over the one on the north. From the one on the south you
enter the older, Arabic building, which is believed to date from the 10th or
11th century. This is a vaulted, rectangular hall flanked by an Arabic
portico, now ruined, and an open courtyard, formerly the court cemetery.
In the garden are remains of an Arabic cistern.

Now return to the Palazzo dei Normanni and turn right along the
southern edge of the wooded Villa Bonanno. At the southeast corner of the
square is one of Palermo's great 14th-century patrician palaces, **Palazzo
Sclafani**. This is a massive, fortress-like building, with dynamic interlacing
arches and black tufa inlays, elegant two-light windows and a fine portal
surmounted by an eagle. The palace was built for Matteo Sclafani in 1330,
but when his bloodline died out it passed into Spanish hands and was made
over as a hospital in 1435. It is at this time that the atrium was painted with
the famous fresco of the *Triumph of Death*, which was detached after World
War II and moved for safekeeping to the Galleria Regionale della Sicilia.
The palace now houses the Regional Military Command.

Continuing eastwards along Via dei Biscottari, you soon come to the
small square and church of Santa Chiara, at the centre of a quarter of
narrow, winding streets whose plan dates back to the Arab period. Perhaps
not by chance, the area is home to a large African community. Beyond the
square, on the right, is **Palazzo Speciale**, another handsome patrician residence erected in 1468 and rebuilt in the 17th and 18th centuries. It
preserves two-light windows and moulding from the original Catalan-
Gothic façade, to which the large doorway was added in the late 17th
century. Salita Raffadali, which is the continuation of Via dei Biscottari,
enters Piazza Bologni beyond the next cross-street; turn left.

This rectangular square was laid out in 1566 on a commission by the
prominent Bologna family, who had built their palace here. It was given its
Baroque appearance later, when the surrounding palaces were built.
Although they are all in poor repair today, they must have looked very
impressive when new. The 18th-century **Palazzo Ugo**, on the south side,
has a loggia over the entrance and marble statues by the Gagini school.
Palazzo Villafranca, on the west, has a long façade with two symmetrical
doorways and a large decorative stucco coat of arms; it was begun in the

17th century, on the site of the demolished Bologna palace, and remodelled in the mid-18th century. **Palazzo Belmonte-Riso**, across Corso Vittorio Emanuele to the north, was the crowning achievement of architect Venanzio Marvuglia; built in 1784, it was gutted by bombs in World War II and is still derelict. The statue of Charles V, by Scipione Li Volsi, was cast in 1630; if you have never heard of Scipione, now you know why.

Turn left in Corso Vittorio Emanuele and return towards the Palazzo dei Normanni. This part of the Corso, the main street of ancient Palermo, was known as the Cassaro Vecchio, a name derived from the Latin *castrum* or the Arabic *kasr* (both of which mean 'castle'). It was extended to the east in 1565 and prolonged to the sea in 1581. Bustling, noisy and badly in need of a facelift, it is lined with shops selling antiques, old books and assorted paraphernalia including *pupi* (see box page 49) and pieces of Sicilian farm carts. It's a good place to keep an eye out for souvenirs as you make your way up the hill.

The **Cathedral** of Santa Maria Assunta (Map 14), rises behind a garden encircled by balustrades adorned with statues of saints. It is a vast edifice of warm, golden stone whose layering of architectural styles faithfully reflects the history of the city. It stands on the site of an earlier church that was transformed into a mosque by the Arabs and again made into a place of Christian worship by the Normans. The present building was begun in 1185 by Palermo's English archbishop, Walter of the Mill (in Italian, Gualtiero Offamilio), when King William II challenged his authority by founding Monreale. Enlarged and altered in the 14th, 15th and 16th centuries, between 1781 and 1801 it was radically redesigned by the Neapolitan architect Ferdinando Fuga, who added the side aisles, the transept arms and the incongruous Neoclassical dome.

The main **façade**, on the narrow Via Matteo Bonnello, preserves its 13th- to 15th-century appearance. Flanked by two slender turrets, it has a 15th-century central portal surmounted by a two-light window and bearing the arms of the Aragonese kings and city senate at the top of its inner arches. The bronze doors, with Old and New Testament stories and episodes from local history, are modern. Two slender ogival arches cross over the street, joining the façade to the Norman tower of the Archbishop's Palace (now the campanile). A carved doorway of the mid-16th century has been incorporated in the 18th-century reconstruction of the north flank; walk all the way around this and you'll reach the striking **east end** of the church, enclosed by corner turrets like those of the façade and presenting three majestic apses with complex interlacing designs and brilliant intarsia work. These are the best-preserved remnants of the original 12th-century building.

The main entrance to the cathedral is now the exquisite Catalan-Gothic **south porch**, in Piazza della Cattedrale. It incorporates a column (on the left) from the earlier mosque, inscribed with a passage from the Koran. The elaborate portal was designed in 1426 by Antonio Gambara; its beautiful wooden doors were carved in 1432 by Francesco Miranda. The mosaic of the Virgin, above, probably dates from the earlier church.

After all the architectural excitement of the exterior, the **interior** of the cathedral is a major disappointment. Although Fuga was a very fine architect, this is one of his least imaginative creations – a sober Latin-cross arrangement with nave and aisles divided by piers incorporating slender granite columns from the earlier church. The first two chapels of the south aisle hold the Norman and Hohenstaufen **royal tombs**, originally located in the choir and now somewhat difficult to see. At the front left is the tomb of Frederick II (died 1250), which also contains the remains of Peter II of Aragon (died 1342); the similar tomb on the right holds the ashes of Henry VI (died 1197). At the back, beneath mosaic canopies, are the tombs of Roger II (died 1154) and his daughter Constance (died 1198), wife of Henry VI, with two porphyry sarcophagi brought from the cathedral of Cefalù. On the left is the sarcophagus of William (died 1338), son of Frederick III of Aragon; the Roman sarcophagus with hunting scenes, on the right, contains the body of Constance of Aragon (died 1222), wife of Emperor Frederick II. Frederick and Constance, incidentally, were wed in the cathedral; he was 14 at the time and she was 24.

In the nave are statues of *Saints* from a high altar by the Gagini family and a 16th-century holy-water stoup. The fourth south chapel holds an altarpiece by Pietro Novelli; the sixth, reliquary urns of saints of Palermo and the tomb slab of St Cosma (died 1160), used as an altar frontal. The seventh chapel on this side has a beautiful 18th-century marble altar. In the south transept are an altarpiece by Giuseppe Velasquez and a bas-relief of the *Dormition of the Virgin* by Antonello Gagini. The adjacent treasury contains the splendid 12th-century crown of Constance of Aragon. The sacristy has two fine portals by Vincenzo Gagini and in the inner sacristy, a *Madonna* by Antonello Gagini. The crypt (closed) contains archbishops' tombs and Roman sarcogphagi. In the chapel adjoining the choir is a 17th-century silver coffer containing the relics of Palermo's patron saint, Rosalia.

In the choir the statues of *Apostles* and *Christ* on the altar are fragments of Antonello Gagini's high altar, dismantled long ago; the Catalan-Gothic stalls date from 1466. Here too are the archbishop's throne and paschal candlestick, both 12th-century creations. The 14th-century wooden *Crucifix*, above the altar, was brought from the destroyed church of San Nicolò la Kalsa. In the chapel on the north of the choir are a 17th-century ciborium in lapis lazuli and the 18th-century funerary monument of Bishop Sanseverino. The north transept holds an early 14th-century wooden *Crucifix*, donated by Manfredi Chiaramonte, and a high relief with scenes from the *Passion of Christ* by Fazio and Vincenzo Gagini. The chapel next to the transept holds a statue of the *Madonna* by Francesco Laurana and his pupils. In the nave on this side is a stoup attributed to Domenico Gagini, of finer workmanship than the one opposite. The second north chapel has an *Assumption* and three reliefs by the Gagini, once part of the high altar.

The **Archbishop's Palace** (Map 14), across Via Bonello from the cathedral, was built in the 15th century by Archbishop Simone da Bologna. His family arms can be seen above the beautiful Catalan-Gothic doorway, one of the few original elements left untouched when the building was restored in the 18th century. Inside the palace is the Museo Diocesano, created in 1927 to preserve sculptures and architectural details from the cathedral and paintings and statues from area churches that had been deconsecrated or destroyed. Unfortunately it has been closed for years and shows no signs of reopening.

From the cathedral square take Via Bonello to Via Papireto and Piazzo Papireto. You are now in the heart of Palermo's colourful **flea market**, with ramshackle stalls selling just about everything you might ever need and a lot of things you might never imagine needing. A network of narrow streets leads eastwards from here to **Sant'Agostino** (Map 10). Its façade, erected in the early 14th century at the expense of the Sclafani and Chiaramonte families (who signed it with their devices), has a Gothic portal inlaid with lava and a fine rose window. The 15th-century doorway on the south side, half-hidden behind the stalls of the lively street-market, is attributed to Domenico Gagini; in the porch are a late Roman sarcophagus and a 16th-century holy-water stoup. The tall, aisleless interior, completely rebuilt in 1671, has gilded stucco decoration by Giacomo Serpotta and his assistants, dating from 1711–29. The church is adjoined by a lovely 16th-century garden cloister.

Via Sant'Agostino continues eastwards to the busy Via Maqueda. You turn left and follow Via Maqueda to the Teatro Massimo, one of the focal points (the other is the Teatro Politeama) around which the 19th-century city developed. Turn right in front of the theatre to reach the first of Palermo's world-class museums, the **Museo Archeologico Regionale** (Map 11).

This excellent museum, in a former convent with two charming 17th-century cloisters, holds one of Italy's more important collections of antiquities. Since its formation in the 19th century, its basic collection has been supplemented by acquisitions – including the Casuccini Collection of Etruscan antiquities, the largest of its kind outside Tuscany – and by finds from excavations in the western part of the island, notably those of Selinunte. Today visitors to the museum can follow the history of western Sicily from prehistoric times to the Roman era and gain insight into developments elsewhere in Italy.

Around the Small Cloister are rooms devoted to underwater archaeology and Egyptian and Punic sculpture. The handsome garden of the Large Cloister has Roman fragments beneath the arcades and in the niches. The rooms at the far end contain finds from Selinunte and Himera. The highlights here are the magnificent *Lion-Head Water Spouts* from the Doric Temple of Victory at Himera, dating from the 5th century BC, and the large *Metopes of Selinunte*, a series of extraordinary beauty and the museum's most important treasure. These panels from the temple friezes date from the early 6th to the late 5th century BC and document the transition from the (abstract) Archaic to the (naturalistic) Classical style of Greek sculpture. In the same room is the lovely and mysterious 5th-century BC bronze *Ephebe of Selinunte*, found in a tomb in 1882. The following four rooms hold the Casuccini Collection of Etruscan Antiquities, whose *pièce de résistance* is the formidable *Wine Jug* of bucchero ware bearing the story of Perseus and Medusa, considered by some to be the finest vase of its kind in existence. It dates from the 6th century BC. There are also several beautiful terracotta and alabaster cinerary urns carved with the effigies of the deceased.

Stairs lead up from the Small Cloister to the first floor and the long North Gallery, displaying finds from Greek and Roman sites in western Sicily. These exhibits continue in the end rooms. The long South Gallery contains a few of the 12,000 terracotta votive figures found in the Sanctuary of Demeter at Selinunte; the West Gallery displays recent finds from sites in and around Palermo. The next room contains another of the museum's treasures, the famous *Bronze Ram of Syracuse*. This is a superb sculpture dating from the 3rd century BC, probably modelled on an original by the famous 4th-century sculptor Lysippus. It was formerly one of a pair (the second ram was destroyed in the 19th century). In the next room, devoted to Greek sculpture, you can see a series of beautiful 5th-century reliefs and stelae. After these, the Roman sculpture and fragments in the following rooms seem commonplace.

The second-floor galleries contain Greek ceramics, Roman mosaics and frescoes, Italiot ceramics, and prehistoric and Early Bronze Age material. Highlights here include some magnificent proto-Corinthian, Corinthian and Attic vases, casts of Palaeolithic graffiti of hooded figures and animals from Addaura, on the outskirts of the city, and the bones of elephants, rhinoceros and hippopotami found beneath the streets of Palermo.

Palermo by the Sea

This walk begins where the first ends, winding seaward through the quarters of old Palermo that developed around the great 16th-century thoroughfares of the Cassaro and Via Maqueda. These main streets cross at the intersection known as the Quatttro Canti di Città, forming four distinct neighbourhoods – the Kalsa (southeast), Amalfitani (northeast), Sincaldi (northwest) and Albergheria (southwest).

Most of your time will be spent in the Kalsa (from the Arabic *khalisa*, 'pure'), the Saracen citadel which grew up by the harbour. In the 9th and 10th centuries this was the walled residence of the emir and his ministers. Later it became an elegant 'gate community' for merchants and nobles. At one point even the Spanish viceroys abandoned the Royal Palace for the choicest morsel of Kalsa real estate, the former family palace of the Chiaramonte. Today this area of the city is decidedly down at heel, having been hit hard by World War II bombs (there are still vast areas strewn with debris) and more recently by the flight of so many Palermitans (four out of five, to be exact) from the old buildings of the city centre to new surburban tower blocks. Walking the badly lit, badly signposted streets after dark is not a good idea; but during the day you should have no problem. Indeed, the area bustles with colourful street markets, and its sights are among the city's finest. Walking time again is about three hours.

The busy Via Roma leads southwards from the Museo Archeologico to **San Domenico** (Map 11), one of Palermo's most renowned Baroque monuments. Its immense, theatrical façade, adorned with stucco statues and flanked by tall bell towers, is preceded by Giovanni d'Amico's equally lofty Colonna dell'Immacolata (1724–27). Founded in 1300 and enlarged in 1458, it was entirely rebuilt in 1640 to plans by Andrea Cirincione. The façade was added in 1726 by Tommaso Maria Napoli, after the new square had been torn out of the fabric of medieval Palermo. Since the mid-19th century, San Domenico has been the burial place of distinguished Sicilians, a role that has won it the nickname: 'Pantheon of Palermo'. The vast Latin-cross interior, with three aisles on robust columns, holds works by Antonello Gagini and his school, notably a statue of *St Joseph* in the third south chapel.

Behind the church, in Via dei Bambinai, is a fine example of the private chapels of Palermo's lay confraternities, the **Oratorio del Rosario di San Domenico**. If it's closed, you can find the custodian at the shop at Via dei Bambinai 16. The interior is a masterpiece of Sicilian decorative art. All around are stuccoes and allegorical statues, cherubs and reliefs by Giacomo Serpotta (a *sirpuzza* or lizard, the artist's trademark, appears on the column of the figure of *Fortitude*). Men, women and children look down from the small dome above the altar; the walls are hung with *Mysteries* painted by Pietro Novelli, Giacomo Lo Verde, Matthias Stomer and Luca Giordano; and the ceiling vault bears a *Crowning of the Virgin* by Pietro Novelli. Over the altar is a magnificent altarpiece of the *Virgin of the Rosary with St Dominic and the Patronesses of Palermo*, by Antony Van Dyck, commissioned in 1624 in Palermo and completed in 1628 in Genoa, where the artist fled to escape the plague.

A few blocks north is the 16th-century church of Santa Zita (or Santa Cita), badly damaged in the war but preserving some fine sculptures by Antonio Gagini. You can gloss over this, but don't miss the **Oratory of Santa Zita** (Map 11), behind the church (reached by Via Valverde). Its interior is among the best of Serpotta's works (if closed, apply in the church). It is entirely covered with magnificent stuccoes executed in stages between 1685 and 1717. Here you will find allegorical statues, lively cherubs, New Testament stories and small representations of the Mysteries of the Rosary. The most astounding work is the *Battle of Lepanto* on the entrance wall, a flamboyant battle trophy teeming with arms, armour and flying putti. The altarpiece of the *Virgin of the Rosary* (1702) is by Carlo Maratta. The benches, with their delicate mother-of-pearl inlays, were for the confraternity brothers.

From Santa Zita Via Squarcialupo continues down to the fine Renaissance church of **San Giorgio dei Genovesi** (Map 8; deconsecrated, now open only for exhibitions), built by Giorgio de Facio for Palermo's Genoese community in 1576–91. Its pleasant façade and lovely aisled interior are among the finest works of Renaissance architecture in the city. The paintings, attributed to Luca Giordano, Bernardo Castello of Genoa and Palma Giovane, were donated by Genoese merchants, whose marble tombstones pave the floor.

Now return along Via dei Bambinai and its continuations through the colourful **Vucciria market**, where fish and produce are sold from stalls in the street. Cross over Corso Vittorio Emanuele and pick up the narrow, winding Via Paternostro. **San Francesco d'Assisi** (Map 12), the church of the Franciscan Order, stands near the centre of what was once the merchant quarter. The present church is the third to stand on this site. It was built in 1255–77, though work has continued practically to the present day. Giacomo Serpotta adorned the interior with his exuberant stuccoes in the 18th century, but these were destroyed in the 1823 earthquake. Afterwards, the church was remodelled along Neoclassical lines; but this interior, too, was destroyed in 1943, and the church was restored to its original 13th-century forms. The façade has a beautiful Gothic portal of 1302, with a shallow porch and zigzag ornamentation; the frescoes in the pediment are modern. The Renaissance portals of the aisles date from the late 16th century; the elaborate rose window is a reconstruction based on that of Sant'Agostino.

The austere Franciscan **interior** has three aisles on cylindrical piers and broad Gothic arches. Eight statues by Serpotta decorate the nave. In the south aisle, above the door, is a beautifully carved arch of 1465; in the second chapel are an altarpiece of *St George and the Dragon* and carved roundels by Antonello Gagini. The *Madonna* in the third south chapel is attributed to Antonio Gagini; the Gothic fourth chapel contains a fine 15th-century Madonna by a Catalan sculptor and the sarcophagus of Elisabetta Omodei (1498), attributed to Domenico Gagini. The altar frontal and bas-reliefs of the sixth chapel were carved by Ignazio Marabitti. The Chapel of the Immaculate Conception, south of the sanctuary, has marble intarsia decoration of the 17th–18th century and eight statues of Sicilian saints by Giovanni Battista Ragusa (1717). The mosaic altarpiece was designed by Vito d'Anna. Fine carved and inlaid stalls (1520) grace the choir.

The four statuettes of Virtues in the north aisle are attributed to Pietro da Bonitate; by the door into the sacristy is a tomb effigy of the young soldier Antonio Speciale attributed to Domenico Gagini (1477). The fourth chapel, the magnificent **Cappella Mastrantonio**, was designed in 1468 by

Francesco Laurana and Pietro da Bonitate; the beautifully carved arch is the earliest and one of the best Renaissance works in Sicily. The first chapel on this side has a fine 16th-century doorway and a *Madonna and Child with St John*, by Domenico Gagini. The substantial treasury has an interesting collection of paintings and furnishings from the 15th–19th centuries.

To the left of the church is the **Oratorio di San Lorenzo** (Map 12; entrance at Via Immacolatella 5; if closed, apply to the custodian of San Francesco), built after 1569 by the Compagnia di San Francesco. The stuccoes of the interior are considered the masterpiece of Giacomo Serpotta's late career (1699–1707). Ten symbolic statues, eight spirited little reliefs telling the stories of St Francis and St Lawrence and a large tableau with the *Martyrdom of St Lawrence* on the end wall, are accompanied by playful cherubs everywhere, making an ensemble of great grace and charm. Around the walls are beautiful 18th-century mahogany and mother-of-pearl benches on carved supports. Caravaggio's large painting of the *Nativity with St Francis and St Lawrence* hung over the altar from 1609 until it was stolen in 1969.

A couple of blocks southeast of San Francesco, at Via Merlo 2, stands the 18th-century **Palazzo Mirto**. Once the residence of the Lanza-Filangeri family, it is now an interesting house-museum. The handsome interiors are furnished with 18th- and 19th-century antiques, Capodimonte porcelain and Murano glass, and include a little sitting room decorated in the Chinese style fashionable in the 18th century. In the stables are the funerary stelae of Giambattista and Elisabetta Mellerio, carved by Antonio Canova around 1820 and purchased by the Region of Sicily in 1978.

Via Mirto ends on Piazza Marina, a shallow inlet of the sea reclaimed by the Arabs in the 10th century. Here the Aragonese held public ceremonies and the Inquisition public executions. The centre is occupied by the beautiful **Giardino Garibaldi**, planted with palms, fig-trees and enormous banyans. The latter are among Palermo's many botanical wonders; there are more in the Orto Botanico (described below).

The east side of the square is dominated by the massive **Palazzo Chiaramonte**, also called **Palazzo Steri** (from *hosterium*, 'fortified palace'). This was home to the most powerful Sicilian feudal family of the 14th century, whose influence rivalled that of the Crown itself and whose last descendant, Andrea, was beheaded in front of the palace in 1396 for rebelling against King Martin I of Aragon. Square in plan with a central courtyard, it was begun in 1307 and completed in 1380. The exterior has lost its battlements but preserves the severe lines of the original design. Oddly enough, this fortress-like palace gave its name to the graceful Chiaramonte style in architecture – best exemplified, perhaps, by the triple-light windows with finely carved roundels, small slender columns, delicate capitals, and characteristic zigzag motifs, in the inner courtyard. In the mid-15th century the palace became the residence of Sicily's viceroys. From 1605 to 1782 it was the seat of the Inquisition (whose victims have left a record of their persecution on the dungeon walls), and from 1799 to 1960 it housed the civil law courts. It was restored in 1984 for the University Rector and is opened to the public from time to time for exhibitions or concerts. If you're lucky enough to get in, take a look at the painted wood ceiling of the Sala Maggiore, on the first floor. It was made in 1377–80 by Simone da Corleone and Cecco di Naro, who took their cue from the ceiling of the Cappella Palatina.

Sicilian Puppets

Sicilian puppets have a specific trait that distinguishes them from other marionettes. The Sicilian *paladini* (paladins), also called *pupi armati* (armed puppets) by virtue of their elaborate shining armour, have a metal staff instead of a string to guide their right hand. This makes it possible for them to fight with particular strength and fury, and to draw and sheathe their swords with surprising skill. The *pupi* appeared on the stages of Sicilian puppet theatres between 1850 and 1860, and the interpretations advanced by the first scholars of popular art link their origins to the persistence on the island of old legends of chivalry – and especially of Charlemagne and his court (the paladins were his knights). In reality, puppet theatre had gained enormous popularity elsewhere in Italy – above all in Rome and Naples – in the early 19th century, and it is probable that the first *opere dei pupi* grew out of Neapolitan puppet shows that travelled to Sicily, and particularly to Catania.

Pupi are the fruit of a painstaking collaboration among craftsmen. The blacksmith and tinsmith fashion the armour, and the sculptor carves the head to traditional figurative canons. But it is the puparo (puppeteer) who establishes the stylistic characteristics beforehand.

Important stylistic and technical differences distinguish the *pupi* of Palermo from those of Catania. The Catanese *pupi* are around 1.5m tall and weigh, on the average, 35kg; their Palermitan counter-parts are just under a metre tall. The sword of the Catanese *pupi* is screwed to the right hand; greaves cover the front part of the legs, but the elbow and knee joints are exposed (the Palermitan *pupi* have elbow and knee plates); the shields tend to be round. The Palermitan *pupi* have particularly elaborate body armour and helmets, movable visors, and insignia embossed on their armour. All *pupi* are dressed, anachronistically, in the battle costumes of 16th-century Italy.

The Turks have no armour, their uniforms are less elaborate and they generally carry a roundish shield – never the triangular one typical of the crusaders. The female figures are cast in demure, dignified attitudes which in no way reflect the warlike appearance of their male counterparts. The leading paladins, in contrast, are strongly characterised: Carlo Magno (Charlemagne) is stern, with long hair and white beard; Orlando (Roland) is cross-eyed; Rinaldo, sly and scornful; Gano di Magonza, grim and sometimes scarred. The show, called *opera dei pupi* or *opra* takes place in special theatres, which in Catania seat about 100, in Palermo 30–40 viewers.

Set back somewhat from the west side of the square is the **Museo Internazionale delle Marionette** (Map 12). This unusual museum possesses more than 3000 displays from the world of puppet theatre, including marionettes, puppets, shadow-play figures, stage equipment and bills. There are *pupi* from Palermo, Catania and Naples; marionettes and puppets from Northern Italy, Spain, France, Burma, India, China and Brazil; Belgian puppets; Indian, Turkish, Greek, Balinese, Malaysian, Thai and Cambodian shadow figures; and stick marionettes from Java and Mali. Regular performances are held in the small theatre, and in spring and autumn the museum sponsors the *Festival di Morgana*, with puppet shows from around the world.

Opposite the museum is the 17th-century Palazzo Branciforti di Butera, where Goethe stayed while in Palermo; and next to it, the former Alberto Trinacria, where Giuseppe di Lampedusa set the death of his hero, Don Fabrizio, in *The Leopard*.

If you have time, walk out of the square from the northeast to the waterfront church of **Santa Maria della Catena** (Map 12), which takes its name from the chain (*catena* in Italian) that was drawn across the old harbour at night. Built in the early 16th century to a design attributed to Matteo Carnelivari, it sublimely mixes Catalan-Gothic and Renaissance elements. Beneath the portico with its fine basket-handle arches are three Classical doorways with low reliefs by Vincenzo Gagini. The three-aisled interior, with slender Renaissance columns, has ribbed vaults in the nave and barrel vaults in the aisles.

From the south corner of Palazzo Chiaramonte, Via Quattro Aprile leads southeast to the narrow Via Alloro and the flank of **La Gancia** (Map 12; Santa Maria degli Angeli), a 15th-century church containing works by Antonello Gagini, Pietro Novelli and Giacomo Serpotta. Turning left here, you immediately come to **Palazzo Abatellis**. This palace was built in 1488–95 by Matteo Carnelivari as the residence of harbourmaster and chief magistrate Francesco Abatellis. Its exposed-stone construction and compact architecture combine late Catalan-Gothic and early Renaissance elements (notice especially the ornate two- and three-light windows with their slender little columns). Severely damaged in World War II, it was restored and adapted in 1954 by Carlo Scarpa to house the **Galleria Regionale della**

Sicilia, the second of Palermo's three great museums. Scarpa is one of postwar Italy's most eminent architects (his special flair for museum design can be seen also at the Fondazione Querini-Stampalia in Venice and the Museo del Castelnuovo in Verona), and this is one of his finest creations, displaying beautifully arranged and well-labelled collections of Sicilian sculpture and painting, particularly of the 14th–16th centuries.

The atrium and graceful courtyard hold sculptures from pre-Romanesque times to the 16th century. In the ground-floor rooms are 12th- to 16th-century wood and 14th- and 15th-century stone sculptures. The former chapel (Room 2) houses the large fresco of the *Triumph of Death* detached from Palazzo Sclafani. Dating from the mid-15th century, this is thought by some scholars to be the work of the Northern Italian painter Antonio Pisanello or his school. Death is shown as an archer on a ghostly horse, cutting down the wealthy and powerful (right) with his arrows, while the poor, crippled and aged (left), among whom are the artist and his patron, pray for release. Beyond this are displays from Arab Sicily and sections devoted to sculptor Francesco Laurana (his 1471 masterpiece, the *Bust of Eleonora of Aragon*, is in Room 4) and the Gagini and their school.

The first-floor rooms are devoted to Sicilian painting from the early Middle Ages to the 16th century. The highlight here is Room 6, with works by Antonello da Messina, including his *Virgin Annunciate* and *St Gregory*, *St Augustine* and *St Jerome*. Antonello's *Virgin*, painted in 1476 after his return from Venice to Messina, is a masterpiece of composed, almost mystical luminosity. Also in this section is the extraordinarily detailed *Malvagna Triptych* by Jan Gossaert (1510), showing the Virgin and Child with Saints Catherine and Barbara on one side, and Adam and Eve on the other. It hangs among the Flemish paintings in Room 9.

At the end of Via Alloro is the 17th-century Baroque church of **La Pietà** (Map 12), by Giacomo Amato, with a splendid façade inspired by Rome's Sant'Andrea della Valle. The beautiful vestibule has stuccoes by Procopio Serpotta and paintings by the Flemish artist Guglielmo Borremans. Within are a fine nuns' choir, at the west end, and four gilded wood cantorie in the nave. The fresco in the vault, a *trompe-l'oeil* composition showing the *Glory of the Dominicans*, is by Antonio Grano (1708). From here, Via Torremuzza and its continuation, Via Cervello, lead southeast past another church by Amato, **Santa Teresa** (with stuccoes and statues by Procopio Serpotta and his father Giacomo, and more paintings by Borremans) to the 18th-century Porta Reale.

Across busy Via Lincoln from here is the **Villa Giulia** or Villa Flora (Map 16), a magnificent formal garden designed in 1777 by Nicola Palma and enlarged and embellished in the late 19th century. It is named after Donna Giulia, the wife of the Spanish viceroy who sponsored its construction, and is the city's first public garden. Laid out on a geometric design of interlacing crosses, it has four Neoclassical exedrae in the Pompeian style and a sundial fountain in the centre. Along the pathways are busts of illustrious Palermitans, and on the seaward side there is a curious statue of the *Genius of Palermo* by Marabitti. Goethe admired the garden's lovely trees and flowers during his visit in 1787. 'It is the most wonderful spot on earth,' he wrote. 'Though laid out formally and not very old, it seems enchanted and transports one back into the antique world. Green borders surround exotic plants, espaliers of lemon trees form gracefully arched walks, high hedges of oleander, covered with thousands of red blossoms which resemble carnations, fascinate the eye. Strange trees, probaby from warmer climes, for they are still without leaves, spread out their peculiar ramifications.' From April to September the garden hosts concerts still financed by a bequest from the music-loving Prince of Paternò in the 1700s.

Adjoining the Villa Giulia on the southwest and linked to it by its design is the **Orto Botanico**, one of the finest botanical gardens in Europe. It was laid out in 1785 on a design by Léon Dufourny and Venanzio Marvuglia and opened to the public some 10 years later. It is famous for its huge collection of rare tropical plants. The main attraction is the century-old *ficus magnolioides* (similar to a baobab), but there are also beautiful palms, lotus trees and bamboos. Dufourny's square, central *Ginnasio*, with its Greek Doric porches, contains the herbarium and library.

Via Lincoln now leads southwest towards the Central Station. Cross over and pass beneath Porta Castrofilippo to reach the large, rubble-strewn Piazza dello Spasimo, devastated by bombs in World War II and still awaiting reconstruction. On its fringes are two interesting churches. **Santa Maria dello Spasimo** (Map 16; 1506), roofless with a lovely garden, is now used for musical and theatrical performances. This is the church for which Raphael painted his *Jesus Falling beneath the Cross* ('Lo Spasimo di Sicilia') now in the Prado in Madrid. **La Magione** is a handsome building standing alone to the west. It was founded before 1151 by Matteo d'Ajello, coun-sellor to regent Margaret of Navarre, as a Cistercian church dedicated to the Holy Trinity. In 1193 it was awarded to the Teutonic Knights as their 'mansion' (in dialect, *magione*). It is a wonderful example of Arab-Norman architecture, with three very unusual doorways and a beautiful tall apse bearing delicate blind arcading. The harmonious interior has a 14th-century stone altar topped by a painted *Crucifix*; Gagini-school statues of *Christ* and the *Madonna and Child*, a 15th-century marble triptych, and a tabernacle of 1528. The custodian shows the charming little garden cloister, with twin columns and carved capitals, and a room containing a detached 15th-century fresco of the *Crucifixion* with its sinopia. The potted palms at the base of the columns offer a delicate counterpoint to those in the delightful garden outside.

A monumental 17th-century gateway admits to Via Magione, which you follow to Via Garibaldi, a run-down street once lined with handsome palaces. The grandest of these, on the right, is **Palazzo Ajutamicristo** (Map 16), built by Matteo Carnelivari in 1490–95. The building's exposed-stone architecture, like that of Palazzo Abatellis, combines late Catalan-Gothic and Renaissance forms. Initially designed for Guglielmo Ajutamicristo, the palace passed a century later to the Moncada di Paternò, who planted the magnificent garden. Today it is privately owned, but you can wander into the courtyard without causing a fuss. From the doorway at Via Garibaldi 23 you cross a first court, then proceed left to the beautiful main courtyard with its magnificent portico of basket-handle arches on columns and its ogival-arched loggia with rondels and lozenges in the pendentives. Beneath the portico are ogival- and round-arched doorways and remains of twin-light mullioned windows.

Via Garibaldi continues northwest to the picturesque Piazza della Rivoluzione, traditionally the centre of a desperately poor area, with a busy market. All three revolts against the Bourbons were begun here – in 1820, 1848 and 1860. You leave the square by Via Divisi, which bears left across Via Roma to Via Maqueda. The building on your left here is **Palazzo Santa Croce-Sant'Elia** (Map 15), one of the most beautiful Palermitan Baroque palaces, built in the mid-18th century. It has large windows with wrought-iron balconies and a fine courtyard. Across the street, on the north corner, is Palazzo Comitini, another sumptuous 18th-century mansion.

Skirt the latter's left flank, then bear north through winding streets to reach the **Chiesa del Gesù**, or church of the Casa Professa, the first church built by the Jesuits in Sicily. Begun in 1564, it was enlarged and reworked in the 17th and 18th centuries. The three-aisled Latin-cross interior, with deep intercommunicating chapels, apsidal transept and sanctuary, and lofty dome, is a magnificent example of Sicilian Baroque architecture. It bears a rich mantle of colourful marble intarsias, stucco reliefs, sculptures and paintings, executed over some two centuries. The only parts of the original pictorial decoration that remain are the frescoes in the first bay of the nave vault, by Filippo Randazzo (1743), and those of the sanctuary vault; the others are modern imitations. The second south chapel has paintings of two *Saints* by Pietro Novelli, and the fourth chapel has a statue of the *Madonna* by the Gagini school. The sanctuary and apse preserve original sculptures by Gioacchino Vitaliano. The Cappella di Sant'Anna, north of the sanctuary, is entirely faced with fine marbles.

Beside the church is the west front of the Jesuit monastery, the **Casa Professa**, with a beautiful doorway of 1685 and an elegant 17th-century columned cloister. Through the latter you can enter the Biblioteca Comunale (Municipal Library), founded in 1760 and transferred here in 1775, eight years after the expulsion of the Jesuits from the kingdom. It has 250,000 volumes and more than 1000 incunabula and manuscripts. The area to the south, the Quartiere dell'Albergheria, is one of the poorest in the city.

Now follow the winding Via Ponticello back to Via Maqueda and turn left. On Piazza Bellini (Map 15), high up in a garden above an old Roman wall,

Agave at the Orto Botanico, Palermo

stand two of Palermo's finest Norman churches. The larger of these, **La Martorana** (Map 15), officially Santa Maria dell'Ammiraglio, was founded in the first half of the 12th century by George of Antioch, the commander of Roger I's navy. Some three centuries later it was given by King Alfonso of Aragon to a Benedictine convent established by Eloisa Martorana (whose kitchen gave us the marzipan fruits, *frutti alla martorana*, which still grace the windows of Sicilian pastry shops), from which it takes its more familiar name. Since 1935 it has shared cathedral status with San Demetrio at Piana degli Albanesi, and if you are lucky you will run into a colourful Albanian wedding, celebrated according to the Greek Catholic rite.

This precious little church has been altered countless times over the centuries, and modern restorations have only partly freed it of later accretions. On the exterior, the Norman structure can be seen in details such as the blind arcading and, of course, the hemispherical dome. The Baroque façade is a 16th-century addition. The present entrance is beneath the splendid 12th-century campanile, which survived the alterations more or less intact. Its decoration of Arabic lava inlays is especially fine; the ogival arches with corner columns and three orders of large twin-light windows were once crowned by a small red dome, now long gone.

The **interior** was originally made up of a square, apsidal space divided to form a Greek cross by the columns bearing the dome. This central plan can still be detected, despite the 16th-century prolongation of the nave and aisles (made by demolishing the Norman narthex and enclosing the atrium) and the 17th-century extension of the chancel. The Baroque marble and frescoes that cover the west end of the church, intricate as they are, are no match for the original mosaic decoration, the overall impression of which is breathtaking. The mosaics, concentrated on and around the cupola, date from the first half of the 12th century. Together with those of the Cappella Palatina, they are the oldest medieval mosaics in Sicily. The iconographic scheme and the distribution of the scenes reflect Byzantine Greek canons; even the style, notwithstanding the diversity of the various hands, suggests the mosaics were made by Greek craftsmen. In the dome is *Christ* surrounded by *Angels, Prophets* and *Evangelists* (the Arabic lettering is a quotation from a Byzantine hymn); on the triumphal arch, the *Annunciation*; in the south apse, *St Anne*; in the north apse, *St Joachim*; in the side vaults, four *Evangelists*, the *Nativity* and the *Dormition of the Virgin*. At the west end are two more original mosaic panels (restored and set in Baroque frames), from the destroyed atrium: to the left, *George of Antioch at the Feet of the Virgin*; to the right, *King Roger Crowned by Christ*. Also here are 18th-century frescoes by the Flemish painter Borremans and a 12th-century carved wooden door, of Arabic workmanship. Vincenzo da Pavia's 1533 *Ascension* stands above the main altar. The transennae in front of the apses, and the mosaic pavement, both survive from the Norman church.

On the same high ground as the Martorana is the **Cappella di San Cataldo**, built around 1160 for Maio of Bari, William I's admiral and chancellor. It preserves its clear-cut Norman form and decoration, including a crenellated moulding at the top of the exposed-stone walls. The number three is important in its design: the tripartite façade is pierced by three single-light lattice windows, and the distinctive roof culminates in three small red domes on tall drums. The interior (ask the custodian of the Martorana for the key) is particularly evocative: it is a simple rectangle divided into three aisles by pointed Arabic arches springing from antique columns with beautiful capitals. At the east end are three small apses, and the nave is crowned by the three small domes. The mosaic pavement is original, as are the altar with its carved cross, lamb and Evangelist symbols. Because of Maio's early death (in a plot by Norman nobles to overthrow William I, in 1160), the bare walls were never decorated. Today the church is the seat of the Order of the Knights of the Holy Sepulchre.

The third church on this square, **Santa Caterina** (Map 11), was part of the huge Dominican monastery that occupies the entire block behind it. Founded in the early 14th century, its late-Renaissance façade and soaring cupola date from a reconstruction of 1580–96. A magnificent decorative mantle of coloured-marble inlay, frescoes, sculpture and altarpieces covers the aisleless interior, which unfortunately is usually closed. If you do manage to get in, glance up at the 18th-century *trompe-l'oeil* frescoes in the cupola, by Vito d'Anna; Antonello Gaggini's 16th-century statue of *St Catherine* stands in the right transept.

Follow the flank of the church northwards and you'll immediately come to Piazza Pretoria (Map 11) so called because it is overlooked by the main front of the Palazzo Senatorio, or Pretorio, the traditional seat of the city's leaders. Founded in 1300 but erected in its present form in 1470, it has a monumental front adorned with a statue of Santa Rosalia and marble eagles here and there, from which it takes its familiar name, **Palazzo delle Aquile**.

At the centre of this square is the **Fontana Pretoria**, the largest fountain in Palermo. It was designed in the mid-16th century by the Florentine Renaissance sculptors Francesco Camilliani and Michelangelo Naccherino for the Tuscan villa of Don Pedro di Toledo, the Spanish viceroy of Naples whose daughter Eleonora married Grand Duke Cosimo de' Medici of Florence. Don Pedro died before the fountain could be installed in his garden, and his heirs sold its 644 marble components to the Palermitan senate for hard cash.

The circular design has two levels joined by four flights of steps, each of which is guarded by rough-carved statues. On the first level are several marble basins: small ones at each staircase, a large one half way between staircases. Crowning the large basins are four marble groups representing the rivers of Sicily, and at the beginning and end of each staircase are four statues of mythological subjects: Bacchus and Hercules, Diana and Apollo, Venus and Adonis, Pomona and Mercury, and so on. All together, there are 16 figures at the sides of the steps. Between one flight of steps and another, at the top, are basins surmounted by niches from which horses, lions, camels, elephants and other animals look out. Within this circular menagerie, one is rather surprised to encounter the fountain proper, embellished by three smaller basins with statues and topped by a shield-bearing putto on a marble stele. The sculptures are traditionally considered so beautiful and the rendering of their nude flesh so voluptuous that the square is known to Palermitans as the *Piazza della Vergogna* (Place of Shame).

Just a few steps away from Piazza Pretoria is the busy intersection of Via Maqueda and Corso Vittorio Emanuele, officially called Piazza Viglieda after the viceroy who conceived it, but better known as the **Quattro Canti di Città** (Map 11). The crossroads was the symbolic centrepiece of the town-planning project which, in the early years of the 17th century, gave Palermo a new lease of life. This project had two goals: to create a new boulevard at right angles to the old Cassaro in order to facilitate circulation of traffic (already hectic at the time), and to create an important meeting point for the city's populace. Under the direction of royal architect Giulio Lasso, the existing town fabric was torn to shreds to build Via Maqueda and this monumental intersection, where the four quarters of the new city came together. The areas that flanked the new street and square were assigned by the viceroy to the nobles, who built luxurious palaces all around, and to the clergy, who here erected more churches and convents.

The concave façades of the Quattro Canti present an elaborate ensemble of balconies, cornices, windows and niches adorned with statues. On the lower level are the Four Seasons with fountains; on the second, the Spanish sovereigns Philip II, III and IV and Charles V; at the top, Palermo's four patronesses, Cristina, Ninfa, Oliva and Agata. In the attic level is the royal escutcheon, flanked by those of the viceroy and the senate. Before the advent of the car these grimy grey walls were a soft buff colour, and right up to World War II the evening promenade came to a halt here, to permit discussions of politics or negotiations between jobless servants and their prospective masters.

Adjoining the southernmost of the Quattro Canti is the great church of **San Giuseppe dei Teatini** (Map 11/15). Legend has it that when the Theatines were granted this ground the jealous Jesuits challenged the decision and did everything they could to have it changed, claiming among other things that part of the land in question was their property. But the Theatines appealed to the viceroy and won out in the end. Their church, begun in 1612 to a design by Giacomo Besio, is among the most splendid Baroque buildings in the city. Its construction took just 33 years, but its decoration required nearly two centuries of constant work. The imposing interior has three aisles divided by 14 monolithic marble columns, a soaring dome on eight colossal twin columns, and small domes along the aisles. Here you can see magnificent holy-water stoups by Marabitti in the nave; stuccoes by Paolo Corso, and frescoes by Filippo Tancredi in the vault; and frescoes by Borremans in the cupola and by Valasquez in the pendentives. The reliefs of the choir ceiling are the work of Procopio Serpotta, and the *Crucifix* in the chapel flanking the choir on the right is by Fra' Umile da Petralìa. In place of a crypt, this upper church stands over an earlier and smaller church, the Madonna della Provvidenza.

The Conca d'Oro

Conca d'Oro, the 'Golden Vale', is the name given to Palermo's hinterland, a broad plain rimmed by limestone hills. Different historical events have shaped its northern, western and southern reaches.

The fertile Piana dei Colli, north of the city, was long a realm of peasant farmers. In the 17th and 18th centuries it was invaded by the Palermitan aristocracy, who here first discovered the pleasure of holidays spent amid the luxuriant greenery of parks and gardens. Around their villas grew up rural settlements that eventually blossomed into populous suburban villages. The construction in 1799 of the royal park of La Favorita, the opening in the late 19th century of Viale della Libertà and the early 20th-century development of the élite beach resort at Mondello, destroyed the area's agrarian character, so that habitation is now continuous all the way north to the land's end at Cape Gallo.

The area west of Palermo has been inhabited since antiquity, but its finest hour came under the Arabs, who transformed its fertile hills and valleys into a vast garden scattered with fragrant fruit orchards and luxurious palaces. It remained a place of delights under the Normans, who in the 12th century turned it into a large hunting reserve studded with lush parks and opulent pleasure palaces, and invited the Benedictines to found convents at Monreale, Castellaccio and Baida in the hills. During the 16th century the western Conca d'Oro fell victim to the same rush of villa-building as the Piana dei Colli, as Palermitan landowners transformed their farms into seasonal residences, covering the entire plain with a tight network of patrician summer houses. After World War II the city grew in this direction too, smothering the area's extraordinary natural and architectural heritage in chaotic suburban sprawl.

The eastern district is a fertile valley traversed by the River Eleutero and enclosed on the east by Monte Catalfano, on whose seaward slopes the Carthaginian settlement of Solunto developed. In this case one trend-setting aristocrat – the Prince of Butera, who built a summer house in the hills here in 1658 – was all it took to convince Palermitan high society to erect the most lavish villas of the Baroque age in the environs. In the mid-18th century the village of Bagheria was born, and in the subsequent decades its intense and uncontrolled development all but overwhelmed the surrounding farms and their elegant manors. In recent years an unending string of holiday estates has assailed the coast, all but erasing the remaining traces of scenic beauty.

North of Palermo

Palermo's most elegant residential quarter, which developed in the late 19th century along Via della Libertà, meets the Conca d'Oro at **La Favorita** (off the map), a beautiful large park at the foot of Monte Pellegrino. The park was laid out by Ferdinand II of Bourbon in 1799, when he and his court fled Naples for Palermo before the advancing troops of Napoleon. It covers a surface of 400 hectares and originally served both as the king's hunting reserve and as a theatre for the agricultural experiments of which he was fond. Today the long, narrow park is home to Palermo's race track and other sports facilities. Its monumental centrepiece is the Fontana d'Ercole, a large rotonda with a great Doric column topped by a copy of the *Farnese Hercules* (the original is in the National Archaeological Museum in Naples).

Within the park is the **Palazzina Cinese**, built for Ferdinand in 1799 by Venanzio Marvuglia. This curious hybrid of Oriental, Gothic and Classical architecture was the favourite residence of the royal family in exile, as well as of their English friends, Admiral Nelson and Lord and Lady Hamilton. A modest annexe houses the **Museo Etnografico Siciliano Pitrè**, founded by the Palermitan ethnologist Giuseppe Pitrè in 1909 and enlarged in 1934–35. The third of Palermo's great museums, it has one of the most interesting ethnographic collections in Europe. The displays document Sicilian life and customs, with objects arranged by activity: hunting and fishing, spinning and weaving (notice especially the fine linens and embroideries, and Siculo-Albanian costumes); grazing and farming; ceramics, toys and musical instruments. There are also some fine carriages and sedan chairs, Sicilian carts, Christmas crèches, ex-votos, a working puppet theatre and a model of the 24m-high, 60-mule-team *Carriage of Santa Rosalia*, drawn through the city in the colourful procession which celebrated the saint's feast day.

A highlight of the museum is its collection of **Sicilian ceramics**, particularly from Palermo. Palermitan ceramicists rose to prominence in the late 16th century. From this period date the extraordinarily beautiful vases of the Lazzaro workshop, the city's most famous. Although the form of these large ornamental vessels can be traced back to that of Siculo-Muslim vases, their decoration bears signs of Tuscan and Umbrian influences. The colours used by the Lazzaro workshop are cobalt blue, yellow, white and red. Compositional schemes that recur almost continuously in the ceramics of Palermo are the *treccia* at the base of the vases (here made up of a series of knots alternating with discs); the *tralcio* (grapevine) and the *cornice dei medaglioni* (medallion cornice), featuring coupled bean-pod decorative elements. The Palermitan workshops declined and, in some cases, disappeared in the 18th century, when those of Burgio, Sciacca and Trapani were nearing the peak of their prestige. Recovery came only at the end of the century, with the establishment of new workshops organised along industrial lines. Today Palermo is an active centre of ceramics manufacture, churning out traditional rustic forms as well as *objets d'art*.

Sicilian Textiles & Embroideries

The famous Incoronation Mantle with which the Holy Roman Emperors were crowned, a semicircular pallium splendidly embroidered at the centre with a palm and a lion felling a camel, can be considered the oldest and most glorious piece of Sicilian textile craft. It was woven and embroidered in Palermo, for the Norman kings, in 1134 by the Ergasterio, the royal mill that brought silk weaving (already thriving in Byzantine Greece) to Sicily and perfected the Arabian technique of spinning and embroidery. Sicily remained a silk-making centre until the 18th century, the damasked fabrics of Messina, in particular, being famous throughout Europe. The splendour of Sicilian apparel, described in great detail in many marriage settlements of the 16th, 17th and 18th centuries, is owed to a considerable degree to the skill and imagination of Sicilian silk workers.

Silk is not the only important fabric produced in Sicily. The *frazzate* of Erice are rugs made by reweaving minute fragments of coloured wool in interlacing or free geometric compositions; and the coarse woollen haversacks and saddlebags once (but, alas, no longer) produced in the Madonie Mountains are much loved by collectors.

The spread and refinement of embroidery techniques went hand in hand, on the island, with the development of the textile industry. After the decline of the latter in the 19th century, embroidery continued to be done, but only in the home, except in some areas (Isnello in the Madonie, Vittoria and Ragusa in eastern Sicily), where it has remained a commercial craft. The most sought-after type of embroidery is still the Sicilian *sfilato*, made by drawing the threads out of an area of the cloth and then creating an ornamental motif.

Towering over La Favorita at the north end of the Gulf of Palermo is the city's sacred mountain, **Monte Pellegrino**. This is thought to have been the ancient *Heirkte*. Goethe called it the most beautiful promontory in the world. Its steep limestone flanks were home to Palermo's earliest inhabitants: above the beach of Addaura, on a spur of the mountain that descends to Punta di Priola, are caves with incised drawings of human and animal figures dating from the Upper Palaeolithic era (closed to the public).

A road and footpath wind up the mountain to the **Santuario di Santa Rosalia**, a cave-sanctuary with a façade carved out of the rock in the 17th century, now barely visible behind the myriad shops and stalls selling religious souvenirs. Rosalia was a young noblewoman, a niece of William I who, following her father's death in the conspiracy of 1160, renounced the world and devoted herself to a life of prayer in this cave, dying in 1166 at the age of 36. In July 1624 her bones were found and carried down to Palermo, where a plague that was raging immediately ceased. She was made the city's patron saint, filling a role once played by Persephone (the water that trickles down the walls of the cave is said to bring fertility). Her feast day is celebrated on 4 September with a solemn procession to her cave. Goethe was particularly fond of the shrine and considered it much more appropriate to the humility of the saint than the pomp of the feast celebrated in her honour: 'In all Christendom, which for eighteen hundred years has founded its wealth, its splendours, its solemn festivities upon the poverty of its first founders and most fervent confessors, there may well be no other sacred spot as naïvely decorated and touchingly venerated as this.'

Spread out along the arched shore of the little bay of Monte Gallo 10km (6 miles) north of the city centre is **Mondello**, the lido of Palermo and one of Sicily's best known bathing beaches. The oldest part of the town is the fishing village with its 15th-century tower, at the north end of the bay. Between 1892 and 1910 the marshland south of this settlement was improved and the area was developed by a Belgian company, which built a garden city in the *finest belle-époque* style, drawing on the atmosphere and architecture of the late Floreal style. Between the two World Wars the town took on the strongly *élitist* character for which it was known until quite recently. Today it is a popular bathing resort whose sandy beach extends for 2km (1¼ miles) from Monte Pellegrino to Monte Gallo. From Valdesi, at the southern tip of the town, the Lungomare Cristoforo Colombo returns towards the centre of Palermo along the rocky coast at the foot of Monte Pellegrino.

West of Palermo

Corso Calatafimi leads west from Palazzo dei Normanni through the densely populated neighbourhood that was once the garden of delights of the Arab emirs and the private park of the Norman kings. As late as the early 20th century this was one of the finest suburbs of Palermo, 'a vast garden of orange and olive trees' in the words of one foreign visitor.

In a neglected park on Piazza Guglielmo il Buono stands **La Zisa**, one of the great Norman pleasure palaces that dotted the once-verdant plain and today the most important example of Arab-Norman secular architecture to survive. La Zisa takes its name from the Arabic *el aziz*, 'the magnificent'. Begun by William I in 1164–65 and completed by his son, William II, it was damaged in the Sicilian Vespers, fortified by the counts of Ventimiglia, and then converted into a mansion at the expense of much of its original interior. It was restored to something near its original form in 1974–90, and there are plans to re-create at least a part of the garden in the near future.

The lighthouse on the outskirts of Mondello

The fine **exterior** appears as a tall, rectangular block flanked by slender towers and scored on all three storeys by shallow blind arches that originally surrounded two-light windows and ended in a cornice with Arabic epigraphs (destroyed to make the crenellations). In William's time the sandstone walls were faced with plaster and decorated with a red and white geometric design.

The three-storeyed **interior** is introduced by a display illustrating the history of the building and its restoration. All the rooms had vaulted ceilings; the pavements were tiled in a herringbone pattern, except that of the great ground-floor hall, which was in marble; and the palace had a sophisticated natural ventilation system (also found in ancient Egyptian buildings) that kept it warm in winter and cool in summer.

Of all the rooms the ground-floor Hall of the Fountain, used for entertainments, is the best preserved. Here many of the original decorative elements – including an Arabic inscription in stucco, a frieze of goldground mosaics similar to those in the Sala di Re Ruggero in the Palazzo dei Normanni, small columns with delicately carved capitals, and stalactite ceilings derived from Islamic architecture – survive inact. A fountain fed by a Roman aqueduct gushed from a wall, its waters collected in the fish

The apse of Monreale Cathedral

pond outside. The faded frescoes were added in the 17th century. Modern steel staircases now lead up to the first floor, where a small collection of Islamic art occupies the former living quarters. On the top floor is a columned central hall, originally open to the sky, flanked by small rooms that may have housed a harem.

South of La Zisa is the 17th-century **Convento dei Cappuccini**, where eminent Palermitans of the 17th to the late 19th century were buried or deposited in eerie catacombs. Writer Patrick Brydone, who visited the convent in 1773, tells what you can expect to find here: 'This morning we went to see a celebrated convent of Capuchins, about a mile without the city; it contains nothing very remarkable but the burial-place, which indeed is a great curiosity. This is a vast subterranean apartment, divided into large commodious galleries, the walls on each side of which are hollowed into a variety of niches, as if intended for a great collection of statues; these niches, instead of statues, are all filled with dead bodies, set upright upon their legs, and fixed by the back to the inside of the nich: their number is about three hundred: they are all dressed in the clothes they usually wore, and form a most respectable and venerable assembly. The skin and muscles, by a certain preparation, become as dry and hard as a piece of stock-fish; and although many of them have been here upwards of two hundred and fifty years, yet none are reduced to skeletons; the muscles, indeed, in some appear to be a good deal more shrunk than in others; probably because these persons had been more extenuated at the time of their death.'

Brydone goes on to explain the rather macabre attitude his contemporary Palermitans held toward the catacombs: 'Here the people of Palermo pay daily visits to their deceased friends, and recal with pleasure and regret the scenes of their past life: here they familiarize themselves with their future state, and chuse the company they would wish to keep in the other world. It is a common thing to make choice of their nich, and to try if their body fits it, that no alterations may be necessary after they are dead; and sometimes, by way of a voluntary penance, they acustom themselves to stand for hours in these niches.'

The monks show the roughly 8000 skeletons and bodies that were mummified in special baths of herbs and vinegar; men, women and clerics occupy different corridors. Giuseppe di Lampedusa, author of *The Leopard*, is buried in the cemetery outside the catacombs.

Laid out on a hill overlooking the Oreto valley and the Conca d'Oro, **Monreale** grew up in the 13th century around William II's splendid **Cathedral**. This great church, begun c 1174 and completed in record time, is the last and most majestic of the Norman churches in Sicily and one of the architectural wonders of the Middle Ages. It was built ostensibly in response to a dream-vision in which the Virgin told the king of a great treasure buried beneath the little hill town. In reality it was probably meant to undermine the authority of Palermo's English archbishop, Walter of the Mill, who had come to Sicily as William's tutor and had skilfully manoeuvred his way into what the king considered a position of excessive power.

The **façade**, tucked between two towers (only one of which was completed), is adorned with interlacing Arabic arches above and an 18th-century Classical portico below. Beneath the latter is a magnificent doorway carved with human and animal figures, surrounding bronze doors with 46 reliefs of Biblical scenes by Bonannus of Pisa (1186). Beneath the Renaissance colonnade on the north side, added in 1547–69 by the Gagini, is a slightly earlier bronze door by Barisanus of Trani (1179) showing battles, saints, animals and scenes from the life of Christ. It is by this door that the church is usually entered.

The simple basilican interior owes its effect to its brilliant gold-ground **mosaics** – like those of the Cappella Palatina, but carried out here on a grand scale. Only the roof (which caught fire in 1811), the transennae screening the choir, and the mosaic-and-marble facing of the lower part of the walls are later additions; the granite and porphyry inlaid pavement was completed in the 16th century following the original design, and the 18 slender columns were salvaged from antique buildings. Stilted Arabic arches spring from their beautiful composite capitals, separating the nave from the aisles. The rectangular crossing with its high lantern is Byzantine in inspiration, whereas the shallow transepts and deep apsidal presbytery recall Cluniac Benedictine churches.

The magnificent **mosaics** cover 6340 square metres – over 2000 more than St Mark's in Venice – making this the second largest mosaic cycle in the world, after St Sofia in Istanbul. Those at the east end are thought to have been made by Greek mosaicists or local craftsmen trained in the Greek tradition, before 1189; those of the nave and aisles appear to be somewhat later and may be the work of Venetian mosaicists. The overall programme, illustrating the themes of Christ's Ascension and the Assumption of the Virgin, by association celebrates the Norman monarchy and emphasises its affinity with the Holy City of Jerusalem.

All the scenes bear detailed mosaic inscriptions in Greek or Latin. Those of the nave, aisles and transepts tell Old and New Testament stories; on either side of the presbytery are scenes from the lives of St Peter and St Paul, who are represented in the side apses. In the main apse the 7m-tall figure of *Christ Pantocrator*, the most imposing of all such figures in Sicily, looms over the Virgin enthroned with angels and apostles, and around the east window, figures of saints. Among the latter stands Thomas Becket, who was murdered by William's father-in-law, Henry II of England; his inclusion, which must have been decided soon after his martyrdom, may have been an expiatory gesture on the part of William's queen, Joanna. William himself appears twice in the mosaics – receiving the crown from Christ, over the royal throne (left), and offering his cathedral to the Virgin, over the episcopal throne (right).

Street in Monreale

The king had intended to make Monreale the burial place of the Norman Hauteville dynasty. In the transept south of the choir, before the entrance to the 16th-century Cappella di San Benedetto, stand the porphyry sarcophagus of William I (died 1166) and that of William II (died 1190) in white marble (1575). On the north of the choir are the tombs (reconstructions of 1846) of Margaret of Navarre, Roger and Henry, William's mother and brothers, and an inscription recording the place where the body of St Louis, who died of plague while crusading in Tunis (1270), lay in state during its return to Paris; the saint's heart remains buried here. Nearby, steps lead up to the the Treasury (fee), which contains precious reliquaries, sacred vestments and liturgical objects; entrance is through the splendid 17th-century Cappella del Crocifisso, where there is a marble tabernacle by the school of the Gagini. From here you can also buy a ticket to the roof, reached by 180 steps from the southwest corner of the nave.

On the south side of the church is the 12th-century garden **cloister**. Once the centre of Monreale's Cluniac Benedictine monastery, this is a small corner of paradise, with pointed arches borne by 228 twin columns of every imaginable design. Many of the colonnettes are decorated with mosaics or reliefs. Their delicate, varied capitals (carved by Romanesque sculptors from Burgundy or Provence) show plants, animals, episodes from myth and scripture, imaginary monsters and, on the seventh from the northwest corner, William offering his church to the Virgin, accompanied by the Lamb of God, with Faith, Hope, Charity and Justice. In the southwest corner a single column, in its own small enclosure, forms a charming fountain shaped like a palm tree without fronds. The north wall is pierced by a doorway and eight two-light windows with an inlaid stone pattern like that of the façade. The south walk is surmounted by a fine Norman wall, possibly pre-dating the cloister, of the ruined dormitory of the monastery.

To see the cathedral's splendid **apses**, decorated with interlacing arches of limestone and lava, walk around behind the church to Via dell'Arcivescovado, where the building opposite the cathedral incorporates some arches and windows of the former Norman royal palace. The medieval streets, in this area and off the central Via Roma, are worth exploring. The town also has some fine Baroque churches.

East of Palermo

East of Palermo lies the sprawling suburb of **Bagheria**. Though largely ruined in recent years by speculative building, it was famous from the 16th to the 18th century as a playground of the wealthy – its gently rolling countryside and splendid sea views encouraging many of Palermo's best families to build magnificent Baroque country houses here. Only two of these old villas are now open to visitors.

Sicilian Baskets

Rushes, osiers (a family of willows from which wicker is made) and reeds are common throughout Sicily, and their pliable stems and twigs are woven together in various ways to make a multiplicity of baskets. The masters of this craft are called *cannistrari*.

Baskets are traditionally sold at village farmers' markets. The most common types are the multi-purpose *cufini* (up to a metre and a half tall), made of reeds and rushes; the relatively small *cartedde*, with rush handles and bases and bodies of various materials; *fasceddi*, the narrow little baskets of tightly woven rushes used to make ricotta cheese; and rush, wicker and reed *panari* (literally, 'breadbaskets', but used to carry food in general). The shape of the latter varies by function: the ones used to carry fish have a flat bottom and tall handle, whereas those for fruit are relatively deep. To this day, basket-making is a common craft throughout the island; the baskets of Monreale are particularly famous.

The extravagant **Villa Palagonia**, located on an untidy little piazza off the main Corso Umberto (ring at the garden gate for the custodian), prompted Goethe to reflect that 'neither tasteless vulgarity nor assured excellence is the creation of one single man or one single epoch; on the contrary, with a little thought, one can trace the genealogy of both'. He was appalled by this house, a 'gauntlet of lunacy' whose 'bad taste and folly' were beyond the wildest imagination. Today we are accustomed to this and more, but the dramatic effect of this singular ensemble of curving forms, designed in 1705 by Tommaso Maria Napoli for Francesco Gravina, Prince of Palagonia, and decorated by the prince's eccentric grandson, Ferdinando Gravina Alliata, is nonetheless quite an experience.

Goethe makes a list of the monstrous statues, of human beings ('beggars of both sexes, men and women of Spain, Moors, Turks, hunchbacks, deformed persons of every kind, dwarfs, musicians, Pulcinellas...') and animals ('deformed monkeys, many dragons and snakes, every kind of paw attached to every kind of body, double heads and exchanged heads...'), that greet the visitor in the overgrown garden. Although the villa itself is now in a state of dusty neglect, the author of the *Italian Journey* gives us an idea of what it looked like when it was inhabited: 'In the house the fever of the Prince rises to a delirium. The legs of the chairs have been unequally sawn off, so that no one can sit on them, and we were warned by the castellan himself not to use the normal chairs, for they have spikes hidden under their velvet-cushioned seats. In corners stood candelabra of Chinese porcelain, which turned out, on closer inspection, to be made up of single bowls, cups and saucers, all glued together. Some whimsical object stares out at you from every corner.' Unfortunately this 18th-century forerunner of Surrealism will soon vanish if steps are not taken to preserve it.

On the Palermo road is the **Villa dei Principi di Cattolica**, a severe building with a gently curving façade approached by a monumental elliptical stair. Completed around 1737, it houses the **Civica Galleria d'Arte Moderna e Contemporanea**, with a collection of 20th-century art mainly by Southern Italian artists. The collection was established in 1973 around a donation of paintings by Renato Guttuso (1912–87), a native of Bagheria and a vigorous crusader first against the Fascists, then against the Mafia. His bright blue tomb, by Giacomo Manzù, is in the garden.

In striking contrast to the Baroque fanfare of Bagheria, the quiet ruins of **Solunto** lie scattered amid wild flowers and aromatic plants in a beautiful setting on the slope of Monte Catalfano, 374m above the sea. They can be approached directly from Bagheria (signposted from Piazza Garibaldi, by the entrance to Villa Palagonia) or by the Palermo road (Highway 113).

This was the Carthaginian town of *Solus*, successor to a city of the same name thought to have been founded in the 8th century BC. The first Solus was destroyed in 397BC by Dionysius of Syracuse, and the city whose remains survive was built no earlier than the mid-4th century BC. It remained in Carthaginian hands until it fell to the Romans, who named it *Soluntum*, in 254BC. After failing to prosper under Roman rule, the city was abandoned by its inhabitants during the 2nd century AD. It was rediscovered in 1825 and has been excavated only in part. Most of the finds are in the Museo Archeologico Regionale, in Palermo.

The city appears to have been laid out over a series of terraces on a regular grid plan similar to that of the Hellenistic cities of Asia Minor. The streets are beautifully paved in brick and stone. There are vestiges of an arcaded **agora**, a small Roman **theatre**, an **odeon** or **bouleuterion**, and numerous houses with plastered and painted walls, mosaic pavements and other interesting details. The many public and private cisterns are part of a complex system for gathering rainwater, made necessary by the lack of natural springs on the site. The view along the coast towards Cefalù and the Æolian Islands from the end of the main Via dell'Agora is breathtaking. At the entrance to the ruins is a small museum displaying capitals, statues, architectural fragments, dies from the town mint, and other material from the ongoing excavations. You can return to Bagheria by the coast road round Monte Catalfano, which is longer (9km/5¹/₂ miles) but considerably more scenic, touching on picturesque small villages and running along a majestic headland amid sheer cliffs.

Ustica

The lovely island of **Ustica** is the tip of a huge submerged volcano rising in a crystal-clear sea c 58km (36 miles) north-northwest of Palermo. It is famous for its rocky shore and beautiful aquatic flora and fauna. In a singularly visionary move to protect these precious assets, the Region of Sicily established Italy's first marine reserve here in 1987, then in 1992 the

Mediterranean's first underwater archaeological park. In addition to its intact marine environment, Ustica is blessed with striking scenery, easily accessible on foot or by donkey. The vegetation includes cultivated fields of wheat and low vineyards, as well as olives, capers, almonds, fruit trees and prickly pear. Wild flowers cover the island except in the hottest months, and there is an abundance of interesting bird life. Farming and fishing are the traditional resources of the inhabitants, though tourism has probably brought the lion's share of income in recent years. Although the wild coastline has magnificent grottoes and rocky coves, there are precious few sandy beaches.

The name *Ustica* comes from the Latin *ustum* (burnt) and is derived from the colour of the black volcanic rock. Excavations suggest that the island was inhabited as long ago as the 2nd millennium BC, as well as by the Phoenicians and Romans. In the Middle Ages it declined under the attacks of Barbary pirates, who defeated all attempts to colonise it. Several attempts to occupy and populate the island were undertaken later by the Spanish, but these ended in failure as every new settlement was destroyed and the population was killed or carried off in slavery by pirates. Only in 1763 was the island fortified and populated by the Bourbons with a hundred families from the Æolian Islands (whose customs and dialect are still dominant on the island), a few Western Sicilians and a garrison of well-armed soldiers. The population grew rapidly until the mid-19th century, when it reached saturation point and the islanders began to emigrate. It was long used as a place of exile and as a prison, and in the Fascist era the Socialist Rosselli brothers and Communist Party leader Antonio Gramsci were held here as political prisoners. In September 1943 Italian and British officers met secretly on the island to discuss details of Italy's change of sides.

Today Ustica is one of Sicily's wildest and most beautiful island resorts. Boats dock at Cala Santa Maria, from where a road winds up to **Ustica town**, laid out in 1763 on a tufa terrace between two little bays dominated by the Capo Falconara headland and the former Bourbon fortress. The houses are brightly painted with murals, the result of a biennial mural competition; and the church of San Bartolomeo is decorated with colourful ceramic saints. A road runs all round the island, and mule tracks and footpaths wind over hill and dale, making for beautiful walks. Donkeys can also be hired.

On the north tip of the island, at Faraglioni, are excavations of a prehistoric fortified village, and on the west coast, from Punta di Megna to Punta Smalmatore, stretches the **Riserva Naturale Marina**. Here fishing is prohibited, boats have to keep offshore, and swimming is restricted. Just to the south, near the lighthouse at Punta Gavazzi, a buoy in the sea marks the underwater archaeological park, with finds from various wrecks left *in situ*. The island has numerous beautiful marine grottoes, notably the 91m-long **Grotta Azzurra**, which like its namesake on Capri derives its colour from light reflected in the water. A popular place to swim and sunbathe is the

Piscina Naturale, a natural sea pool near the southern tip of the island. There are also some fantastic volcanic rocks. The lighthouse at Punta dell'Uomo Morto (Dead Man's Point) stands over a cave where the island's prehistoric inhabitants buried their dead. Boats can be hired at the harbour.

Erice

Erice is a beautifully preserved medieval town on top of an isolated hill 751m above the sea, at the extreme tip of western Sicily. On this splendid site, visible for miles around, it was one of the great landmarks in the Western Mediterranean. When shrouded in mist (which it is most of the time), it feels totally isolated from the rest of the world; but on clear days it enjoys wonderful views – north to the sheer red cliffs of Monte Cofano, and south over Trapani and the Egadi Islands to Cape Bon in Tunisia. Its grey stone houses, hidden behind their high courtyard walls, and the beautifully paved streets, unusually clean and deserted, give the town a Central Italian air, more like the hilltop villages of Tuscany or Umbria than like other Sicilian towns. Its triangular shape (which has sparked some interesting symbolic interpretations) makes it difficult to find your bearings, but its

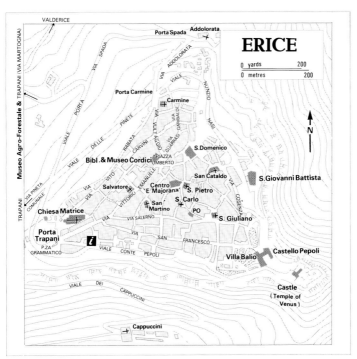

steep maze of winding streets and alleys, sometimes so narrow that only one person at a time can get down them, and its small courtyards, almost all graced with flowers and evergreen plants, are well worth exploring. Don't come up to Erice without bringing something warm to wear: on average the town is 10° cooler than the coast below.

The ancient *Eryx* was known far and wide in the Classical world for its temple dedicated to the goddess of love – the Phoenician Astarte, Greek Aphrodite or Roman Venus, the orgiastic goddess of the Western Mediterranean surnamed Erycina, 'of the heather'. This temple, mentioned by Virgil in the *Æneid*, was the holy of holies of the Elymians, the mysterious mountain people who also founded Segesta (see page 76). Virgil tells that Venus Erycina married Anchises and became the mother of Æneas, the hero of the Trojan race, from whom the Elymians claimed descent; and an old Sicilian myth tells that to make her lover Adonis jealous, she spent several nights in Lilybæum with Butes, thus becoming the mother of Eryx, king of the Elymians, who founded her cult on this mountain. Excavations suggest that an altar was first set up here by the Sicani, and the sanctuary became famous during the Elymian and Phoenician period.

Taken by Pyrrhus, king of Epirus, in 278BC and destroyed by the Carthaginian general Hamilcar (Hannibal's father) in 260, Eryx fell to the Romans in 248BC. It was at this time that the cult of Venus Erycina reached its maximum splendour, as seamen and pilgrims climbed the mountain to lie with the *ierodule*, priestesses of the goddess who practised sacred prostitution here as they did at the sanctuaries of Venus in Corinth and Cyprus. The Saracens called the place *Gebel-Hamed* (Mohammed's Mountain). The Norman Count Roger, who had seen St Julian in a dream while besieging it, rechristened the town *Monte San Giuliano*, a name it kept until Mussolini's time. The city reached its greatest expansion in the 18th century when the population touched 12,000; today it is around 600.

The women of Erice have long been noted for their beauty – as well as for their brightly coloured cotton rugs, called *frazzate*. Modern Erice is home to a scientific study centre, the 'Centro di Cultura Scientifica Ettore Majorana', hosting a calendar of important international congresses every year. It also offers numerous cultural events throughout the year: the 'Giornate delle Arti', during which international contemporary artists make site-specific works for the town (January); the 'Procession of the Mysteries' on Good Friday (see box page 81); and festivals of medieval and Renaissance music (in July) and folk music (in December).

If you are driving, leave your car by the **Porta Trapani**, where buses also stop. This is one of the three gates in the old town walls; like the others, it was built by the Normans over foundations dating from the 8th–7th century BC, with Roman additions. Beyond, Via Vittorio Emanuele, the former Via Reggia along which the main civil and religious buildings were built, climbs steeply. To the left, on a square just inside the walls, stands the

Chiesa Matrice (Santa Maria Assunta), the most important of Erice's ten churches. Its free-standing campanile, with Gothic double-light windows in the Chiaramonte style, may have been built by Frederick of Aragon as a watchtower. The church was begun in the early 14th century; its Gothic façade and porch date from 1426. The dimly lit interior, with its elaborate cream-coloured vault, was remodelled in 1852. A huge marble altarpiece by Giuliano Mancino (1513) fills the apse, but the chief treasure is a beautiful *Madonna and Child* on the south side, carved in 1469. Once attributed to Francesco Laurana, it is now thought to be by Domenico Gagini.

Via Vittorio Emanuele continues steeply uphill past several old shopfronts and characteristic courtyards, bearing left at the fork with Via Salerno to enter the central Piazza Umberto. Here are a few cafés, a pretty palace now used by a bank, and the long 19th-century building that houses the town hall. The latter includes the **Biblioteca and Museo Comunale Cordici**, named after the local historian Antonino Cordici (1586–1666). In the entrance hall are a beautiful relief of the *Annunciation* by Antonello Gagini (1525) and a number of inscriptions. Upstairs, the well-arranged small museum houses local archaeological finds, including an Attic *Head of Aphrodite* of the 5th century BC and coins from ancient Eryx inscribed with doves, the bird sacred to the goddess. Erice's cafés are known especially for their sweet almond pastries, which have been made to traditional recipes since the time of Frederick II and represent a curious blend of the German and Arabic culinary traditions.

From the north end of the square Via Guarrasi, the stepped Via Argentierie and Via Vultaggio lead out of town to a fine stretch of the ancient walls. These are made of huge rough-cut stones (probably Elymian) and smaller, square-cut blocks (Carthaginian), reinforced during the Roman period and in the Middle Ages. They protected the only side of the hill that had no natural defences: on all the other sides the sheer rock face made the town an impregnable fortress. The stepped Via Addolorata continues to the church of the **Addolorata** (or Sant'Orsola; closed), where the 18th-century sculptures of the Misteri (see page 81), borne in procession through the streets on Good Friday, are kept, and to the Norman Porta Spada.

From Piazza Umberto, Via Antonio Cordici leads east, past a few shops, to Piazza San Domenico with a pretty Baroque palace. The church of San Domenico, with a classical porch, has been restored as a lecture hall. From its square, Via Guarnotti (on your right) leads up to the church of **San Pietro**, with an 18th-century portal. The beautiful white interior by Giovanni Biagio Amico (1745; open for services) has a worn tiled pavement. The former convent next door is the headquarters of the 'Centro Internazionale di Cultura Scientifica Ettore Majorana'.

Stick with Via Guarnotti as it winds past the closed church of San Carlo and the post office and you'll come to a pleasant piazza with a statue, behind which rises the church of **San Giuliano** with its distinctive 18th-century campanile. The road continues down past a very old shopfront and

The Cathedral at Erice

crosses Via Porta Gervasi. A flight of steps leads up right to the **Villa Balio**, a shady English garden laid out in 1870 by Count Agostino Pepoli on the summit of the hill, with magnificent views. Its usual entrance is by the monumental double staircase at the top of Via San Francesco. Above is the **Castello Pepoli** (no admission), a Norman castle reconstructed in 1875–85 by Count Pepoli, with a 15th-century tower.

Walk down beside the castle to Viale Conte Pepoli, on the southern edge of the hill, to reach the 17th-century **Castello di Venere** on the edge of the rock. The ruined Norman walls surround the sacred area, once the site of the famous Temple of Venus. When Count Roger conquered Erice he ordered the temple's destruction, and his Normans did their work well, taking the stone for their walls and this castle. Now only the base of the Temple of Venus Erycina remains, on the northeast side. Unlike most Greek temples, which are built on an east-west axis, this temple was aligned northeast-southwest, perhaps with the rising of the midsummer sun. The historian Diodorus Siculus wrote that the base and walls of the sanctuary were strengthened by the mythical architect Dædalus.

Gibellina Nuova, or Utopia Manquée

North of Segesta extends the basin of the River Belice, known as the *Valle del Belice* after the violent earthquake of 14 January 1968, which levelled scores of villages and took thousands of lives. If you pass through this area today you will see the ruins of the old towns, the half-abandoned shanty towns built immediately after the disaster, and the ghastly new villages of the government reconstruction programme, perhaps even more tragic than the ruins themselves. Less obvious are the alterations made in the agrarian landscape, where wine, fruit and vegetables have replaced the traditional cereal crops.

The town most symbolic of the Belice tragedy is *Gibellina Nuova*, built 18km (11 miles) away from the ruins of the old medieval village now known as Gibellina Vecchia. Here numerous Italian contemporary artists have been called on to embellish the town with works of beauty and originality, in an effort to counter the desolation of post-earthquake reconstruction. The artists who have participated in the project to date are all quite accomplished; several (Pietro Consagra, Fausto Melotti, Giuseppe Uncini, Nino Franchina) are Sicilian. Each has sought, with his or her thought and creativity, to enhance the town's spaces and to transform Gibellina into a 'living museum' in which works of art enjoy a direct, affirmative relationship to their social and physical context. The operation takes in Gibellina Vecchia as well: to a plan by internationally known abstract expressionist Alberto Burri, the ruins of the medieval village have been covered with a huge sheet of cement, which spreads through the landscape at a uniform height, lacerated by what were once the town's streets.

Burri's piece is in fact the most successful, for it stands in romantic isolation miles from the nearest new building, striking a daring balance between the relentless, erosive power of nature and the forceful, constructive impetus of human imagination. The pieces sited in Gibellina Nuova, in contrast, sadly succumb to the squalor of the overall town plan, fruit of the warped fantasy of a government committee. There is nothing human about this place, with its straight streets, prefabricated houses, and parched, treeless gardens. To add expensive and – let's face it – obscure works of art to an architectural context that seems to have been planned and executed with the express intention of humiliating its inhabitants, is to add insult to injury.

Segesta

Segesta is an indescribably romantic site rising in glorious isolation amid the rolling countryside of western Sicily. Known for its theatre, set high up on a hill and commanding stunning views out to sea (especially remarkable in the afternoon), and for its windswept Doric temple, it has been admired by travellers for centuries.

Like Erice, Segesta is one of the principal settlements of the Elymians, a people of uncertain origin thought to have come from the Eastern Mediterranean. The Greek historian Thucydides says they were born of intermarriage between the Trojans and the Sikans, and the Roman poet Virgil claims *Egesta*, as the city was first called, was founded by the Trojan hero Acestes (Egestus). Certainly the date of its establishment, the 12th century BC, fits the traditional fall of Troy. Whatever the case, the Elymian settlement grew up on a spot inhabited since prehistory, dominating a vast area from the slopes of Monte Barbaro (400m) to the sea.

Ancient sources tell of its century-old rivalry with its powerful neighbour, the Greek city state of Selinus (Selinunte). The trouble began in the 6th century BC, with a border dispute. When Selinus allied itself with Syracuse, the Egestans negotiated a mutual defence treaty with Athens (426BC). In 416 the Athenians dispatched a fleet to destroy first Syracuse and then Selinunte; but their action was checked and the fleet destroyed by the Syracusans in 414. Left without protection, the Egestans turned for aid to the other great power of the Mediterranean, Carthage, which annihilated Selinunte in one of the most devastating battles of ancient history (409), then defended Egesta from the attacks of Dionysius of Syracuse (397). In 307, however, the tyrant Agathocles captured the city for Syracuse, slew most of its inhabitants and sold the rest into slavery. In its place he established a Greek colony, *Dikoeopolis*, which in a singular act of political opportunism resumed the alliance with Carthage and cast off its new name. But the Carthaginians, too, would soon be betrayed by the wily Segestans: during the First Punic War, when the latter realised the tables in the Mediterranean had turned, they boldly switched sides, becoming the first city in Sicily to ally itself to Rome. Regaled with special privileges, Segesta prospered in the Roman period, only to wither away after the fall of the empire.

Only a few vestiges remain of the ancient city. The **Temple** (58 x 23m), a peripteral hexastyle building in the purest Doric style, is particularly well preserved. Perhaps the grandest and most inspiring of all Sicily's ancient monuments, it rises on the western summit of Monte Barbaro, in a wild natural setting that underscores its magnificence. The Romantic Goethe was particularly impressed by the building and its location. 'The site of the temple is remarkable,' he wrote. 'Standing on an isolated hill at the head of a long, wide valley and surrounded by cliffs, it towers over a vast land-scape, but, extensive as the view is, only a small corner of the sea is visible. The countryside broods in a melancholy fertility; it is cultivated but with scarcely a sign of human habitation. The tops of the flowering thistles were alive with butterflies; wild fennel, its last year's growth now withered, stood eight or nine feet high and in such profusion and apparent order that one might have taken it for a nursery garden. The wind howled around the columns as though they were a forest, and birds of prey wheeled, screaming, above the empty shell.'

He rightly noticed that the great sanctuary, begun after 430BC, was never finished. 'One sign that the temple was never completed is the condi-tion of the temple steps. The peglike projections to which ropes were attached when the blocks were transported from the quarry to the site have not been hewn off. But the strongest evidence is the floor. Here and there slabs indicate where its edges must have been, but the centre is natural rock which rises higher than the sides, so that the floor can never have been paved. In addition, there is no trace of an inner hall, and the temple was never coated with stucco, though one can presume that this was intended.' The incomplete state of the temple has led to a great deal of speculation about its original function. Some scholars suggest it was built to solemnify a holy precinct used by an indigenous Elymian cult and left deliberately open to the sky; others believe that construction was interrupted when war broke out with Selinus in 416. The latter hypothesis appears most accept-able today, even if certain details (such as the rock eminences which emerge above the floor line within the peristyle) leave considerable room for doubt.

The **Theatre**, which dates from the mid-3rd century BC, stands on the second and highest summit of the mountain, in a position dominating the town. It has a singular characteristic: unlike other ancient theatres, it faces north for an extraordinary view over the hills and distant sea. With a diam-eter of 63m and 20 rows of seats, it could hold 3200 spectators. The upper

Temple at Segesta

part of the cavea, now lost, was carried by a robust wall; the surviving tiers of seats go only as far as the upper diazoma, beyond which the structure has vanished. Little or nothing remains of the skene, which archaeologists believe was adorned with piers and columns. Beneath the theatre, excavations have brought to light remains of a sacred grotto datable to the 10th century BC. The half-hour walk up to the theatre takes you through the recent excavations of a residential neighbourhood; for the less energetic a shuttle-bus makes the run every 15min. Classical drama performances are held here in the summer.

Outside the city, at the foot of Monte Barbaro to the east, is Segesta's third ruin (overgrown and difficult of access), a large **Archaic Sanctuary** surrounded by an imposing temenos. Thought to date from the 7th century BC, the 83 x 47m sanctuary must have contained several sacred buildings, as the discovery of numerous architectural fragments (capitals, columns) and pottery sherds suggests.

Trapani and the Egadi Islands

As you make your way through western Sicily, you'll see signs of the region's ties to Spain and Africa and of its remoteness from Greece and mainland Italy – a geographical peculiarity that profoundly influenced patterns of settlement and social organisation here. The proximity of the African coast made this part of Sicily a bridgehead for North African invaders, from the Carthaginians to the Arabs; and the nearness of the

Iberian peninsula facilitated political and trade relations, first with Aragon, and later with united Spain.

These cultures have left their mark on the region. The maze-like street plan of Trapani, for instance, derives from North African models. Such a plan not only offered protection from the wind, it also provided a formidable defence against invasion, especially where natural barriers were lacking. The enemy would be lured into the narrow winding streets, then attacked from above with stones, firewood and boiling oil. In the countryside you can still see the fortified farm complexes known as *baglie*, another Arabic invention, meant to protect lord and vassal alike from marauding bandits by clustering homes and outbuildings together inside a robust wall with just one gate, which was closed at night. Later, the Spanish moved the region's population off the land and into large, compact towns. These early concentration camps were built so that peasant farmers could be kept under their thumb by the forerunners of the Mafia – the often unscrupulous agents of absentee landlords. The classic village was revived only in the 18th century, when the large feudal properties of the Spanish era were broken up into smaller lots given to farmers in emphyteusis.

Trapani

Occupying a low plain and narrow promontory at the foot of Mount Erice, **Trapani** is the most important city on the west coast of Sicily. It's not a particularly attractive place, and most visitors pass right through on their way to the Egadi islands, which are usually visible offshore. This is unfortunate. The old district has some interesting medieval buildings, Baroque churches by the local architect Giovanni Biagio Amico (1684–1754) and a Corso lined with dignified palaces. The extensive modern city, with its eerie, slightly surreal air, is home to the delightful Museo Pepoli, which boasts one of the best collections of decorative arts on the island. These vestiges of a glorious past – when Trapani was a busy port, its silversmiths and jewellers were known throughout Europe (particularly for their works in coral), and the precious harvest of the salt marshes was shipped as far afield as Norway – seem sadly anachronistic now, for Trapani is one of the poorest places in Italy, and the Mafia has become increasingly important to economic survival.

A Carthaginian and later a Roman city, *Drepana or Drepanon* (the name means 'sickle') grew up on the gently arched promontory at the west end of town. It was an important emporium and naval base in antiquity. It thrived as a trading centre under Arab and Norman rule, and during the Crusades it acquired strategic importance as the maritime crossroads between Tunis, Anjou and Aragon. After the destruction of the rival harbour of Marsala, in the 16th century it enjoyed a period as western Sicily's most important port. Since the Middle Ages slow decline has reduced the city to a sleepy backwater. All hope is not lost, however: the ancient industry of

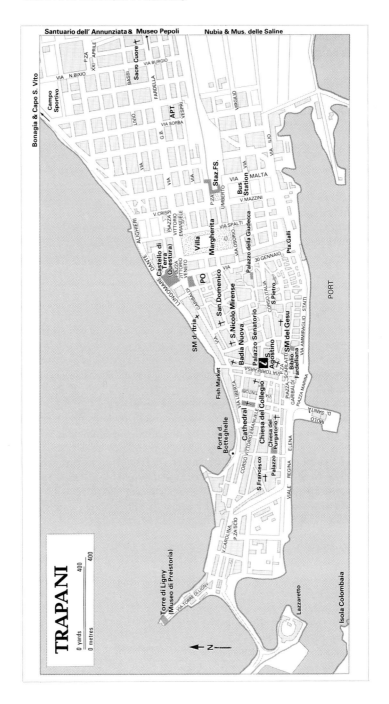

TRAPANI

0 yards   400

0 metres   400

extracting salt from the marshes has recently been revived, and conversion of some of the salt pans to fish-farming has introduced a new source of wealth.

Holy Week in Sicily

Novelist Leonardo Sciascia called the religious feasts of Sicily a 'collective existential explosion', observing that 'it is in the feast alone that the Sicilian abandons his solitary condition, the condition of his vigilant and sorrowful super-ego, to discover that he is part of an order, a class, a city'. Throughout Sicily, and particularly in the more remote areas where tradition is still strongly rooted, the period before Easter represents the high point of religious feeling, for (to paraphrase Sciascia) it provides the opportunity for a contemplation of death in the memory of the Passion of Christ. The Holy Week ceremonies in Sicily, which reach their most melancholy and sorrowful heights on Good Friday, are equalled only by those of southern Spain. And this is not surprising, for from Spain came the legacy of ancient rites which established clear parallels between the suffering and sacrifice of Christ and the hardship and privation of an impoverished peasantry.

The **Processione dei Misteri** (Procession of the Mysteries) in Trapani is one of the island's more important Holy Week ceremonies. The 'mysteries' are 20 near life-size wood-and-canvas sculptural groups representing scenes from the Passion of Christ. They were made in the 18th century to replace the disorderly and sometimes violent groups of amateur actors who, in prior centuries, had re-enacted the drama of the Saviour's last days. The procession begins in the early afternoon of Good Friday and winds through the city streets without pause until midday Saturday. Each *mistero*, splendidly decked out with flowers and lights, is borne on the shoulders of *portatori* (bearers) representing the various trade associations, preceded by *consoli* (patrons of the pageant), standard-bearers, adults and children with lighted candles, and a band.

The streets of Enna are invaded during Holy Week by the town's lay confraternities in the traditional **Rituale dei Sepolcri** (Ritual of the Sepulchres). This ceremony dates from the time of Holy Roman Emperor Frederick II, but its most interesting development took place during the passage of power from the French Angevins to the Spanish Aragonese in the 14th and 15th centuries. At that time the conservative aristocracy, slow to accept the new political order, was exiled to the lower town, while loyal subjects of the Spanish crown were allowed to settle on high ground, around the Castello di Lombardia.

The town's three confraternities reflected this strict separation, one siding with the Angevins, and two with the Aragonese. Their members suspended hostilities only during the Easter period, for the Feast of the Resurrected Christ and the Virgin Mary. The truce remained in force until the Sunday after Easter.

Today the ceremony is performed by 15 confraternities whose participation is governed by a strict hierarchy. All in all, some 2000 people roam the streets and alleys of Enna in a week-long pageant of processions, performances and curious culinary events. For instance, the bearers of the Urn of the Dead Christ and of the Simulacre of Our Lady of Sorrows are fed wine and boiled beans as a reminder of how frugal the foods of the people once were; wild-vegetable luncheons are served in evocation of the Jews' meagre diet in the desert; and the special Easter cakes and pastries recall pagan offerings to Ceres, the Greek goddess of grain, fertility and the seasonal renewal of life.

The old quarter stands quietly on its promontory, west of the station and the public gardens of Villa Margherita. Just a few blocks in is **San Domenico**, a 14th-century church with a delicate rose window awaiting restoration. Here are kept the 'Misteri', 20 groups of wood-and-paste figures carved in the 17th and 18th century that provide the high point of the town's Easter celebrations (see box). Along the wide, handsome Corso Vittorio Emanuele is the **Cathedral** of San Lorenzo, with an unusual porticoed façade built by Giovanni Biagio Amico in 1743. The Corso continues past some interesting palaces to Via Caterina and Via Torre di Ligny, which ends at a fortress built on the point by the Spanish viceroy in 1671. Here is the **Museo Trapanese di Preistoria**, with prehistoric finds from sites in western Sicily and Tunisia, and displays devoted to the Palaeolithic drawings and Neolithic paintings at Cala dei Genovesi on the isle of Levanzo (see page 84).

In the rebuilt district of San Pietro, near the harbour, stand Sant'Agostino, with a Gothic rose window like that of San Domenico, and **Santa Maria del Gesù**, a 16th-century church with a Gothic-Renaissance façade. Inside is an enamelled terracotta *Madonna* by Andrea della Robbia beneath a marble baldachin by Antonello Gagini. Further east, in the former Jewish quarter, is the 16th-century **Palazzo della Giudecca**, one of the few surviving examples of medieval Jewish architecture in Sicily. Its rusticated stone tower and elaborately decorated windows and doors recall the fanciful Plateresque style, current in Spain in the 15th and 16th centuries and brought from there to Sicily.

Trapani's most important monument, the **Santuario dell'Annunziata**, is situated at the landward end of the town c 4km (2¹/₂ miles) from the centre. It was founded in 1315 to house the much venerated *Madonna of Trapani*, a lovely marble sculpture carved by one of the sculptors of the great medieval Pisan school. The statue was left here by a Pisan Knight of Jerusalem returning from the Holy Land, in gratitude for deliverance from a storm. Little remains of the original structure except the façade, with a Norman Gothic door and rose window of the early 15th century. The powerful Baroque campanile beside it, dating from 1650, is emblematic of the continuous reconstruction that has marked the history of the complex. The aisleless interior holds several interesting chapels. The 15th-century Cappella dei Pescatori (Fishermen's Chapel, south) has an octagonal fres-coed dome and shell-shaped niches around the walls. The 16th-century Cappella dei Marinai (Mariners' Chapel, north) is built of warm golden tufa. The Chapel of the Madonna, in the sanctuary, stands behind a bronze gate of 1591 by Giulio Mussarra; its walls and pavement sparkle with coloured marbles. The marble arch with reliefs of *Prophets, Sibyls and God the Father* was carved by Antonino and Giacomo Gagini in 1531–37. The celebrated statue of the *Madonna and Child* stands over the altar.

The huge 17th-century Carmelite convent adjoining the sanctuary is occupied by the **Museo Regionale Pepoli**. It offers a thorough overview of the history of art and culture in Trapani and its territory from antiquity to the 20th century, with fine collections of antiquities, paintings, sculpture, deco-rative arts, coins and historic mementos. The entrance is through the cloister, planted with palm trees.

Highlights of the ground-floor collections include a statue of *St James the Great* by Antonello Gagini (1522) and a holy-water stoup of 1486 from the Annunziata, resembling those in Palermo Cathedral. On the first floor, the painting collection includes works from the 14th to the 18th centuries, notably a serene 15th-century panel of the *Madonna and Child* by the 'Master of the Trapani Polyptych', a *Pietà* by Roberto di Oderisio (c 1380), a triptych by Antonio del Massaro, and *St Francis Receiving the Stigmata* attributed to Titian. The most distinctive feature of the museum, however, is the **collection of decorative arts**, featuring objects made by local craftsmen in the 17th–19th centuries. Here are many fine examples of jewellery and sculpture, largely from the collection of the museum's benefactor, Count Pepoli.

Notice especially the elaborate objects in coral, a skill for which Trapani is particularly famous. The art reached its apex during the Baroque period (17th century) when, according to the accounts of historians and travellers, it employed more than 500 people. Set and shaped in various ways, coral was used to make religious articles (monstrances, pyxes, reliquaries, chal-ices, even holy-water stoups) and secular ornaments (cameos, necklaces, brooches). The advent of mechanised production in the late 19th century and the depletion of local coral reefs led to a gradual decline in the activity – a trend that has been reversed in recent years by a cooperative which brings together old *corallari* and young craftsmen.

Trapani was also famous in the past for its ceramics; its workshops were active from the 17th century to the last years of the 19th. They made objects of great value and extraordinary quality – and always in small numbers, which means that Trapani ceramics were never abundant. They were particularly sensitive to continental Italian influences, notably those of 15th-century Tuscany (many Trapani vases present a reinterpretation of the Tuscan Gothic cartouche) and Faenza (profiles of figures). The distinctive colours of Trapani ceramics range from cobalt blue to green, white, black and yellow. This lively chromatic gamut is most evident in the large peacock-feather vases, similar in form to those of Faenza. Another field in which Trapani craftsmen worked was the fabrication of large-scale pavements and panels. Some especially beautiful examples of this activity, representing maritime life in Trapani, are preserved here.

The museum's archaeological section has finds from Erice, Selinunte and Lilybæum. Here too is the flag of *Il Lombardo*, the ship used by Garibaldi and the Thousand.

The Egadi Islands

The **Isole Egadi** are three small islands lying just off the coast between Trapani and Marsala. They formed the western tip of Sicily until melting Ice Age glaciers raised the level of the sea just 5000 years ago. In recent years tiny **Levanzo**, secluded **Marettimo**, and the main island, **Favignana**, have become burgeoning resorts. The archipelago has been designated a Marine and Landscape Reserve in an attempt to slow development and safeguard the natural environment.

Paleolithic incised drawings and Neolithic paintings found in a cave on Levanzo prove that the islands were inhabited in prehistoric times. Their location on a major trade route between Carthage and Europe made the islands attractive to the Phoenicians, although they were never as important as Motya just to the south. During the First Punic War they witnessed the great sea battle in which 200 Roman warships defeated a Carthaginian fleet of twice the size, taking 10,000 prisoners (241BC). Although the inhabitants were Romanised after the debacle, some inscriptions in Punic characters from the 1st century BC found in Favignana's caves suggest their Phoenician heritage remained strong. After the decline of Rome the Isole Egadi vanish from history, reappearing in the 16th century when a financially embarrassed Spanish crown sold them to the Pallavicino-Rusconi family of Genoa.

Quarries of fine-grained Quaternary shell tufa, an excellent building material, have long been among the islands' main assets. The vast quarries of Favignana, especially, have yielded blocks of tufa known as *cantuna* with which whole towns in Sicily, Tunisia and Libya have been built. But the principal resource of the Egadi has always been the sea. These charming islands block the course of tuna on their way from the cold Atlantic to the warmer breeding waters around Sicily. Together with the rocks of Formica and Maraone, they serve as huge markers for the fish, which in late spring approach the coasts to reproduce and are captured in complicated systems of nets known as *tonnare* (see box).

The Art and Science of Tuna Fishing

'Meat of the poor', tuna was called in Sicily, because of its abundance and its nutritional value: like anchovies, sardines and mackerel, it is rich in protein and polyunsaturated fats, and its firm flesh is easy to preserve in oil or salt for long periods.

Thunnus thynnus is a powerful swimmer that can weigh up to 400kg and reach a length of two metres. Like all migratory animals, it tends to follow the same route each spring, when it leaves its deep-water home and approaches the coasts to mate. In Italy the tuna arrive by the thousand in April and May, skirting the shores of western Sicily around Trapani, Marsala and the Egadi Islands.

Sicilians use the Spanish term *mattanza* to designate the capture and slaughter of the fish. The method utilises special traps, called *tonnare*, and has been around for as long as anyone can remember. Sturdy vertical nets are used to intercept entire shoals of fish and convey them toward the so-called death chamber. Here, trapped by the hundreds in a few square metres, they thrash about until they knock each other senseless. The stunned fish float to the surface and are harpooned, their blood splashing over the fishermen and their 'weapons': the scene, unaltered over time, is so bloody that the Greek poet Æschylus compared it to the slaughter of the Persians at Salamina.

Of the 50 or so *tonnare* which once existed in Sicily, only that of Favignana is still working today, processing 1000–1500 tuna each year. The system of nets, or *impianti a mare*, is divided into *tonnare di corso*, situated on the north and west shores to trap inward-bound fish, and *tonnare di ritorno*, on the southwestern coast, along the route followed by outward-bound fish. There is also a series of support structures, the *impianti a terra*, on the shore. Here nets, boats and harpoons are stored, and the tuna is processed and packaged. The fishermen (*tonnaroti*) and crew-master (*rais*) live in humble dwellings around the central courtyard (*bagghiu*) of the processing plant.

The decline of the industry, which began in the period between the two World Wars, has accelerated since the 1960s, for a number of reasons: the competition of Japanese tuna-fishing ships, the intense urbanisation of the coasts, the difficulty of finding specialised labour, and the increasing economic advantages of deep-sea fishing. The Favignana tonnara is today almost a symbol, the last vestige of an antique culture in need of study and preservation.

The Phoenician *Katria*, the Greek *Ægusa* and the medieval *Faugnana* (from 'Favonio', the name of a wind), **Favignana** is the largest (19 sq km/7 sq miles) and most populous (3500 inhab.) of the Egadi. Long, low Monte Santa Caterina (417m) dominates this otherwise flat island, which offers very few shade trees but plenty of rocky coves and crystal-clear water. The sun-baked little town, around the harbour, was last rebuilt in 1637 by the Pallavicini; its most important buildings are the town hall, a former mansion designed in 1876 for Ignazio Florio by Giuseppe Damiani Almeyda, and the huge and rather bleak tuna fishery across the harbour, due to be recycled as a marine research centre. A short walk west of the town, by the Punta San Nicola, are the Grotta del Pozzo, with the late Punic inscriptions mentioned above as well as some signs left by early Christians, and the Grotta degli Archi, with Christian tombs from the 4th and 5th centuries.

Four kilometres north of Favignana and clearly visible from its harbour lies **Levanzo**, the smallest of the islands in terms of surface area (10 sq km/4 sq miles) and population (200 souls), but the most interesting historically. In a magnificent dark cave at Cala dei Genovesi, on the island's west shore, are drawings of 29 animals, scratched with light but exceptionally perfect lines, and four human figures in ritual dance, left 10,000 years ago, when Levanzo was still attached to Sicily. The drawings are as fragile as they are magnificent; the beautiful deer beside the entrance is under a protective glass because the slightest touch causes the stone to crumble. Less skilful are the confused rows of stylised black paintings of men and women, unfinished animals and tuna fish, added 5000 years later, in the Neolithic era. A pretty footpath winds its way to the cave from the harbour, but it is more impressive to arrive by sea, as the Genoese merchant ships of yore did. Before setting out from Levanzo town, be sure to make an appointment with the cave's custodian, who lives by the dock (Via Calvario 11; tel. 924 032).

The most remote and best preserved of the Isole Egadi, **Marettimo**, lies 38km (24 miles) from Trapani. The Greeks called it *Iera* ('sacred'); the Arabs, *Malitimah* (from which the present name comes). It is a wild, mountainous island, with abundant freshwater springs and beautiful grottoes. Its lovely little Arab-like village has a population of just 800. There are no hotels, but a few seasonal restaurants, and the inhabitants love to take paying guests. In *The Authoress of the Odyssey*, Samuel Butler claimed Marettimo was the Ithaca of the *Odyssey* and the islets of Le Formiche were the rocks hurled by Polyphemus at Odysseus. The fishermen will take you for boat rides along the coast, and footpaths meander through the rocky interior. The most interesting of these wind westwards amid splendid scenery to **Cala Nera**, where you can swim off the rocks; and northwards through the Aleppo pines, holm oaks and fragrant Mediterranean *maquis* of Monte Falcone (686m) to the **Castello di Punta Troia**, on a precipice high above the sea.

Pantelleria

Although the sea around the island abounds with fish, the inhabitants of **Pantelleria** (83 sq km/32 sq miles, 80km/50 miles from Africa and 110km/68 miles from Sicily) are not fishermen. Fishing fleets from the Sicilian mainland must work the sea around here, for the *Panteschi* are primarily farmers. Their vineyards produce the delicious white wine *Moscato di Pantelleria* and its sweet dessert variant, *Moscato Passito*. Another big crop is capers, which are produced by the tonne and highly prized for their intense flavour. The quality of these products of the earth is due to the island's volcanic origin – it was formed by two explosive eruptions on the sea floor, which here lies at the bottom of an abyss 2000m deep.

The **Montagna Grande** (836m) is the oldest of the island's extinct cones; of the several lesser cones, **Monte Gibelè** (700m) has maintained its crater shape, and **Monte Cuddia Attalora** (560m) has created an extraordinary lava landscape. Minor volcanic activity still goes on here and there on the island. It accounts for phenomena such as the *favare*, steam geysers that roar forth from fissures in rocks; *bagni asciutti* or *stufe*, natural caves with vapour emissions sometimes used for thermal cures; *caldarelle*, hot springs that rise at temperatures of up to 70°C and *mofette*, carbon dioxide exhalations.

Pantelleria enjoys an excellent climate, with summers cooled by gentle breezes and warm, dry winters. The natural vegetation is Mediterranean *macchia* (mainly heather) and *gariga* (low-growing shrubs like rosemary), with small forests of Aleppo pine.

The earliest inhabitants of the island were a mysterious Neolithic population of hunters, fishers and gatherers who probably came from Tunisia or Libya. They settled on the island's rugged east coast, some time around 1800 BC. Although they did not have a written language, they left signs of their passage in the cyclopic boundary wall which once defended their village, and in the hemispherical funerary monuments called *sesi*, made of large, regular stone blocks enclosing one or more cells. There were once more than 500 of these imposing prehistoric constructions, but today only one, the great 'Sese del Re' or 'Sese Gigante', survives intact.

Due to its strategic position, Pantelleria was frequented by Phoenician and Carthaginian merchants until it came under the influence of Rome, in 217BC. The Phoenicians called the island *Hiranin* (Isle of Birds), but the Romans adopted its Greek name, *Cossyra*. After the Romans, the island was taken by the Vandals, the Byzantines and the Arabs, who over their 400-year tenure completely reshaped Pantelleria or *Bent el-Rhia* (Daughter of the Wind) as they called it, introducing the cultivation of cotton, barley, citrus fruit, grapes and figs. The Arabic language lingers in many place names and in the local dialect, and a distinctly North African influence can be seen in the cube-like domed houses called *dammusi* and in their lush gardens, whose high drystone walls rise like tiny bastions against the wind.

Here as elsewhere the Normans brought an end to Arab rule, adding Pantelleria to their Sicilian possessions in 1123. During World War II the island was a Fascist naval base; it was heavily bombed in May 1943. It has been used as a place of exile for political prisoners and has hosted Italian and US military installations. Today it is a fashionable place to have a summer house.

Ferries dock at **Pantelleria** town, a dull modern place rebuilt after the Allied bombardments. From here a circuit of the island (35km/22 miles) can be made by car or moped (rentals are available), or by bus and on foot. The town spreads out around its little harbour; on the left is the Castello Barbacane or Relegati, several times destroyed and rebuilt but dating in its present form from Norman times. Proceeding clockwise around the island, you come first to the **Specchio di Venere** (Venus' Mirror), a lovely small crater lake fed by hot springs, then to the villages of **Tracino** and **Khamma**, with their characteristic *dammusi*. A turning leads down to the pretty little fishing village of **Gadir**, and to the coves of Cala Levante and Cala Tramontana, the island's best bathing spots. Nearby is the 'Arco dell'Elefante', a rock formation resembling a reclining elephant.

Scauri, on the island's south shore, has been the second port on the island since Phoenician times, although the town itself stands on a cliff almost 100m above the sea. Continuing northwards you round the Punta Fram, with its prehistoric obsidian mines, to reach the **Sese del Re**, in a beautiful natural setting unfortunately close to the beach resort of **Mursia**, 3km (1³/4 miles) south of Pantelleria town.

Motya and Marsala

The low, marshy coast between Trapani and Marsala has a particular charm that merits special attention. Here lie Trapani's famous **salt pans**; century-old windmills still pump sea water into a vast network of shallow pools where salt is extracted by evaporation. The Arabic geographer Al-Idrisi marvelled at this dreamlike landscape at the time of Roger I, and it is hardly less captivating today, especially in the golden light of the setting sun. To see it at its best, take the local road to Marsala, which leads out of town from the harbour and runs on the seaward side of the railway and Highway 115. All around are the beds into which sea water is pumped by the conical Greek-type windmills, decreasing in depth from one basin to the next to allow the salinity of the water to increase. In midsummer you can even see the newly harvested salt piled up and protected from humidity by tiles. At Nubia, a few kilometres south of Trapani (signposted), a **Museo delle Saline** was established in 1988 to illustrate the various stages of this age-old industry. The marshes became a bird sanctuary in 1991.

Motya

Eleven kilometres (7 miles) north of Marsala, in a shallow lagoon protected from the sea by the long, low Isola Grande, lie the ruins of the Phoenician colony of **Motya**, in Italian *Mozia*. This city was founded in the late 8th century BC on the islet today known as San Pantaleo, which had been the site of a prehistoric village. Because of its location – close to Africa, and on the principal trade routes with Spain, Sardinia and Central Italy – Motya soon became one of the more important Carthaginian trading centres in the Mediterranean, as well as the chief Punic bulwark against Greek expansion in this part of the island. Despite its well protected position (the waters of the lagoon were too shallow for warships) and its sturdy walls, it was destroyed by Dionysius the Elder of Syracuse in 397BC. Its survivors moved to the mainland, where they founded Lilybaion (Marsala). Motya remained buried until the curiosity of an English wine merchant, Joseph 'Pip' Whitaker, reawoke interest in the site at the end of the 19th century. Excavations have revealed part of the city, including the walls with their towers and gates, the rectangular Punic harbour, a sacred precinct, several houses, and a causeway (still visible beneath the waters of the lagoon). The latter joined the isle to its necropolis on the mainland, near Birgi Airport, whose traffic now disturbs the quiet of this otherwise enchanting place. Finds from the site are displayed in the former Whitaker mansion, now a museum. The island is accessible by boat.

In the sacred precinct is an open-air sanctuary, the *trophet*, where remains of human sacrifices to the god Baal Hammon were deposited in vases. The Phoenician religion in fact required Motya's families to offer their first-born male to the god. Every offering was marked by a stele, with carved or painted symbolic markings that reveal Egyptian and indigenous as well as Phoenician influences. Also well preserved is the *cothon*, the only known Phoenician dry dock other than that of Carthage. It was used both for merchant vessels (the manufacture of ceramics seems to have played an important role in the economy of Motya) and warships (the city was home to a large naval fleet). Diodorus Siculus mentions the elegant homes and palaces of Motya, but only a few foundations and rudimentary mosaics have been unearthed to date.

The **Museum** was established by Mr Whitaker in a wing of his villa, and its recent rearrangement has not impaired its 19th-century charm. It holds some 10,000 pieces, notably the magnificent marble *Ephebe of Motya* representing a young man, perhaps a charioteer, dressed in a long tunic. It is certainly a Greek original of the 5th century BC. Probably war booty, it bears witness to the continuity of relations between western Sicily and the Eastern Mediterranean.

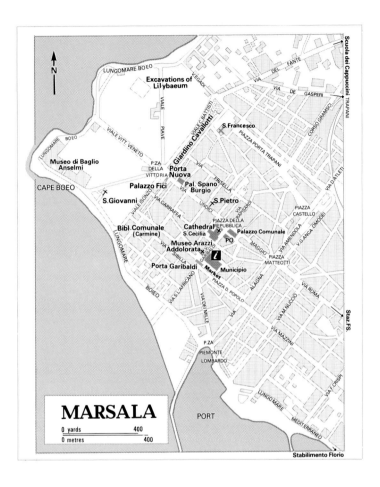

Marsala

The few Phoenicians who survived the destruction of Motya in 397BC migrated to Cape Boeo on the Sicilian mainland, where they joined with the native Elymians and Sikans to found a new settlement called *Lilybaion*. The new city quickly became the chief Carthaginian stronghold in Sicily, a position it maintained until the Second Punic War, which brought an end to all Phoenician influence on the island. In 214BC Lilybaion was taken by the Romans, who renamed it Lilybæum and made it their main port in the central Mediterranean and ultimately their chief administrative centre in western Sicily. The city flourished again under the Arabs, who were so struck by its beauty that they called it *Marsa Alì* or *Marsa Allah* ('port of God'). It continued to prosper under the

Normans and Aragonese, but its fortunes plummeted in the 16th century when the emperor Charles V, in an ill-advised attempt to protect it from pirate attacks, deliberately destroyed its harbour.

Today **Marsala** is a pleasant agricultural town whose economy is based on one product, its famous mellow dessert wine. Marsala, in fact, is the most important wine-producing centre on the island, and its affluence is clearly visible in its beautifully preserved historic centre. The heart of the town is the ancient *kalsa*, a regular square area possibly laid out as early as Carthaginian times but redesigned in the Baroque period. Its hub is Piazza della Repubblica, where the main civil and religious monuments stand. On the east is **Palazzo Senatorio**, the town hall, a 16th-century building with an 18th-century clock tower and interesting lamps. To the south rises the **Cathedral** of San Tommaso di Canterbury, begun in 1628 over a Norman foundation of 1176 and largely rebuilt following the collapse of the dome in 1893. The Baroque front, with its statues and two small campanili, was completed in 1957. There are some sculptures by Antonello Gagini inside, but the cathedral's most important treasures are the eight precious 16th-century Flemish tapestries now displayed in the **Museo degli Arazzi**, behind the church in Via Giuseppe Garraffa. They were given to the church by Antonio Lombardo, archbishop of Messina (1523–95), who was born in Marsala and is buried in the cathedral. Beautifully restored and displayed in special low lighting (to avoid fading) they depict the *Conquest of Jerusalem* and were given to Lombardo by Philip II of Spain when the archbishop was ambassador to the Spanish court.

A Short History of Marsala Wine

The fame of Marsala wine is owed largely to an Englishman, John Woodhouse, and to a freak of chance. Woodhouse, caught in a violent storm at sea in 1773, sought shelter in the harbour at Marsala. Here he tasted the local wine, which he found so delicious that he sent a large quantity home, adding a bit of brandy as a preservative. His countrymen not only found the wine quite palatable, they also realised it had an important trait in common with the prestigious Spanish wines so popular at the time: like these, Marsala could travel by sea for long periods without spoiling and so be provisioned to the Royal Navy. The many English merchants who came to Marsala to engage in the wine trade included Joseph Whitaker, the amateur archaeologist who assembled the collection of antiquities now in the museum at Motya. They were joined in 1832 by the Italian Vincenzo Florio, whose economic fortune became inextricably tied to that of the city: today the Florio firm is the leading producer of Marsala wine and the principal employer in town. Numerous 18th- and 19th-century wineries of the *baglio* type survive along the coast as mementos of the early days of the activity.

From Piazza della Repubblica, the main Via XI Maggio leads northwest, passing through a 16th-century town gate. Just beyond, on the right, is the **Giardino Cavallotti**, a luxuriant public garden with giant ficus trees, magnolias and other ornamental plants. The area between here and the seafront, planted with lawns and trees and closed to motor traffic, is the protected district of **Cape Boeo**, where you can see some scanty remains of Roman Lilybæum, including a 3rd-century bath complex with interesting mosaic pavements.

On the tip of the promontory the excellent **Museo Archeologico di Baglio Anselmi** occupies two huge vaulted warehouses around the garden courtyard of an old *baglio* once used to make and store Marsala wine. The well-labelled displays (which begin in the hall on the left) include prehistoric material from Marsala and its environs, Phoenician objects from Motya and Lilybaion, Roman finds from Lilybæum, a large coin collection, and Early Christian and medieval material (including some beautiful Siculo-Norman ceramics and finds from a Norman wreck found offshore in 1983).

The museum's most outstanding attraction has an entire hall to itself (right). This is a **Punic ship** found off the shore of Isola Longa in the Stagnone lagoon by underwater archaeologist Honor Frost in 1971 and carefully restored under her supervision. It is the only known example of a *libruna*, a sleek, swift warship 35m long, which was manned by 68 oarsmen. It is particularly important because of the light it casts on Carthaginian shipbuilding techniques, which seem to have used prefabricated pieces assembled in the shipyard. It is thought to have been sunk on its maiden voyage during the First Punic War, and to this day no-one knows why the iron nails didn't rust, notwithstanding they were underwater for hundreds of years. Cases at the end of the hall display objects found on board, and amphoras and other underwater treasures line the walls.

Not far from the Baglio Anselmi is the lonely little church of **San Giovanni**, from which you can enter the so-called *Antro della Sibilla Lilibea*, the cave of the Lilybæan Sibyl according to legend, but more probably the shrine of a Roman water cult. It is usually open in summer.

Selinunte

Selinunte is quite simply one of the most impressive archaeological sites in the Mediterranean. Perched on a rocky headland overlooking the sea, it stands majestically among fragrant Mediterranean *macchia* interspersed with wild acanthus, capers and parsley – from the latter (*selinon* in Greek) it took its Greek name, *Selinous*.

The ancient historians Thucydides and Diodorus Siculus claim that Selinunte was founded in 7th century BC by colonists from Megara Hyblea (near Syracuse). The westernmost Greek colony in Sicily, it quickly became one of the most prosperous cities of Magna Græcia, reaching the apex of its development in the 6th–5th centuries BC. Its sudden and remarkable success, however, brought it into conflict with Elymian Segesta over questions of territorial supremacy, and in 409BC the Segestans, allied for the occasion with the Carthaginians, marched on the city 100,000 strong. Before reinforcements could arrive from Syracuse and Agrigentum, they had sacked and destroyed Selinunte and put the inhabitants to the sword in one of the most terrible massacres of the ancient world. The Syracusan Hermocrates later attempted to found a new settlement, but this effort was likewise repressed by Carthage, in 250BC; this time the population was resettled at Lilybaion. Thereafter Selinunte was used as a garrison town by the Carthaginians. Its destruction was completed, at the end of the First Punic War, by the Romans; what they left standing is thought to have been toppled by earthquake in the Middle Ages.

Systematic excavation of the site began in 1822–23 under the English archaeologists William Harris and Samuel Angeli, who unearthed, among other things, the famous metopes in the Palermo museum. Today archaeologists are still digging. The many magnificent temples are designated by letters, as their dedications are still uncertain. All except Temples B and G are peripteral and hexastyle, and all face east. The measurements given in the text refer to the temple stylobates.

The archaeological site encompasses four distinct districts. From the new car park and entrance pavilion, a dirt track leads up to the **East Group of Temples**, which stand on high ground above a marshy depression now called the Gorgo di Cottone. These are the most important temples of Selinunte. Probably surrounded by a single enclosure at one time, they provide a clue to the opulence of the Greek city in the 6th and 5th centuries BC. **Temple E**, possibly dedicated to Hera or Aphrodite, dates from 490–480BC. It is a Doric building measuring 6.7 x 25.3m; four of its metopes, now in the Palermo museum, give an idea of the beauty of its sculptural decoration. Its 1958 reconstruction makes extensive use of moulded concrete – a technique that (fortunately) was later abandoned. Just to the north lie the remains of **Temple F**, the oldest (560–540BC) and smallest (61.8 x 24.4m) on this hill – and also the most pillaged. It may have been dedicated to Athena or Dionysus. Further north, beyond a dirt track, lie the impressive remains of **Temple G**, one of the larger temples of Classical antiquity. It measures 110.4 x 50.1m; the fallen capitals give some idea of its colossal scale. Probably dedicated to Zeus or Apollo, it was begun some time after 550BC and was still unfinished when the Carthaginians took the town. Today just one colossal column, 16m high and 3.5m in diameter, emerges from the overgrown ruins. The cella, preceded by a pronaos of four columns, had three aisles, the central one open to the sky. Away to the west is a restored farmhouse, the Balio Florio, which may soon become a museum.

Temple E at Selinunte

From the east group of temples an old road winds its way across the Gorgo di Cottone (site of one of the ancient harbours, now silted up) to the **Acropolis**. The road may be walked or driven as far as the second car park, below the acropolis. The acropolis stands on a sloping terrace directly above the sea, with splendid views in all directions (that to the east is marred somewhat by the modern resort of Marinella). Have a look, as you walk up, at the massive walls, erected in the 6th–5th centuries and rein-forced in 307–306BC. The ruins are criss-crossed by two main streets which divide the site into four quarters. If you are not careful you walk right by **Temples A** and **O**, identical in form and dimension (40m x 16m) and thought to have been dedicated to Castor and Pollux. Built in 490–480BC, they were the latest and probably the most perfect of the temples of Selinunte. Devotees had to step up to reach the cella from the pronaos, and step up again to reach the adytum; the roof could be reached by two spiral staircases set between the pronaos and the cella. Some traces of propylaea exist to the east, and a sacred area believed to pre-date the cataclysm of 409 has been found near Temple O. In front of Temple A is a mosaic pave-ment with a representation of the Punic goddess Tanit.

Temple C (63.7 x 24m), across the street, dates from the early 6th century BC and is thought to have been dedicated to Apollo. This is where the most famous metopes in the Palermo archaeological museum were found. Fourteen immense columns (the smallest are nearly 2m in diameter at the base) were reconstructed along the north side in 1925–27, and you can still see part of the sacrificial altar. Crosses carved on some of the archi-

Temple C on the acropolis at Selinunte

tectural fragments suggest the temple was still standing in the Christian age, and there are traces of a Byzantine village in the area which may have been destroyed in the medieval earthquake. To the south of the temple is a megaron (17.6 x 5.5m) dating from 580–570BC. In the east corner of the temenos a stoa has been excavated which was probably built at the same time as the acropolis walls. To the right is the small **Temple B**, a prostyle aediculum with pronaos and cella. It may have been erected in honour of Empedocles, the famous philosopher and scientist of Agrigento who is said to have engineered (and paid for) the drainage and improvement of the Cottone marshlands.

Turn right on the acropolis's north-south thoroughfare to reach **Temple D**, which flanks the road. It dates from 570–554BC and is thought to have been dedicated to Poseidon or Aphrodite. The stylobate, which carried 34 columns, measures 56 x 24m; the entrance, like that of the other temples, was on the west. Some of the stone blocks of this temple still display the bosses used for manoeuvring them into place. Fronting a road near the temple is a row of modest constructions thought to have been shops, each with two rooms, a courtyard, and stairs up to the living quarters on the first floor. Nearby are the foundations of the **Temple of the Small Metopes**, so called because it is thought the six small metopes now in the Palermo museum belong to it; it had a simple cella and adytum and measured 15.2 x 5.4m.

Continuing northwards you enter the **Ancient City**, the third archaeo-logical area, by the well preserved **North Gate**. This is one of the main gates of the city, part of the original 6th-century walls. Outside is a sophis-ticated defence system once thought to date from the time of Hermocrates but probably constructed somewhat later, using material from the acrop-olis. The fortifications include three semicircular towers and a second line of walls c 5m outside the earlier ones. The ancient city itself is still being excavated: there are remains of streets and foundations of a few houses. Recent research has suggested it may originally have extended beyond the (later) perimeter wall to the north and into the valleys of the Cottone and Modione rivers. After 409BC the few surviving Selinuntines, who lived on the acropolis, may have used it as a necropolis.

To visit Selinunte's fourth and most recent dig you have to return to the acropolis and descend the track at the end of the main east-west street, then cross over to the right bank of the River Modione. In just a few minutes you reach the unimpressive but important remains of the **Sanctuary of Demeter Malophoros** – an area sacred to the goddess of fertility and of the harvest (literally, Demeter the Apple Bearer), now approached by a 5th-century propylon and portico. In the centre is a huge sacrificial altar, and beyond, the temple, a megaron, thought to have been built c 560BC. Nearby are the scant remains of two other sacred precincts, one of them dedicated to **Zeus Meilichios** with two altars, where numerous stelae carved with a male and female head were discovered. Very well known in antiquity, the Sanctuary of Demeter Malophoros survived the decline of the city, being frequented by Carthaginians and Byzantine Christians. Thousands of terracotta figurines of the goddess have been found in the vicinity. Another temple is being excavated to the south. Near a spring, some 200m north, a sacred edifice has recently been excavated and called **Temple M**. This may in fact be an altar or a monumental fountain of the 6th century BC. Two inhumation necropolises excavated nearby have yielded proto-Corinthian and Corinthian artefacts. A cinerary necropolis, northwest of the Sanctuary of Demeter Malophoros, has yielded pottery of the 5th century BC.

If you still have your legs after visiting Selinunte, a very pleasant 6km (3 ³/₄-mile) walk leads west along the beach to the **Rocche di Cusa** (also reached by bus), the ancient quarries from which the column drums for the temples were drawn. Surrounded by olive and orange plantations, the quarries have not been worked since the destruction of Selinunte, and you can still see several huge drums half-hewn out of the rock or lined up awaiting shipment. It is thought that wooden frames were constructed around these 100-tonne stones, which were transported to Selinunte on wheels of solid wood strengthened by iron bands and pulled by oxen or slaves.

Sciacca and Eraclea Minoa

Between Selinunte and Agrigento lies some of the more pleasant, peaceful landscape in western Sicily. Citrus plantations, vineyards and fields of artichokes line the road, which meanders through low hills offering occasional glimpses of the sea. Along this coast lie medieval Sciacca, on a hillside above its harbour, and Eraclea Minoa, a Greek site in a breathtaking position above a beautiful (and deserted) white beach.

Sciacca

Sciacca is a pretty but neglected town of 40,000 souls, which seems to tumble down a hillside to the sea. Since antiquity it has been known as a spa: the Greeks called it *Thermai Selinuntinai* and the Romans, *Thermæ Selinuntinæ*. Both took the waters of its hot sulphur springs to cure their rheumatism. The Romans also introduced a system of intensive cultivation that relaunched the town economically and made it an important stop on the road from Syracuse to Lilybæum. Its present appearance was modelled mostly by the Arabs and Normans; the name Sciacca is Arabic, although its origin and meaning are unknown. In the 15th and 16th centuries Sciacca was notorious for the feud between the local Perollo clan and the Spanish Luna family. Known as the *Caso di Sciacca* (the 'Sciacca Affair'), it ended only after half the population lay dead. Today as in the past, Sciacca's livelihood comes from fishing, thermal cures, and traditional **pottery**. Its ceramic artists are among Sicily's finest; their shops are concentrated along the busy Via Licata and around the harbour. A characteristic decoration of the ceramics of Sciacca is made up of two facing, convex plant motifs joined by a rosette. Distinctive colours are deep red, dark green and brown. Some very fine examples of Sciacca ceramics are preserved in the museums of Palermo and Trapani.

Sciacca is one of those towns whose ambience is more important than its single monuments. The city centre is made up of three distinct neighbourhoods, each of which occupies a terrace on the hillside. At the top of the town is the medieval quarter, a maze of narrow streets and stepped walkways. Next comes the narrow strip of churches and palaces on either side of the main street, Corso Vittorio Emanuele. Below this, the fishermen's and artisans' quarter descends to the picturesque harbour. A promenade planted with palm trees skirts the clifftop to the east, before the Art Nouveau-style Nuovo Stabilimento Termale and the Grand Hotel (open June–October for thermal baths and mud therapy); modern suburbs extend to the west.

Dress to be seen if you visit Piazza Scandaliato after six; this splendid garden terrace overlooking the sea is where the townsfolk meet for the evening promenade. The church of San Domenico is an 18th-century remake of the 1534 original; the former Collegio dei Gesuiti, now the town hall, has a lovely 17th-century courtyard. Just a block east, along the Corso, are Piazza Duomo and the **Cathedral** (locally known as the Basilica), founded in 1108 but rebuilt in 1656. The apses are all that is left of the original Norman church; the unfinished Baroque façade has marble statues by Antonino and Gian Domenico Gagini in niches. In the hilltop medieval quarter are the **Palazzo Steripinto**, a Catalan-Gothic palace of 1501 with diamond-point rustication, and the 14th-century church of **Santa Margherita**, with a beautiful portal sculpted by Francesco Laurana and his school (1468). The 16th-century Porta San Salvatore, the main gate of Sciacca, is adorned with Plateresque carvings.

In the oldest part of town, reached by Via Santa Caterina, are the Romanesque churches of San Nicolò la Latina, with a simple façade and triple apse, and Santa Maria delle Giummare (or Valverde), with two Norman towers and 18th-century stuccoes inside. The 14th-century Castello Luna, along Sciacca's eastern walls, is in ruins.

Eraclea Minoa

Midway between Sciacca and Agrigento a turning leads seawards to the ruins of **Eraclea Minoa**, magnificently situated at the mouth of the ancient Halykos (now the Platani). The beautiful, meandering river (which the road follows for c 4km/2¹/2 miles), the low hills planted with vineyards, and the white limestone cliffs plummeting down to an enchanting crescent-shaped beach make this site well worth a visit even if you have had your fill of ruins. The wooded shore here was saved from development in 1991 when part of it was purchased by the World Wide Fund for Nature; no refreshments are available, but it is a beautiful place to picnic.

Although there is fragmentary evidence that the settlement may date as far back as the Neolithic age, the oldest certain signs suggest it was founded by the Phoenicians: the city is mentioned in documents as *Macara* (from Macar, the Phoenician Hercules), and the Phoenicians made the oldest coins that have been found on the spot.

The name *Minoa* recalls the mythical version of the city's origin. As the story goes, Dædalus, builder of the Labyrinth, escaped Crete with the help of his man-made wings and came here, hotly pursued by his former master, King Minos. Minos discovered Dædalus at the court of the Sicilian Cocalus, but he was murdered there and his fleet destroyed; *Minoa*, according to the legend, was founded by the few sailors who survived. This story is picked up by Diodorus Siculus, who records that Theron of Akragas found the bones of Minos at Minoa and returned them to Crete. Whether fact, fiction or a mixture of both, the tale gave the Greeks of Selinunte sufficient claim to establish a colony here in the 6th century BC; the name *Heracleia* is thought to have been added later by Spartan émigrés.

Because the Halykos formed the boundary between the Greek and Carthaginian territories in Sicily, the city held immense strategic value for both sides and was captured and recaptured until the advent of the Romans in 210BC. By the time of Augustus, however, it seems to have been abandoned, possibly because of a landslide that swept the southern part of town and its walls into the sea.

Excavations begun in 1907 have brought to light part of the **residential quarter**, where different layers show traces of Greek and Roman houses, including wall paintings and mosaic pavements. You can also see a stretch of the **defensive walls**, ending in a square Roman tower. The beautiful **theatre**, with its view over the sea, has been covered with plexiglass to protect the soft sandstone from eroding. Constructed in the 4th century BC, it is one of the finest extant examples of a Classical Greek theatre in Sicily. A small **museum** displays finds from the excavations.

Agrigento

Agrigento, a large provincial capital on high ground overlooking the sea, is the *Akragas* of the Greeks and the *Agrigentum* of the Romans. Although a legend claims it was founded by Dædalus, it seems to have been established by colonists from Rhodes and nearby Gela, in the early 6th century BC. In alliance with Syracuse it defeated the Carthaginians at Himera in 480BC, captured Carthage, and so extended its wealth and power that Pindar (who lived here) described it as 'the fairest city of men'. Its population was then about 200,000. Its breed of horses was famous throughout the ancient world, and the racing chariot found on coins minted here may derive from their many successes at the Olympic Games. In 406BC the Carthaginians took the city and burned it after a siege of eight months. The Greeks under Timoleon won it back in 340 and rebuilt it, but in 261 and again in 210 it was taken by the Romans, in whose possession it remained until the fall of the empire. It fell to the Saracens in 827 and was renamed *Kerkent*; in 1087 it was conquered by the Normans, who developed it as a centre of trade between Sicily and Africa. The present town (called *Girgenti* until Mussolini's time) occupies only the acropolis of the Greek city. The archaeological area, known as the 'Valley of the Temples', is particularly beautiful in early spring, when the almond trees are in bloom. Natives of Agrigento include Empedocles (c 490–430BC), the poet, scientist and philosopher, and Luigi Pirandello (1867–1936), the playwright. Pirandello's birthplace, in the country, can be visited.

The Ancient City

In *A Tour through Sicily and Malta* (1773) writer Patrick Brydone recalls that 'Plato, when he visited Sicily, was so much struck with the luxury of Agrigentum, both in their houses and their tables, that a saying of his is still recorded: that they built as if they were never to die, and eat as if they had not an hour to live'.

The ancient city extended from the high hill where the modern town now stands to the lower ridge somewhat capriciously called the Valley of the Temples. It had a regular, chequerboard plan, with long east-west main streets intersected at right angles by narrower cross-streets. Its fortifications, partly cancelled by new building, ran along the ridge known as the Rupe Atenea, then dipped down into the valley of the Akragas River (today the San Biago), turning west along the line of the temples and north along the Hypsas River (now the San Leone), returning to the ridge top beyond the so-called Valley of Empedocles. The temples of Agrigento all belong to the Doric order and are entirely made of locally quarried limestone which time has turned to a rich golden brown. Traces of pigmented marble dust on some surfaces suggest that the soft stone was given a protective coating of plaster and brightly painted above the capitals. Agrigento is Sicily's most popular archaeological site, and in peak season can be quite crowded.

The most convenient way to visit the ruins is to make a circuit beginning at the upper (east) end of the Valley of the Temples. The Strada Panoramica takes you to the southeast corner of the ancient city, a stone's throw from the beautifully situated **Temple of Hera**. Set just inside the city walls in the vicinity of Gate 3 and dating from the late 5th century BC, it is one of the city's oldest temples. For a long time it was confused with the temple dedicated to Hera on the Lacinian promontory at Croton – hence its popular name, the 'Temple of Juno Lacinia'. It is a peripteral hexastyle building (in layman's terms, a construction surrounded by a colonnade, with six columns on the main west front), and it measures 38 x 16.8m at the stylobate. Twenty-five of its 34 columns are still standing; the walls of the cella collapsed in a medieval earthquake. There is a large sacrificial altar at the east end of the temple, and a cistern at the west end. If you look closely at the columns you can see traces of a fire in 406BC.

The road to the temples now runs parallel to the ancient city walls, riddled with Byzantine tomb recesses, which Goethe believed must have been reserved for the Brave and the Good ('what fairer resting place could they have found as a memorial to their glory and an immortal example to the living?'). Almond and olive trees grow all around. Some 500m along, on a little rise on the left, stands the **Temple of Concord**, one of best preserved of all Greek temples. The harmony of its proportions and the majesty of its forms are matched only by the Theseion in Athens. Erected in the mid-5th century BC and possibly dedicated to the Dioscuri, Castor and Pollux (the present name appears in a Latin inscription found here, but has no real connection with the temple), it stands on a stylobate of 39.3 x 16.9m and is peripteral and hexastyle in form. The cella has a pronaos and opisthodomus, both *in antis* (front and rear porches, both projecting outward). The arches in the side walls of the cella were knocked out in the 6th century AD when the temple was made into a Christian church.

The Villa Aurea (opened to the public for temporary exhibitions, but otherwise closed) was the home of Alexander Hardcastle, an eccentric Englishman who financed the excavations of Agrigento in the early 20th century. Across the road is an extensive burial ground that remained in use for many centuries. It includes a Roman necropolis, an Early Christian catacomb, and a Byzantine cemetery.

The adjacent **Temple of Herakles**, a heap of ruins (67 x 25m at the stylobate) with nine columns standing upright, dates from c 500BC – which makes it the oldest of the temples in this area. It was a peripteral hexastyle building of 38 columns, with a central cella, pronaos and opisthodomus *in antis*. In antiquity it was known for its statue of Herakles and for a painting of the infant Herakles strangling the serpents, by Zeuxis.

Outside Gate 5 – the main gate or Porta Aurea of Akragas – is a Roman funerary monument mistakenly called the **Tomb of Theron**, a two-storeyed edifice with blind doors in its massive limestone walls, a Doric entablature and Ionic corner columns. It stands on the edge of a large Roman cemetery which extends eastwards below the line of the walls. From here, Highway 115 and a dirt track lead east to the little **Temple of Asklepios** (visible in the fields to the right) which, according to Cicero, contained a statue of Apollo by Myron. It dates from the 5th century BC.

The ruins of the **Temple of Olympian Zeus**, or Olympieion, lie 'scattered far and wide like the disjointed bones of a gigantic skeleton', as Goethe remarks, in an enclosure west of the café and car park. The immense building is thought to have been begun by the Carthaginian prisoners taken at Himera and left unfinished in 406. It is the largest Doric temple known

Temple of Hera, Agrigento

(110.1 x 52.7m), and in the plans of the tyrant Theron it was to have been one of the largest of all Greek temples. Its design was unique in the ancient world. Archaeologists call it pseudoperipteral heptastyle – meaning the seven columns at each end and the 14 along the sides were engaged in the walls to form a false portico. The half-columns were 16.7m high and 4m wide at the base. Goethe observed that 'it would take twenty-two men, placed shoulder to shoulder, to form a circle approximating in size to the circumference of such a column'; when he stood in one of the flutes, his shoulders barely touched both edges. Between the half-columns were 38 colossal telamones; their exact arrangement is still under discussion, and there are drawings detailing the various hypotheses in the archaeological museum. Also in the museum is a recomposed telamon, a cast of which lies at the centre of the cella here.

Further west, in the vicinity of Gate 5, are several shrines that formed a **Sanctuary of the Chthonic Divinities**. They were enclosed in a single precinct, the wall of which is visible to the west. The most famous building here is certainly the 'Temple of Castor and Pollux', which for its artful combination of columns and trabeation is often taken as *the* symbol of Classical Sicily. Oddly enough, no-one really knows to whom it was dedicated, and its present appearance is a spurious 19th-century reconstruction using material from other temples. It is known to have been erected in the late 5th century BC, damaged by the Carthaginians, and restored to its peripteral hexastyle form by the Greeks, only to be destroyed, ultimately, by earthquake. Nearby is a complex believed to be a Sanctuary of Demeter and Kore, constructed in the 6th and 5th centuries BC. The oldest structures – two sacred enclosures with an altar within – stand at the north end; the other altars and three small temples are somewhat later.

Approached through the 15th-century cloisters of the former Cisterian abbey of San Nicola, the **Museo Archeologico Regionale** is one of Sicily's finest. It stands in an area of the ancient city that was used for public assemblies – as the 3rd-century ekklesiasterion, through which you must walk to reach the museum, attests. In one corner is the so-called Oratory of Phalaris, probably a late Hellenistic shrine, which was later made into a chapel. The abbey church contains a magnificent Attic or Roman sarcophagus of the 2nd or 3rd century AD, portraying four episodes in the story of Hippolytus and Phædra.

The museum itself is brilliantly arranged in a contemporary building utilising a part of the former monastery. Among its many treasures are Bronze Age material from sites near Agrigento; a superb pottery collection, including Corinthian and Rhodian ware and Attic black- and red-figured vases; many fine architectural fragments; the famous Giant, one of the telamones from the Temple of Zeus, and several other telamon heads; a 5th-century statue of Apollo (or the river-god Akragas) known as the *Ephebe of Agrigento*; and a large 5th-century red-figure krater from Gela, beautifully painted with a representation of *Battling Amazons*.

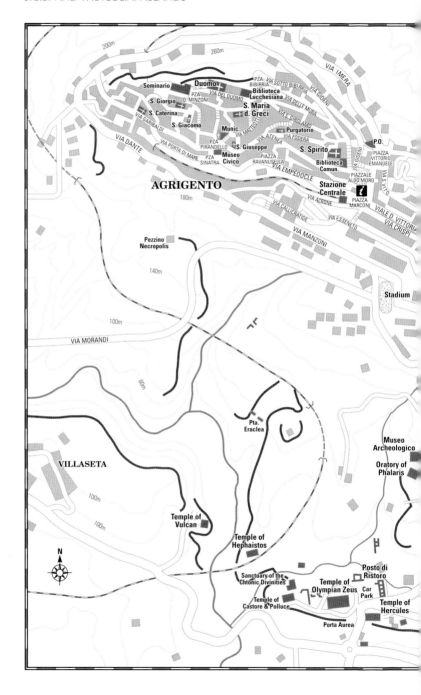

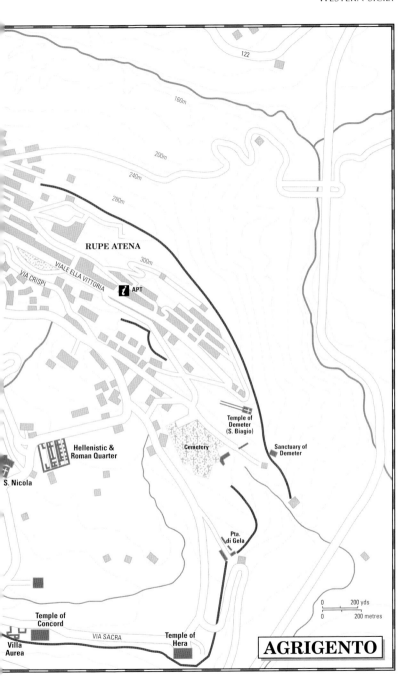

122

160m

200m

240m

280m

RUPE ATENA

300m

VIALE ELLA VITTORIA

VIA CRISPI

i APT

Temple of
Demeter
(S. Biagio)

Cemetery

Sanctuary of
Demeter

Hellenistic &
Roman Quarter

S. Nicola

Pta.
di Gela

0   200 yds
0   200 metres

Temple of
Concord

VIA SACRA

Temple of
Hera

Villa
Aurea

AGRIGENTO

Telamone from the Temple of Zeus now in the Archaeological Museum, Agrigento

Across the Via dei Templi from the museum is the entrance to the **Hellenistic and Roman Quarter**, with some of the best-preserved ancient houses in Sicily. The street system, in keeping with the precepts of Hyppodamos of Mileto, is composed of a regular network of avenues (*plateiai*) crossed at right angles by secondary streets (*stenopoi*); it dates from the late 4th century BC. The Romans built over the foundations of the Greek houses here and embellished their new homes with mosaic pavements and stucco and fresco wall decorations. Generally speaking you can distinguish the Greek houses from the Roman because the Greeks' rooms were arranged around a peristyle, whereas the Romans preferred to dispose their rooms around an atrium and ambulatory. The water pipes and sewers also date from the Roman period. The civic life of the quarter probably lasted until the early Middle Ages, when Agrigento's diminished population withdrew to the acropolis hill.

What may be oldest temple at Agrigento is actually *in* rather than on the

Byzantine tomb recesses in the ancient city walls, Agrigento

hill. This is the **Rock Sanctuary of Demeter**, near the modern cemetery. It is traditionally thought to pre-date the foundation of Akragas, although a current interpretation dates it to the 5th century BC. A steep flight of steps leads down through gardens to the natural caverns in the rock, where numerous statuettes of Demeter and Kore have been found, and to a man-made tunnel which carried spring water from deep within the mountain to a sacred fountain. Not far from the sanctuary is the little church of **San Biagio**, built by the Normans over the remains of a temple of Demeter and Kore dating from 480–460BC: you can still see some of its foundations behind the apse.

The Medieval and Modern City

The Normans 'delivered' Agrigento from the Arabs only to make it the hub of their extensive trade relations with North Africa. To give power and authority to the new centre, they also made it the seat of a wealthy diocese. Today Agrigento is a pleasant medieval town overlooking the Mediterranean and the Valley of the Temples from its high hill.

Goethe was particularly struck by the view from the town when he visited *Girgenti* in 1787. 'I swear that I have never in my whole life enjoyed such a vision,' he commented. 'The new Girgenti stands on the site of the ancient citadel, which covers an area large enough to house a city. From our windows we look down over a wide, gentle slope, now entirely covered with gardens and vineyards, so that one would never guess this was once a densely populated urban quarter. All one can see rising out of this green and flowering area is the Temple of Concord near its southern edge and the scanty ruins of the Temple of Juno to the east. All the other sacred ruins, which lie along a straight line between these two points, are invisible from this height. At the foot of the slope, looking south, lies the shore plain, which extends for about two miles till it reaches the sea'.

But Agrigento's historic centre is interesting for more than its view. From the main Via Atenea, Via Porcello and the stepped Salita Santo Spirito lead up to the church and convent of **Santo Spirito** (if the church is closed, ring at the convent), founded by the powerful Chiaramonte family for Cistercian nuns in the 13th century. The nuns' modern successors still make marzipan fruit and other delicious sweets, and if you manage to get up here you should not leave empty handed. The church has a composite façade with a Gothic portal and 14th-century rose window, and 18th-century stuccoes attributed to Giacomo Serpotta inside. The convent has a beautiful cloister and a chapter house with 14th- to 16th-century frescoes. Since 1990 it has housed the **Museo Civico**, with modest collections of antiquities, paintings and ethnographical material.

Near the top of Via Atenea, by the church of San Giuseppe, Via Bac-Bac and the stepped Via Saponara mount to **Santa Maria dei Greci**, a small basilica built over a Doric temple of the 5th century BC. The smooth, simple façade, tightly bound all around by houses, has a beautifully carved Chiaramonte-style portal. You can see remains of the antique building in the church interior and in a passage below the north aisle, entered from the little courtyard.

The narrow alleys to the north lead to Via del Duomo and the **Cathedral**, dedicated to Agrigento's first bishop, St Gerlando. The original Norman church was built in the late 11th century (some say over a Greek temple), but altered in the 14th, 16th and 17th centuries. It's somewhat upstaged by the unfinished 15th-century campanile, with beautiful Catalan-Gothic arches and balustrades and Arab-Norman zigzag moulding. Steps lead up to the Latin-cross interior, which has three aisles separated by ogival arches on tall piers, a 16th-century painted wood ceiling at the west end and 16th-century coffers to the east. The chapel of the patron saint, in the south transept, contains a fine silver reliquary of 1639. A singular acoustic phenomenon allows a person standing in the apse to hear what is said, even in a whisper, beside the main doorway 85m away. The cathedral museum has been closed since it was damaged by a landslide in 1966.

The Mafia

Some years back, the Mafia was defined by the *Oxford English Dictionary* as 'often erroneously supposed to constitute an organised secret society existing for criminal purposes'. By the time the *New Shorter* version was published, the first five words had been deleted from the definition. The dictionary's erudite editors were not the only ones who were late to acknowledge the Mafia's existence: the first use of the term in the Italian penal code dates only from 1982.

The development of the Mafia in Sicily can be linked to centuries of external rule, misrule, exploitation and injustice – which did little to encourage regard for the State. Among the factors which contributed to its growth were the failure of Sicily's foreign governments to establish equitable rule by law, the resistance to democratic social organisation by the island's feudal aristocracy, and the impulse among the peasantry to organise an efficient defence against oppression.

The first *mafiosi* were companies of armed men hired by wealthy landowners to enforce the law as they saw fit. Against them arose peasant self-defence groups, often supported by rival aristocrats who wished to strengthen their local influence by weakening that of their neighbours. These bands were organised along the lines of the extended family, with sons, brothers and cousins forming a small army. Members owed allegiance only to the family head, or *don*, who in turn was bound by a code of honour to live austerely, donate money to charity, look after his own, protect women and children, etc. The integrity of each *cosca*, or family was assured by a strict code of silence and secrecy, violation of which was punished with death.

This, the old-style Mafia, was essentially a rural phenomenon. It filled the vacuum left by the absence of efficient State institutions, and it flourished until the time of Mussolini, who found its authoritarian hold over the populace a threat to his own and conducted a number of anti-Mafia purges.

The end of World War II and the advent of the Cold War, however, brought a resurgence of Mafia activity. The liberation of Sicily was rendered swift and relatively painless by the collaboration of the Mafia with the US Army. The mediator in this singularly cynical alliance was the American gangster Lucky Luciano. In return for their help in assuring the smooth progression of the Allied landings and occupation, the Mafia bosses were aided by the Ango-American postwar administration. The US administration was also prepared to re-establish the Mafia's authority in Sicily in order to prevent the Communists from gaining control.

The end of the war saw the beginning of the new-style Mafia, in which the power of money thoroughly eradicated all old-fashioned notions of honour. At this time the Mafia made a move to the cities from the country and became involved in building speculation, protection rackets, prostitution and, eventually, drug processing and trafficking. Also at this time, they infiltrated the central government by making an alliance with the leading figures of the majority coalition. This powerful alliance is one of the factors that allowed the Christian Democrats to remain in power for more than 45 years.

Things went from bad to worse when the Mafia, or *Cosa Nostra* ('Our Business'), came under the ruthless, authoritarian sway of Salvatore Riina. He came from the Corleonese family and eliminated all opposition to gain control of the highly lucrative heroin trade.

Riina's was a reign of terror and he is thought to have been responsible for at least 150 murders. His policy, however, contained the seeds of his undoing, as other *mafiosi* such as Tommaso Buscettta turned against him. Riina was behind the killing of at least four members of Buscetta's family, including two of his children. Buscetta sought revenge by turning State's witness and testifying against Riina. He was the first important *mafioso* to turn, and in so doing he started an avalanche of confessions that resulted in the 'maxi-trials' of the 1980s, which led to hundreds of convictions. The Mafia fought back by targeting journalists, politicians, judges, lawyers and police chiefs. In 1992 violence in Palermo reached new levels with the assassination of public prosecutors Giovanni Falcone and Piero Borsellino. In spite of this violent reaction, the confessions continued and resulted in the arrest and imprisonment of Salvatore Riina in 1993.

Supposedly on the run for the previous 24 years, Riina had been living at home in Corleone. He was turned in by his driver, who thought things were getting too dangerous and confessed. The political fallout following his arrest was enormous. It became obvious that the head of the Mafia could not have lived openly in Corleone, sending his children to school, etc, without a very high level of protection. That protection is now believed to have come from a top-level Christian Democrat: at the time of writing one of the party's most influential politicians, Giulio Andreotti, seven-times Prime Minister and a member of every postwar government in which his party participated, has been accused of association with the Mafia. If found guilty, he is likely to spend the rest of his life behind bars.

The end of the story is unclear. The Italians view the Mafia as a many-headed monster – as one head is chopped off, another grows in its place. However, huge steps forward have been taken in recent years and, most importantly, the invincibility of the Mafia has been shown to be a myth.

The Isole Pelagie

Set like rare jewels in the southernmost territorial waters of Italy, Lampedusa, Lampione and Linosa are much closer to Africa than to Sicily. The name under which they are collectively known, **Isole Pelagie**, is curiously tautological: *pelagos* means 'sea' in Greek. The three small islands have different geological profiles: Lampedusa and Lampione are made of limestone and are part of the African continental shelf; Linosa is volcanic and is part of Sicily.

Traditionally considered too small and exposed to serve as military bases notwithstanding their location on the busiest sea route in the Mediterranean, the Isole Pelagie have always been isolated. On one hand this has favoured the development of an independent economy on the islands; on the other it has preserved them from the devastating effects of mass tourism. Their untamed natural beauty has therefore survived intact, and today the islands enjoy a wide reputation for their extraordinary flora and fauna. Sea turtles nest on their beaches, seals sun on their reefs, and migratory birds pause on their rocks.

The largest and most popular of the islands is **Lampedusa** (20 sq km/7³/4 sq miles, 5100 inhab.), once known for its sponges. It appears as a long, sloping rock rising out of the sea like a whale. The coast is honeycombed with caves and reefs, and interspersed with small sandy coves. Although there are traces of the passage of Phoenicians, Greeks, Romans and Arabs, its real colonisation dates from 1843, when Ferdinand I of Bourbon discovered it was a convenient place to send his enemies. Now, the island's trendy hotels are concentrated at the southern tip, in and around Lampedusa town.

Lampione, northwest of Lampedusa, is a rock with an automatic lighthouse. **Linosa**, 48km (30 miles) from Lampedusa and 161km (100 miles) from Sicily, was once a volcano. There are three extinct cones on the island – Monte Rosso, Monte Vulcano (the highest peak, 195m) and Monte di Ponente. They have not shown signs of activity for at least 200 years. Like Lampedusa it has a mild climate, with warm, sunny winters and hot summers which are usually made bearable by cooling breezes. Unlike the white limestone of Lampedusa, however, Linosa's black volcanic soil retains the heat, and when there is no breeze summer temperatures can exceed 40°C (104°F).

Linosa was sparsely inhabited in the Roman and Arabic periods, probably as a logistical base for slave ships. It was not formally settled until 1845, when the Bourbon governor Bernardo Maria Sanvisente landed here with 40 colonists from Agrigento. Its pleasant little village is a jumble of brightly coloured houses. Farming and fishing are the main livelihoods, and its rocky bottoms are popular with divers. Until recently the island also held a prison, used especially for terrorists and *mafiosi*.

Practical Information

Getting There

BY AIR
Palermo's **Punta Raisi Airport** lies 30km (18 miles) west of the city. From here it is easy to reach most destinations in Western Sicily. Highway S113 and Autostrada A29/E90 connect the airport to central Palermo in about 30min. There are direct flights to Palermo from Bari, Bologna, Florence, Lampedusa, Milan, Naples, Pantelleria and Rome; most international flights connect through Rome. The airlines that serve Palermo all have free-phone numbers: *Alitalia*, 1478 65643; *Meridiana*, 323 494; *Alpi Eagles*, 167 555 777. Lampedusa is connected by daily flights to Catania, too; contact *Alpi Eagles* for details.

BY RAIL
Intercity trains run from Messina to Palermo several times daily, covering the 232km (144 miles) in c 3hr 20min. They stop at Milazzo, Sant'Agata di Militello, Cefalù and Termini Imerese. There is frequent local service between Catania and Palermo (243km/150 miles in c 3hr 20min, stopping at Enna and Caltanisetta), Palermo and Agrigento (138km/85 miles in c 2hr), and Palermo and Trapani (126km/78 miles in c 2hr 10min, stopping

at Segesta; a branch line from Alcamo serves Marsala).

BY ROAD

The motorway from **Messina to Palermo** has yet to be completed. At the time of writing you must follow Autostrada A20/E90 to Torre del Lauro, switch to Highway S113, then return to Autostrada A/20-A19/E90 at Castelbuono. The total journey of approximately 230km (143 miles) takes 2hr 40min.

Here are some of the fastest routes from point to point in western Sicily; travel times, of course, are based on posted speed limits and do not take account for heavy traffic: **Palermo–Monreale**, 8km (5 miles) in 20min by S186; **Palermo–Bagheria**, 18km (11 miles) in 20min by A19/E90; **Palermo–Erice**, 85km (53 miles) in 1hr 10min by A29/E90 and S187; **Palermo–Trapani**, 97km (60 miles) in 1hr by A29 and A29dir; **Palermo–Segesta**, 64km (40 miles) in 40min by A29 and A29 dir; **Segesta–Erice**, 41km (25 miles) in 30min by S115, S113 and S187; **Palermo–Marsala**, 91km (56 miles) in 50min by A29 and A29dir; **Palermo–Selinunte**, 106km (66 miles) in 1hr 10min by A29/E90, S115/E931 and S115d; **Selinunte–Sciacca**, 34km (21 miles) in 40min by S115 and local roads; **Agrigento–Eraclea Minoa**, 36km (22 miles) in 40min by S115/E931 and local roads.

If you are travelling by car you can make a circuit of Sicily, touching upon the major places along the coast and one or two of the important inland sights. The western portion of the circuit can be made as follows: **Palermo–Erice**, 85km (53 miles) in 1hr 10min; **Erice–Segesta**, 41km (25 miles) in 30min; **Segesta–Marsala**, 48km (30 miles) in 40min; **Marsala–Selinunte**, 88km (55 miles) in 1hr; Selinunte–Sciacca, 34km (21 miles) in 40min; **Sciacca–Agrigento**, 60km (37 miles) in 1hr. To continue, see Chapters 6 and 7.

BY SEA

Ferry service to **Palermo** from Genoa and Livorno (daily except Sun) is operated by *Grandi Traghetti*, Via Mariano Stabile 53, Palermo (tel. 091 587 939, fax 091 589 629); from Naples (daily) and Cagliari (Friday), by *Tirrenia Navigazione*, Calata Marinai d'Italia, Palermo (tel. 091 333 300, fax 091 602 1221). There is also a catamaran that makes the run between Naples and Palermo (daily, Mar–Oct); contact *Navitalia*, Calata Marinai d'Italia, Palermo (tel.091 584 535).

From Palermo you can reach the **Æolean Islands** by hydrofoil, daily Jun–Sep (1hr 50min); information and tickets from *Aliscafi SNAV*, Agenzia Barbaro, Piazza Principe di Belmonte 51/55 (tel. 091 586 533, fax 091 584 830). There are also daily connections for **Ustica** by ferry (2hr 30min) and hydrofoil (1hr 15min); contact *Siremar*, Via Francesco Crispi 118, Palermo (tel. 091 582 403).

Trapani is connected to the **Egadi Islands** by ferry (daily, from 1hr to 2hr 45min) and hydrofoil (daily, from 15min to 1hr); contact *Siremar*, Agenzia Mare Viaggi, Via Staiti 61/63 (tel. 0923 540 515, fax 0923 20663); and to Cagliari (Tue), by *Tirrenia Navigazione*, Agenzia Salvo, Corso Italia 48/52 (tel. 0923 21896, fax 0923 28436). There are also ferries to **Pantelleria** (daily, 4hr 45min) and Tunis; contact *Siremar*, Agenzia Mare Viaggi, Via Staiti 61/63 (tel. 0923 540 515, fax 0923 20663); on Pantelleria, the phone number is 0923 540 122.

Lampedusa is linked by ferry to **Porto Empedocle** (daily in 8hr 15min – no service Fri in winter); for information and tickets, contact *Siremar* in Porto Empedocle, Via Molo 13 (tel. 0922 636 685); or on Lampedusa, Via Luigi Rizzo (tel. 0922 970 003).

During the summer (Jun–Sep, Thu, Fri and Sat), hydrofoils run from **Cefalù** to the **Æolian Islands** in 1hr 30min; information and tickets from *Aliscafi SNAV*, Agenzia Barbaro, Corso Ruggero 76, Cefalù (tel. 0921 21595).

Tourist Information

AGRIGENTO Via Cimarra (tel. 0922) 604 284.

ERICE Viale Conte Peopoli 11 (tel. 0923 869 388, fax 0923 869 544).

MARSALA Via Garibaldi 45 (tel. 0923 714 097).

PALERMO Piazza Castelnuovo 34 (tel. 091 583 847, fax 091 331 854); Punta Raisi Airport (tel. 091 591 698); Stazione Centrale, Piazza Giulio Cesare (tel. 091 616 5914).

SCIACCA Corso Vittorio Emanuele 84 (tel. 0925 21182, fax 0925 84121).

TRAPANI & EGADI ISLANDS Villa Aula, Via Sorba 15 (tel. 0923 27077, fax 0923 29430); Piazza Saturno (tel. 0923 29000).

Hotels

AGRIGENTO
Jolly dei Templi, Contrada Angeli (tel. 0922 606 144, fax 0922 606 685). Modern and comfortable, with views of the Valley of the Temples; moderate.
Kaos, Contrada Pirandello (tel. 0922 598 622, fax 0922 598 770). An aristocratic villa with fine gardens, a lovely pool, and good views of the Temple of Concord; moderate.
Tre Torri (tel. 0922 606 733, fax 0922 607 839). Calm and functional, at the beginning of the Valley of the Temples; moderate.
Villa Athena, Via dei Templi (tel. 0922 596 288, fax 0922 402 180). An

18th-century aristocratic villa with gardens, orchards and views of the Temple of Concord; moderate.

ERICE
Edelweiss, Cortile Padre Vincenzo 3 (tel. 0923 869 420, fax 0923 869 252). Simple, friendly, and centrally located; inexpensive.
Elimo, Via Vittorio Emanuele 75 (tel. 0923 869 377, fax 0923 869 252). Elegant and comfortable, with a Middle Eastern air; moderate.
Moderno, Via Vittorio Emanuele 63 (tel. 0923 869 300, fax 0923 869 139). In a 19th-century townhouse with panoramic terrace and excellent kitchen; moderate.

ISOLE EGADI
Egadi, Via Colombo 17, Favignana (tel. 0923 921 232; seasonal). Simple, with just 11 rooms; inexpensive
Pensione dei Fenici, Via Calvario 18, Levanzo (tel. 0923 924 083; seasonal). A small family-run place; inexpensive.

LAMPEDUSA
Cavalluccio Marino (tel. 0922 970 053, fax 0922 970 767; seasonal). Inexpensive.
Guitgia Tommasino (tel. 0922 970 879, fax 0922 970 316; seasonal). Half pension only; inexpensive.
Martello (tel. 0922 970 025, fax 0922 971 696; seasonal). Inexpensive.

MARSALA
Cap 3000, Via Trapani 161 (tel. 0923 989 055, fax 0923 989 634). Modern, with good views of the Egadi islands; inexpensive.
President, Via Nino Bixio 1 (tel. 0923 999 333, fax 0923 999 115). Modern, quiet and comfortable; moderate.

MONDELLO
Mondello Palace, Viale Principe di Scalea 2 (tel. 091 450 001, fax 091 450 657). Comfortable and elegant, with a tropical garden and pool on the sea and an excellent restaurant; expensive.
Splendid Hotel La Torre, Via Piano di Gallo 11 (tel. 091 450 222, fax 091 450 033). Modern, on a headland with fine views and another first-rate restaurant; moderate.

PALERMO
Astoria Palace, Via Monte Pellegrino 62 (tel. 091 637 1820, fax 091 637 2178). A grand hotel with comfortable rooms and an excellent restaurant, enjoying beautiful views over the Sanctuary of Monte Pellegrino; expensive.
Centrale Palace, Corso Vittorio Emanuele (tel. 091 336 666, fax 091 334

881). A beautifully renovated patrician villa in the heart of Palermo; moderate, excellent value.

Cristal Palace, Via Roma 477/d (tel. 091 611 2580, fax 091 611 2589). Modern and functional; moderate.

Europa, Via Agrigento 3 (tel./fax 091 625 6323). Centrally located and comfortable; moderate.

Excelsior Palace, Via Marchese Ugo 3 (tel. 091 625 6176, fax 091 342 139). Furnished with genuine antiques, outstanding restaurant; expensive.

Grand Hotel Villa Igiea, Salita Belmonte 43 (tel. 091 543 744, fax 091 547 654). The city's most stately and renowned hotel: Art Nouveau décor, magnificent gardens and unrivalled views of Palermo and its harbour; fine restaurant; luxury.

Jolly del Foro Italico, Foro Italico 22 (tel. 091 616 5090, fax 091 616 1441). An elegant, comfortable place on the waterfront by the gardens of Villa Giulia; expensive.

Mediterraneo, Via Rosolino Pilo 43 (tel. 091 581 133, fax 091 586 974). Near the Archaeological Museum; moderate.

President, Via Crispi 230 (tel. 091 580 773; fax 091 611 1588). With a rooftop restaurant overlooking the harbour; moderate.

Villa Archirafi, Via Lincoln 30 (tel. 091 616 8827, fax 091 616 8631). A quiet 19th-century villa located near the Orto Botanico; inexpensive.

PANTELLERIA
Khamma (tel. 0923 912 680, fax 0923 912 570; seasonal). Moderate.
Port (tel. 0923 911 299, fax 0923 912 203; seasonal). Moderate.

SCIACCA
Grand Alberbo Terme, Lungomare Nuove Terme (tel. 0925 23133, fax 0925 21746). A spa, widely known for its mineral-water treatments; moderate.

Torre Macauda, Highway S115 (tel. 0925 997 000, fax 0925 997 007; closed Nov–Easter). 9km (5¹/₂ miles) southeast of town; quiet and comfortable, with indoor and outdoor pools; moderate.

SELINUNTE
Garzia, Via Pigafetta 6 (tel. 0924 46024, fax 0924 46196). At Marinella, 1km south; in a panoramic location on the beach, within walking distance of the temples; inexpensive.

TRAPANI
Crystal, Via San Giovanni Bosco 17 (tel. 0923 20000, fax 0923 25555). New and functional; moderate.

Vittoria, Via Crispi 4 (tel. 0923 873 044, fax 0923 29870). Modern, in a good location near the Villa Margherita gardens; inexpensive.

Restaurants

AGRIGENTO
Cioffi (tel. 0922 606 333; closed Mon, except May–Sep, and two weeks in Nov). A family-run place with summer seating on a terrace, 8km (5 miles) southeast on Highway S115; moderate. **Le Caprice**, Strada Panoramica dei Templi 51 (tel./fax 0922 26469; closed Fri and two weeks in Jul). A country restaurant with panoramic terrace overlooking the Valley dei Templi; delicacies include *involtini di melanzane, cavatelli al cartoccio, aragosta gratinata and torta di ricotta;* inexpensive.
Leon d'Oro (tel./fax 0922 414 400). At San Leone; good seafood and other local dishes; inexpensive.

ERICE
Cortile di Venere, Via Sales 31 (tel. 0923 869 362; closed Wed). An 18th-century patrician villa with large patio providing outdoor seating in summer; moderate.

ISOLE EGADI
On Favignana:
Guccione, Via Colombo 17 (tel. 0923 921232; closed Oct–Apr). Excellent local dishes, especially tuna, in a simple setting; inexpensive.
Rais (tel. 0923 921 233). Genuine local ambience and seafood; inexpensive.

LAMPEDUSA
Gemelli (tel. 0922 970 699; closed Nov–May and midday in Jul–Aug). Moderate.
Lipadusa (tel. 0922 971 691; closed Nov–Mar). Moderate.

MARSALA
Delfino, Lungomare Mediterraneo, 4km (2 1/2 miles) south (tel./fax 0923 998 188; closed Tue, except Jun–Aug). Skilfully prepared local cuisine served on a garden terrace in summer; moderate.

MONDELLO
Al Gabbiano, Via Piano Gallo 1 (tel. 091 450 313; closed Wed and Jan). Right on the rocks, with splendid views of the sea and Monte Pellegrino; inexpensive.
Casablanca, Via Piano di Gallo 32 (tel. 091 454 685; closed Mon). Rustic Mediterranean architecture and cuisine; inexpensive.
Chamade, Viale Regina Elena 45 (tel. 091 450 512; closed Mon in winter). A waterfront establishment serving delicious local specialities; try the *conchiglia Gazebo con ruchetta, linguine alla mondellana and giardinetto gelato;* moderate.

Charleston le Terrazze, Viale Regina Elena (tel. 091 450 171; closed Oct–May). Summer home of Palermo's famous Charleston restaurant, with Art Nouveau décor, a terrace on the sea, and the usual fine food and service; specialities include *insalata di mare mille isole, pasta in melanzana, fettuccine all'ammiraglia, ricciola all'acqua di mare, pesce spada in crosta;* expensive.

MONREALE
La Botte, 3km (2 miles) southwest on Highway S186 (tel. 091 414 051; closed Mon and Jul–Aug; open evenings only except Sat–Sun). Summer seating outdoors; moderate.
Taverna del Pavone, Vicolo Pensato 18 (tel. 091 640 6209). In a historic 18th-century palace; inexpensive.
Villa Tre Fontane, 2km (1 1/4 miles) northeast on Highway S186 (tel. 091 640 5400, fax 091 640 5206; closed Tue and two weeks in Aug). Sicilian cuisine, especially fish, served in summer in a garden with lemon and orange trees; moderate.

PALERMO
'A Cuccagna, Via Principe Granatelli 21/A (tel. 091 587267; closed Mon and two weeks in Aug). Fine Sicilian cuisine and ambience, with terrace and gardens; moderate.
Charleston, Piazzale Ungheria 30 (tel. 091 321 366, fax 091 321 347; closed Sun and Jun–Sep). *Pasta con le sarde, risotto al basilico, fusilli caserecci alla palermitana, fagottino di vitello cerdese, parfait di mandorle e salsa di cioccolato calda* are the house specialities; the décor is turn-of-the-century Art Nouveau; expensive.
Friend's Bar, Via Brunelleschi 138 (tel. 091 201 066; closed Mon and two weeks in Aug). Best in summer, with seating in a large, lush garden; moderate.
Gourmand's, Via della Libertà 37/e (tel. 091 323 431, fax 091 322 507; closed Sun and two weeks in Aug). Modern ambience, classic Sicilian cuisine; recommended dishes are the *fettuccine alla Nelson, involtini di pesce spada, entrecôte Conca d'Oro, and semifreddo di mandorle;* expensive.
L'Approdo Ristorante Renato, Via Messina Marine 224 (tel. 091 630 2881; closed Sun and two weeks in Aug). Known for its antique furnishings, seaside terrace and extensive wine cellar; try the *Bummi ca sarsa pipiràta, cappone di galera alla siciliana and pastizzu di jaddina;* expensive.
La Scuderia, Viale del Fante 9 (tel. 091 520 323, fax 091 520 467; closed Sun evening). Excellent Sicilian cuisine, notably *magliette alla Donnafugata, involtini di spigola e spada and torta di fico d'India;* expensive.
Regine, Via Trapani 4/a (tel. 091 586566; closed Sun and Aug). Good Sicilian fare, especially fish; inexpensive.

Ristorantino, Piazza De Gasperi 19 (tel. 091 512861; closed Mon and Aug). Especially well known for its *semifreddi*; moderate.
Stella, Via Aragona 6 (tel. 091 616 1136; closed Sun and Aug). A simple but excellent trattoria, with outdoor seating in summer; inexpensive.
Trittico, Via Principe di Paternò 126/b (tel. 091 345 035; closed Sun and Aug). Traditional Sicilian cuisine, especially *risottino affumicato, fagottini di spada alla mentuccia and cestini di vitello alle verdure;* moderate.

SCIACCA
Le Gourmet, Via Monte Kronio 7 (tel. 0925 26460; closed Tue, except Jun–Sep, and in Nov). A family-run establishment serving local food and wine, 4km (2$^{1}/_{2}$ miles) northeast on the road to San Calogero; moderate.

SELINUNTE
Il Vigneto, near Menfi, in the country (tel. 0925 71732; closed evenings, except Fri and Sat, and Mon Oct–Jun). Inexpensive.
Pierrot, at Marinella, 1km (half a mile) south (tel. 0924 46205; closed Jan and Feb). Local dishes, especially fish; inexpensive.

TRAPANI
P&G, Via Spalti 1 (tel. 0923 547 701; closed Sun, 27 Dec–1 Jan and Aug). Small and intimate, with good seafood; moderate.
Peppe, Via Spalti 54 (tel. 0923 28246; closed Mon and Aug). Small, with summer seating in a gazebo adorned with flowers; moderate.
Trattoria del Porto da Felice, Via Ammiraglio Staiti 45 (tel. 0923 547 822; closed Mon). An unpretentious place with great seafood; inexpensive.

Museums and Monuments

AGRIGENTO
Valle dei Templi and Antiquarium di Villa Aurea: daily 9.00–dusk.
Museo Archeologico Regionale: daily 9.00–13.00, 15.00–18.00.
Museo Civico: daily 9.00–12.00, 15.00–17.00.
Museo Diocesano: closed indefinitely.

BAGHERIA
Civica Galleria d'Arte Moderna e Contemporanea: Tue–Sun 10.00–18.00.

ERACLEA MINOA
Antiquarium e Zona Archeologica: daily 9.00–13.00.

ERICE
Museo Cordici: Mon–Sat 8.30–12.30, Sun and hols 9.00–12.00.

MARSALA
Museo degli Arazzi: daily 9.00–13.00, 16.00–18.00.
Museo Archeologico di Baglio Anselmo: Mon, Tue, Thu, Fri 9.00–14.00; Wed and Sat also 15.00–18.00; Sun 9.00–13.00, 15.00–18.00.
Museo Whitaker (Mozia): daily 9.00–13.00, 15.00–dusk.

MONREALE
Chiostro del Convento Benedettino: winter, Mon–Sat 9.00–14.30, Sun 9.00–12.30; summer, Mon–Sat 9.00–12.30, 16.00–19.00.

PALERMO
Cappella Palatina: Mon–Fri 9.00–12.00, 15.00–17.00; Sat 9.00–12.00; Sun 9.00–10.00, 12.00–13.00.
Galleria Regionale della Sicilia: daily 9.00–13.00, odd afternoons.
Museo Archeologico Regionale: daily 9.00–13.30, Tue and Fri also 15.00–16.00
Museo Etnografico Siciliano Pitrè: Sat–Thu 9.00–13.00.
Museo Internazionale delle Marionette: Mon–Fri 9.00–13.00, 16.00–19.00; Sat 9.00–13.00.
Orto Botanico: Mon–Fri 8.00–13.00, Sat 8.00–12.00.
San Giovanni degli Eremiti: daily 9.00–12.30; Mon, Thu also 15.00-18.00.

SCIACCA
Pinacoteca del Museo Scaglione: Mon–Sat 8.30–13.00, 15.00–19.00.

SEGESTA
Zona Archeologica: daily 9.00–dusk.

SELINUNTE
Zona Archeologica: daily 9.00–dusk.

SOLUNTO
Zona Archeologica: daily 9.00-dusk.

TRAPANI
Museo Regionale Pepoli: Mon, Wed, Fri, Sat 9.00–13.30;
Tue, Thu also 15–18; Sun and hols 9.00–12.30.
Museo delle Saline (Paceco, frazione Nubia): 9.00–12.00, 15.00–18.00.
Museo Trapanese di Preistoria: daily 9.00–13.00, 16.00–20.00.

6. SOUTHEASTERN SICILY

The southeastern corner of Sicily coincides largely with the *Val di Noto*, one of the three Arab divisions of the island. Here you'll find a beautiful and varied landscape, from the flat plain of Catania to the Hyblæan hills and the vast rolling highlands of Enna – a land of contrast and contradiction, but also a complete microcosm of the island. You'll also notice the imbalances of Sicily's recent development – hectares of luxuriant orange groves and large estates left uncultivated; high-tech chemical plants rising above the ruins of ancient cities; century-old carob trees casting their shadows over state-of-the-art greenhouses; dark oil wells ranging like great iron animals over green pastures. These and other paradoxical images reveal the economic disparities that have come to characterise the area over the last century. But as always in Sicily, there is hope: reawakened awareness of the area's unique environmental heritage has brought a change of conscience, and the keyword today is conservation, not exploitation.

Ragusa and the Ragusano

The history of the territory here called the *ragusano* is as diversified as its landscape. What ties the region together is its exclusion from the island's economic mainstream – traditionally around Palermo, Catania and Syracuse. For centuries this economic isolation has spelled poverty for the *ragusani*. But in recent years the tables have turned, as locals and outsiders alike have begun to understand the advantages of compatible growth. In this part of Sicily large areas of the countryside have been preserved from indiscriminate use: for instance, in the hinterland of Modica and Ragusa, where Mediterranean *macchia* still grows wild along crystalline streams; or around Chiaramonte Gulfi and Caltagirone, where the hills look today much as they did to the Greeks. Where the sea is concerned, it is the underwater beds of *posidonie* – the seaweed so beautiful that it bears the name of the god of the sea – that have captured attention. So far, the waters here have been spared from overfishing; in addition, they have been cleansed since the dawn of time by unusually strong currents – the same currents that in past centuries wrecked whole fleets, making the sea floor one of the region's most interesting and least explored archaeological sites.

Ragusa

There are really two Ragusas: Ragusa Superiore, the more modern of the two, with its straight, regular streets; and the old Ragusa Ibla, a maze of narrow, winding, often stepped alleys. Each stands on its own hilltop. The old city was probably the site of the Siculan *Hybla Heræa*, and excavations in the area have brought to light a Greek necropolis of the 6th century BC; in the environs are traces of settlement that go back as far as the 3rd millennium BC. Almost totally destroyed in 1693 by southeastern Sicily's most devastating earthquake, Ibla was rebuilt, stone upon stone, in the 18th century, in keeping with the late Baroque aesthetic then in vogue. The new town was constructed on the adjoining hill at the same time.

Occupied first by the Romans and then by the Byzantines, Ibla fell in 848 to the Arabs, whose superior agricultural skills allowed them to repopulate the countryside and introduce new methods of farming. Under Norman rule, which began in the late 11th century, and under that of the powerful Chiaramonte and Cabrera families in the centuries that followed, the city took on its medieval aspect, as settlers were brought in from the Italian mainland to replace the Arabs who had fled, and the great religious orders established their houses in the city to save the newcomers' souls – and help them redistribute their wealth. Meanwhile the introduction of emphyteusis (the perpetual right to a piece of land in exchange for rent paid to the landowner) changed the face of the agrarian landscape: as the fields were placed in the hands of those who farmed them, the region's large agricultural estates were broken into small lots marked out by drystone walls. Today these walls are the most distinctive feature of the countryside in this area of Sicily, the postcard symbol of the *ragusano*.

Most of Ragusa's businesses are located in **Ragusa Superiore**, which for this reason has become the undisputed centre of civic life. The gateway to the upper city is **Piazza Libertà**, a striking example of Rationalist town planning created by the leading Italian architect of the inter-war period, Marcello Piacentini. Better known for his creations in northern Italy (the spacious lower town of Bergamo, Piazza della Vittoria in Brescia, Corso della Libertà in Bolzano), Piacentini was the favourite architect of Mussolini, whose ghostly presence can still be discerned here in the stern, military aspect of the buildings and the weathered slogans stencilled on their walls. The Fascists were particularly proud of this square, which they called *Piazza Impero*.

Across the Ponte Nuovo is the high street of Ragusa, Via Roma. Next to

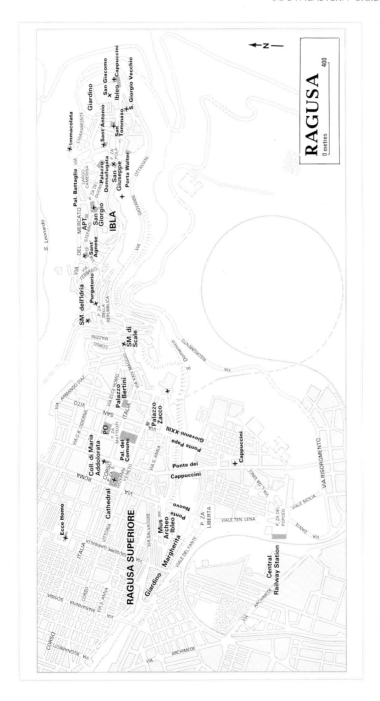

the department store on the left, steps lead down to the **Museo Archeologico Ibleo**, tucked beneath a lofty viaduct. Here you'll find a chronological arrangement of finds from Ragusa and its province, dating from prehistoric to Roman times. The beautifully displayed collection comprises six sections: prehistoric sites, the Greek colony of Camarina, Siculan centres, Hellenistic centres, Roman and late Roman centres, and acquisitions from private collections. Some of the exhibits are complemented by full-scale reconstructions of the excavations – a nice touch, especially for children. The utensils from the Bronze Age civilisation known as the Castelluccio Culture are particularly important for their number and rarity.

Via Roma continues to the focal point of the upper town, the tidy Piazza San Giovanni. Here the 18th-century **Cathedral** (San Giovanni Battista) stands on a broad terrace supported by a loggia. It has a monumental façade with engaged Corinthian columns and ornate Baroque windows high up on the walls, and an imposing campanile. The Latin-cross interior features two orders of columns in locally quarried asphaltite.

Corso Italia, the handsome, tree-shaded main street, descends steeply from the cathedral square to the edge of the hill above Ibla. Four blocks down, on the left, the 18th-century **Palazzo Bertini** has interesting masks on the keystones of its windows. These, according to local lore, form a sort of pre-Marxian primer on the relationship between class and power – the first represents the power of the poor, based on lack of concern; the second, that of the aristocrat, placed by birth above the law; and the third, the power of the bourgeoisie, derived from the arrogance of wealth.

At the end of the Corso, Via XXIV Maggio leads left to a balcony offering marvellous views over Ragusa Ibla. Next to the terrace stands **Santa Maria delle Scale**, which takes its name from the 242 steps that join the two cities. It was built in the 15th century over a Norman-period Cistercian church and rebuilt after the 1693 earthquake. Remnants of the 15th-century building include the Gothic doorway and pulpit at the foot of the campanile. The interior (usually closed) is a curious combination of Baroque architecture on the north side, and Catalan-Gothic and Renaissance elements on the south. The coloured-terracotta relief of *The Dormition of the Virgin*, over a side altar, was made in 1538 by the Gagini school.

To reach Ibla from Santa Maria delle Scale you can follow Corso Mazzini, which winds its way down in switchbacks, or take the stairs – called Discesa Santa Maria (St Mary's Descent) at the top, and Salita Commendatore (The Commander's Climb) at the bottom. The steps dip beneath the road and descend through arches and along buttressed walls past the pretty little Palazzo della Cancelleria, built in 1760 and seat of the town Chancellery of Ibla until the 19th century; the church of Santa Maria dell'Idra, founded in 1626 by the Knights of Malta and rebuilt in the 18th century with a pretty majolica dome; and Palazzo dei Cosentini, an early 18th-century palace with fabulous balconies supported by little monsters. Here you rejoin Corso Mazzini and turn right to enter the quiet and evocative atmosphere of **Ibla**.

Frankly, the town has become a bit too quiet in recent years, as many of the inhabitants have moved away to more comfortable quarters, leaving its streets and squares to their destiny. Nevertheless, it remains a uniquely peaceful place, particularly suited to exploration on foot. Narrow streets and stepped lanes lead up to the palm-lined Piazza del Duomo and the magnificent golden curves of the cathedral of **San Giorgio**, which stands to one side, slightly askew of the main axis of the square. Built in 1744 by Rosario Gagliardi, the brilliant architect of Noto (see page 147), its three-tiered convex façade, rhythmically marked by engaged columns bearing bold projecting cornices, rises above a flight of steps enclosed by a 19th-century balustrade. Climb the steps on the left to enter the church. The three-aisled Latin-cross interior is bathed in light, thanks to the 43m-high Neoclassical dome added in 1820 and the 13 modern stained-glass windows (1926) in the nave, telling the story of the martyrdom of St George. Statues of the saint in various attitudes abound, and the organ is one of the most original creations of the famed Serassi brothers. Around the square are the Palazzo la Rocca, home of the Tourist Board, with seven beautiful balconies and a double asphaltite staircase; Palazzo Arezzi, with another good balcony over a side street; and other fine palaces. Palazzo Donnafugata, at the lower end of the square, has a little 19th-century theatre where public performances are sometimes held.

The church of **San Giuseppe**, in the adjacent Piazza Pola, looks like a sibling of San Giorgio, and it comes as no surprise that its design is ascribed to Gagliardi or his school. It too has a three-tiered façade, with Corinthian columns and statues. The elliptical interior is delicately adorned with stuccoes; the cupola was frescoed with a depiction of the *Glory of St Benedict* by Sebastiano Lo Monaco in 1793. The asphaltite pavement, nuns' galleries and painted glass altars all merit a glance.

Corso Venticinque Aprile continues downhill past the churches of San Tommaso and (reached by a turning on the right) San Giorgio Vecchio, with a fine 14th-century Catalan-Gothic doorway surrounding a relief of St George and the Dragon, to the **Giardino Ibleo**, a beautiful 19th-century public garden with lush tropical vegetation and magnificent views over the hills. In the grounds are several churches in various states of preservation, notably the Cappuccini, which contains a large altarpiece of the *Assumption of the Virgin* by Pietro Novelli and an anonymous 16th-century *Nativity* with a representation of a medieval town thought to be Ibla. The convent next door houses the Museo Diocesano, usually closed.

A panoramic view of Ragusa

Around Ragusa

The countryside around Ragusa is extraordinary even for Sicily. The arid limestone hills are riddled with caves, inhabited from remotest antiquity well into the Middle Ages, and the rocky soil seems to have crystallised in strange linear patterns – in reality the system of low walls erected by the peasant farmers of times past. Except for a few large, sprawling towns the land is virtually deserted. Few and far between rise the fortified farm complexes that were once the region's most characteristic form of rural settlement, their regular geometric volumes standing like lonely sentinels of human reason in the midst of overpowering nature. Many of these have been left to the elements, for only the Arabs, with their sophisticated irrigation systems, were able to make the dusty soil bear fruit. Today cultivation is concentrated near the coast, where the rainwater soaked up by the porous rock returns to the surface. Here market gardens and citrus orchards abound, battling one another for control of the fertile bottom land, while lush tropical gardens bloom in the private parks of one-time feudal lords.

Regardless of whether you take the new highway, which threads its way through the low hills on a series of lofty viaducts (including Europe's highest at 186m), or the old local road, which descends the picturesque Irminio valley, the 15km (9 1/2 miles) that separate Ragusa from **Modica** make one of the most beautiful drives on the island. Like Ragusa, Modica is divided into two parts, Modica Bassa and Modica Alta. Travellers of the past tend to describe it as a place carved out of the rock – probably because

Fortified Farms of the Southeast

As you travel through the countryside between Ragusa and Syracuse you're bound to notice the large, fortified farms that lie scattered among the pastures and fields. These are the *masserie iblee* – tiny hamlets huddled around a central courtyard and presenting a single, impenetrable wall to the outside. The *masseria* was not just a home shared by landed gentry and peasant farmers, it was the economic and social centre of rural life in this area, of all farming and craft activities. It customarily included a *bagghiu* (atrium), a *carrittaria* (where carts parked), a *stadda* (stable), a *casa ri mann:ra* (rustic kitchen), a *casa ri stari* (living quarters) and a *stanza ro travagghiu* (for spinning and weaving). When the massive wooden gate was closed at night, the *masseria* offered its inhabitants a safe haven from marauding bandits and pirates. Its singular architectural structure seems a natural outgrowth of the *mura a siccu*, the drystone walls so characteristic of the area, which were the boundary and the threshold of peasant culture and of its traditions of life and labour.

Many *masserie* have recently been converted into farm-holiday complexes or restaurants; among those that are still working farms are the **Fattoria Musso** and the **Fattoria Rizza**, which can be visited on request (apply at the Information Office in Ragusa). The former is a small village with a church. The large courtyard is bounded by low houses; at the sides are stables and storerooms. The latter has a regular courtyard defined by a *palazzotto padronale* (owner's residence), its chapel and two low symmetrical farm buildings at the sides. The nature of life on these farms can be gleaned from the **Museo Ibleo delle Arti e Tradizioni Popolari** in Palazzo dei Mercedari in Modica, where there are excellent reconstructions of 18th- and 19th-century interiors with original furnishings and equipment.

of its location, in a deep ravine at the confluence of two river torrents (now covered) and on the steep spur between them.

Archaeological evidence suggests that the area has been inhabited for some 20 centuries, and Latin sources mention the existence of a Roman town called *Motyka*. The Normans made it the capital of a powerful county – a status it retained under its subsequent lords, the Chiaramonte, Cabrera and Henriquez-Cabrera. Rebuilt after the earthquake of 1693 in the fashionable Baroque style, it remained one of the island's more populous cities right up to the end of the 19th century. It was the birthplace of the Nobel prizewinning poet Salvatore Quasimodo (1901–68).

The main attraction of Modica Bassa is the fascinating **Museo Ibleo delle Arti e Tradizioni Popolari**, a private museum opened on request. It occupies lovely vaulted rooms on the top floor of the huge former Convento dei Padri Mercedari (Palazzo dei Mercedari) on Via Mercè. The museum is famous for its perfect reproductions of old farms and craftsmen's shops, including those of a *scarparu* (shoemaker), *firraru e firraschecchi* (smith and farrier) and *mastru ri carretta* (cartmaker). There is also an outstanding collection of Sicilian carts. The 18th-century monastery houses the municipal library and museum, where you can see displays of archaeological material from prehistory to Roman times, found in Modica and its environs; this is where you ask to have the ethnographic museum unlocked.

Visible from all over town is Modica's cathedral, **San Giorgio**, a building reminiscent of San Giorgio in Ragusa and probably designed by the same architect, Rosario Gagliardi. To get there, take the stepped alley at the top of the arch formed by Corso Umberto I. Its splendid curved façade soars upwards atop a staircase of 250 steps, in a spectacular marriage of architecture and urban theatricals. It was consecrated in 1738, and the staircase was completed in 1818. The interior has five aisles with transept and dome and a wealth of artworks, none of which is as memorable as the church itself. The silver high altar dates from the early 18th century; the huge polyptych above, ascribed to the local painter Bernardino Niger, goes back to the end of the 16th. The treasury holds an urn with relics of St George, made in Venice in the 14th century, and there is a 19th-century sundial traced in the pavement of the transept. The beautiful Serassi organ dates from 1888. Streets and alleys continue steeply uphill to Modica Alta, which merits a glance if you have the time.

Between Modica and the sea is **Scicli**, a lovely little Baroque town that most tourists drive right by. It is a very ancient place, famous for a bloody battle between the Arabs and the Normans (1093) commemorated each year on the last Sunday in June. The interesting old town has a number of fine palaces and churches, notably **Sant'Ignazio**, founded before the 1693 earthquake but rebuilt in 1751. Inside is the *Madonna delle Milizie*, a papier-mâché work representing the Virgin on a white horse with drawn sword, valorously fighting the Saracens – two of whom are being trampled beneath the horse's hoofs. If you're prepared for a hike you can climb up to the oldest settlement at Scicli, the 11th-century fortified village of **San Matteo**; it stands abandoned and in dire need of restoration. Higher up, in an impregnable position, are the ruins of the triangular **Castle**, which probably pre-dates the Arab conquest of 864. The church and convent of **La Croce** stand on another hill, enjoying wide views; the façade is decorated by the Catalan-Gothic insignia of Scicli and of the Henriquez-Cabrera.

Reached by a byroad west of Scicli is **Donnafugata**, a huge country house with a magnificent park, which amply repays a visit. Built in an eclectic style around the end of the 19th century by Baron Corrado Arezzo De Spuches, senator and mayor of Ragusa, it was acquired by the city in 1982 and is now open by appointment. Reservations are taken at the town hall in Ragusa. There are over a hundred rooms with period furnishings (only a few of which are shown), and you can wander through the delightful gardens to the intriguing labyrinth, Neoclassical coffee house and small chapel. The huge ficus trees alone merit a trip. Giuseppe di Lampedusa borrowed the name 'Donnafugata' (but not the place) for the country house of his Salina family in the novel *The Leopard.*

Camarina, on the coast west of Marina di Ragusa, near the beautiful beach and forest preserve of Cava di Randello, was once one of the Greeks' most important outposts in southeastern Sicily. It was founded by Corinthians from Syracuse in 598BC and, after a long and violent history chronicled by Thucydides, Herodotus and Diodorus, destroyed by the Romans in 258BC. Little remains of Camarina today, though the foundations of a 5th-century Temple of Athena can be made out, together with several *insulæ* with their houses and part of the wall. Several treasure-laden necropolises (mostly dating from the early 6th century) have been dug up in the environs; finds are on display in the small musum on the acropolis, where you can also see Greek, Punic, Roman and medieval material from wrecks found offshore. Close by to the east are the remains of the medieval harbour town of **Caucana** – some 20 houses and a small church with a mosaic pavement in the apse – where the fleets of the Byzantine general Belisarius and the Norman Count Roger put in.

Syracuse and Its Territory

The particular geological structure of Sicily and its position at the meeting point of the European and African continental plates have made it the theatre of devastating earthquakes since the beginning of time. The 1693 earthquake, in particular, completely changed the appearance of the southeastern corner of the island. Both in the cities that were completely destroyed and in those that were just damaged, reconstruction gave rise to a new Baroque architectural style which is unlike anything you find in Naples, Rome or Northern Europe. Not content with the self-satisfied decorative grace of the Rococo style, which had come into vogue elsewhere in Europe, Sicilian architects launched themselves into new feats of engineering, producing forms of unprecedented complexity that were masterfully realised by their expert stonemasons. The chief material of this architectural revolution was a soft local limestone particularly suited to bold forms such as arcs and curves, and easily carved in elaborate designs. The need for total reconstruction created an occasion for cities such as Noto to redesign their urban image from the ground up, by moving to new sites that were considered safer or healthier and by developing town plans based on the ideal cities of the Renaissance. These cool, rational town plans, with their streets at right angles and spacious squares, were spiced up with Sicilian theatricality – in a word, with dramatically modelled buildings strategically placed where their visual impact would be greatest: at the top of tall staircases, the end of long streets, etc. Similar ambitions underlay the reorganisation of cities that had been only partly damaged, such as Syracuse, where skilful stonemasons and metalsmiths were asked to give new zip to the drab urban fabric of the medieval city centre. Today the complex forms of these Baroque cities dazzle us still, thanks to the fascinating golden aura of the native stone and the supreme skill of the artists and artisans who worked it.

Syracuse

Syracuse, in Italian *Siracusa*, is one of the highlights of a visit to Sicily. Rising on the lovely islet of Ortygia and on the adjoining coastal plain, it is the cultural and administrative capital of southeastern Sicily. Despite modern industrial development and the accompanying urban sprawl, it remains one of the island's more pleasant cities – especially now that a renewal of interest in the architectural heritage of its historic centre has led many residents to move back to Ortygia from the modern suburbs, reversing a trend towards depopulation that had threatened the island's integrity in recent decades. As beautiful as the city and its environs appear from the terra firma, the ideal way to approach Syracuse is by sea, sailing slowly past the gold-tinted palaces, campanili and church domes of Ortygia against their backdrop of low rolling hills culminating in the white limestone plateau of Euryelos, with Ætna steaming in the distance.

Syracuse is the modern successor of the Greek *Syrakúsai*, which once rivalled Athens as the most powerful city of the Greek world. It was established in the 8th century BC by colonists from Corinth, on a site that seems to have been inhabited earlier by Sicels or Phoenicians. The first Greek settlement arose on Ortygia and on the adjacent area of the mainland known as Achradina; in later centuries it expanded to include the outlying districts of Tyche, Epipolis (the 'city above') and Neapolis (the 'new city'). Near Achradina ran a torrent, the *Syrakò*, from which the name *Syrakúsai* probably derived.

The Greek colony prospered quickly and immensely, extending its influence throughout Sicily. It became the most powerful city in the western Greek orbit, particularly after it came under the rule of Gelon, tyrant of Gela (c 485–478BC), who in alliance with Theron of Akragas defeated the Carthaginians at Himera. Eventually it came into conflict first with Athens (on which it inflicted a terrible defeat in 414BC) and then with Carthage which, despite numerous attempts, never breached its walls. The city enjoyed several periods of successful democratic government (notably under Timoleon of Corinth in 343–336), but its moments of greatest splendour came under the absolute rule of its tyrants – Hieron I (478–467BC), architect of the Greek victory over the Etruscans at Cumæ (474) and patron of Æschylus and Pindar; Dionysius the Elder (405–367BC), who defeated the Carthaginians under Himlico in 397; Agathocles (316–289), the first Greek to carry the war with Carthage to Africa; and Hieron II (c 275–215BC), who preserved the city's primacy in the Mediterranean by striking an early alliance with Rome. Plato visited the city c 397BC, and probably wrote the *Republic* on the invitation of Dionysius II.

When Hieronymus, successor to Hieron II, switched the city's allegiance to Carthage in the First Punic War, a Roman army under Marcus Claudius Marcellus moved against Syracuse, taking the city in 212BC after a two-year siege – notwithstanding the ingenious inventions of Archimedes (287–212), who was killed during the sack of the town. Its ties with the Eastern Mediterranean made the Roman *Syracusæ* a fertile field for Christianity, especially after St Paul stopped there for three days on his way from Malta to Rome (*Acts* xxviii, 11–12).

Syracuse declined after the Roman period, though one of the Eastern emperors, Constans II, moved his capital here from Constantinople in 662–68. The city was besieged and destroyed by the Saracens in 878, held for a time by the Byzantines under George Maniakes (1038–40) and definitively reclaimed by Count Roger in 1105. Under the Normans, Syracuse recovered some of its former economic prosperity, political security and cultural liveliness. After the brief Angevin domination, it drew substantial economic advantages from the Aragonese, thanks to its extensive trade relations in Europe and the East. This affluence left its mark in the great architectural development of the Middle Ages: the town's ramparts and many of its palaces date from this period. The semi-independent Sicilian Regional Assembly had its capital at Syracuse from 1361 until 1536, but the importance that derived from that position failed to be maintained, and for a while in the 19th century Syracuse even lost to Noto its primacy as provincial capital. An important naval base in World War II, the city was bombed first by the Allies and then by the Germans. The supposed enmity of Syracuse and Ephesus provides the background of Shakespeare's *Comedy of Errors*.

The Terra Firma

The best way to approach Syracuse and the most coherent, from a historical viewpoint, is to begin with the ancient remains on the mainland and work gradually towards the splendid medieval and Baroque centre of Ortygia.

The most impressive ancient ruin is undoubtedly the **Castello Eurialo** – an authentic masterpiece of military engineering, considered the only true fortress in Europe at the time of the Greek domination. The 'castle' stands on the barren ridge of Epipolæ, 8km (5 miles) northwest of the city. To get there, take the Catania road from central Syracuse and turn off for the town of Belvedere; the entrance to the site, on the edge of the town, is sign-posted.

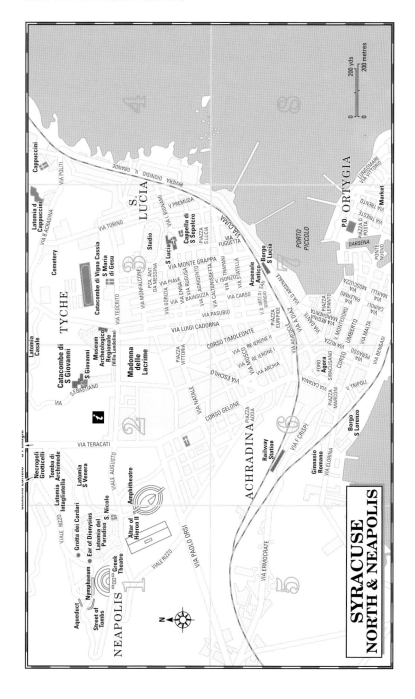

SYRACUSE
NORTH & NEAPOLIS

Thousands of slaves working under the personal supervision of Dionysius the Elder took five years to build this great fortress, which was begun in 402BC in the wake of the Carthaginian sack of Agrigento. The fortress stood at the highest point of the ancient city, on a knoll or knob (*euryelos* in Greek) where the north and south walls met – a point considered particularly vulnerable to enemy attack. In antiquity, as today, it dominated the coast from the Gulf of Augusta to well beyond the harbour of Syracuse. The only level approach, from the west, was protected by the strongest fortifications – three ditches alternating with advanced walls and crossed by drawbridges, some piers of which can still be seen. This, the principal defence of the fortress, was later reinforced with five square towers connected to a powerful curtain wall. From here a maze of passages and casemates led all over the fort, the longest running along the north flank to the Epipolæ Gateway (see below). The gallery to the south leads to a ditch outside the castle wall and to another advanced outwork. The castle proper consisted of a keep where the troops were garrisoned, and a triangular outer court to the east. On the northeast side of the outer court was the main gate from the town; on the southeast stood a tower connected with the southern segment of the city walls. The northern segment of the walls is linked to the keep by an ingenious system of underground passages and surface works that included the Epipolæ Gateway, a pincer-like entranceway into which enemy troops could be lured, enclosed and then massacred.

Syracuse's most famous monument, the **Greek Theatre,** stands in an archaeological park in the modern city (Map 1) together with other important remains. It is among the largest Greek theatres known (the cavea measures 138m in diameter). The first theatre on this spot dates from the 6th century BC; it was a simple construction where farmers and shepherds came to sing the praises of the goddess Artemis. What you see today is largely the consequence of an enlargement made under Hieron II in 230BC of an intermediate construction dating from the 5th century. Here Epicharmus (540–450BC) worked as a comic poet and Æschylus (525–456BC) probably produced his *Persæ*; but the theatre was used also, throughout the Greek period, for public assemblies. Under the Romans the orchestra and scena of Hieron's theatre were altered, possibly for the production of gladiatorial games and aquatic performances (*colymbetra*). Today Classical plays are performed in the theatre on alternate years, in June.

Completely hewn out of the rock in a natural setting which offers stunning views over the city, the coast and the sea, it is composed of three distinct parts: cavea (auditorium), orchestra and scena (stage). The cavea has 67 rows of seats divided into nine wedges by eight staircases, intersected by a corridor (the *diazoma*) half-way up. The north wall of the diazoma retains its moulding, inscribed with the names of divinities (Olympian Zeus, Heracles, Demeter) and important citizens (Hieron, his queen Philistis) to

San Giorgio, Modica (p 126)

Ancient drama in the Greek theatre, Syracuse

whom the blocks of seats were dedicated. A second corridor served the lower cavea, where the flat profile of the first 12 rows of seats suggests they were faced with another material. In the central wedge, between the 4th and 6th rows, was a special tribune for the tyrant and his guests. The orchestra, which originally held an altar of Dionysus around which the chorus performed, was paved with marble. Little remains of the scena, other than the recess for the curtain. The abandonment of the monument began with invasions by Vandals and Goths in AD440, which marked the twilight of Classical culture, and culminated in the partial destruction of the edifice in 1526 by Charles V, who had the scena and topmost part of the cavea removed and reused for his fortifications.

Carved out of the rock wall at the top of the theatre is an artificial cave with a fountain where a branch of the Greek aqueduct ended. It may have been used as a nymphaeum. From the northwest end of the wall the **Via dei Sepolchri** (Map 1; Street of Tombs, a Byzantine burial ground) rises in a curve c 150m long cut in the hillside. In the Hellenistic age, probably at the time of Hieron II, the entire hilltop was enclosed by a monumental U-shaped portico measuring 110 x 90m, the purpose of which was to connect the religious sanctuary with the theatre below, and with the streets of Neapolis above. The sanctuary of Demeter and Kore, which Cicero mentions as lying in the upper part of Neapolis, probably stood at the east end of this portico. Immediately southwest of the cavea, excavations have brought to light a sacred precinct identified as the **Santuario di Apollo Temenite**, which Thucydides mentions as an important theatre of action in the war with Athens. The oldest part of the sanctuary dates from the 7th century BC.

Immediately southeast of the theatre lies the **Altar of Hieron II**, probably dedicated to Zeus Eleutherios (The Liberator). At the north and south ends of this immense (198 x 23m) sacrificial altar were two symmetrical ramps mounting to the central platform, where the ritual victims – in the case of the *Eleutheria*, 450 bulls – were slaughtered. Each ramp had its own entrance: that on the north was flanked by two telamones, of which the feet of one survive. It is important to remember that this was just the foundation of the building, which must have been quite tall; the limestone blocks on the east side belonged to the roof coping. Fronting the altar on the west was a large square planted as a garden, surrounding a large rectangular piscina and surrounded in its turn by a portico with 14 columns on the short sides and 64 on the long sides.

The **Roman Amphitheatre** (Map 2), built in its present form in the 1st century BC, occupied a prime location next to the altar of Hieron II and the theatre. It is one of the largest (140 x 119m) buildings of its kind, just slightly smaller than the Arena of Verona. Of the two entrances at the extremities of its longer axis, that on the south connected directly to the city. At the centre of the arena was a large underground chamber probably intended for the machinery used during games and events. A raised podium separated the arena from a covered corridor (*crypta*) from which the gladiators and animals entered the arena, and above which the seats reserved for important citizens were located, as inscriptions on the marble balustrade attest. Parallel to the crypta, but higher up, were two more vaulted corridors; a third, with a colonnade, ran around the top of the monument. From here a series of radial passageways gave access to the seats of the cavea. Below the little church of San Nicolò nearby, you can see the cistern that held the water with which the arena was flooded for the staging of naval battles.

The **latomie** are the ancient quarries from which came the greyish-white limestone used to construct Syracuse's buildings and walls. Once dark caverns whose roofs have been brought down by earthquakes, they now form a luxuriant garden. The white limestone walls, corroded by the elements to form strange, bizarre shapes, provide a dramatic backdrop to groves of citrus trees, immense ficus trees, magnolias and delicate maidenhair ferns. Within the archaeological area is the most famous group of quarries, with heights that vary from 25m to 47m; the complex they form, just below the Greek Theatre, is called the **Latomia del Paradiso** (Map 1). Here is the famous **Orecchio di Dionisio** (Ear of Dionysius) – an S-shaped artificial cavern 65m long, 5–11m wide and 23m high. The painter Caravaggio gave it its colourful name in 1586, picking up on a 16th-century legend according to which the tyrant kept his captives here and from a small fissure in the roof listened to their laments, amplified by the echo (snap your fingers to hear it). There may be some truth in this story: that the *latomie* were worked by forced labourers is known from the writings of Thucydides, Cicero and Diodorus. Nevertheless, the unusual shape of the cave is due solely to the fact that its excavation began at the top and followed the serpentine course of an aqueduct. On the walls you can see traces of the stone-cutters' tools and the horizontal lines of detachment of the blocks extracted.

In the northwest wall of the Latomia del Paradiso is the vast artificial cave supported by piers cut in rock known as the **Grotta dei Cordari**, from rope-makers who, exploiting the cave's abundant humidity (an essential condition for manufacturing good cord) made the rigging of Syracusan ships.

The nearby **Museo Archeologico Regionale Paolo Orsi** is located in a modern building opened in 1988, in the splendid gardens of the Villa Landolina on Viale Teocrito (Map 3). It contains one of the more fabulous archaeological collections in Italy, with statuary, coins and antiquities from the excavations of the Græco-Roman city and from prehistoric and Classical sites of eastern Sicily. The building itself is shaped like a honeycomb, each cell of which houses a separate section of the collection. Section A is devoted to **Prehistory and Protohistory**; Section B to the **Greek Colonies of Eastern** Sicily; Section C to **Sub-Colonies and Hellenised Centres**.

Section A begins with an introduction to the geology, flora and fauna of the ancient Mediterranean and particularly of eastern Sicily. Highlights of this section include the exhibits from the Castelluccio Culture, which spread throughout eastern Sicily from the 19th to the 15th century BC; the Thapsos Culture (15th–13th centuries BC), which was strongly influenced by Mycenæan civilisation; and the Pantalica Culture (13th–7th centuries BC), which has left important evidence of the Siculan migration from the Italian mainland to Sicily: particularly interesting are the bronze implements, which demonstrate the high degree of specialisation achieved in the working of metals.

The outstanding exhibits of Section B are the extraordinary statue of an earth-goddess suckling twins *(Kourothrophos)* from Megara Hyblæa (mid-6th century BC); the beautiful 5th-century BC marble *Kouros* from Leontinoi, which may have been sculpted in Greece; the *Venus Anadyomene* (also called the *Landolina Venus*) from Syracuse, a Roman adaptation of a Hellenistic original of the 2nd century BC; and the many fine tomb treasures from the Greek necropolises of Syracuse, which testify to the city's extensive trade relations with partners as far afield as Egypt and Asia.

Important displays in Section C include the enthroned *Demeter* or *Kore* from Terravecchia di Grammichele, the largest terracotta figure of a female divinity in the museum (late 6th century BC); the extraordinary trove of refined terracotta *pinakes* representing male and female divinities (470–460BC) recently unearthed at Francavilla di Sicilia, near Naxos; and three rare wooden statuettes *(xóana)* of the late 7th century BC, from Palma di Montechiaro, near Agrigento.

Adjoining the archaeological museum is the recently established **Museo**

del Papiro, with displays documenting the natural history of papyrus and its many uses, especially in papermaking. From the plant's slender stalk are cut long strips that are first softened in a special solution, then spread out and arranged in horizontal and vertical rows, pressed under a roller and joined with a glue made from the stem of the plant itself. The papyrus plant is one of the many natural treasures of Syracuse: to see the only spot in Europe where it grows wild, visit the source of the River Cyane (see page 145).

The vicissitudes of the Catholic Church in Syracuse have had an important role in the history of Christianity, bearing witness to the continued importance of the city even after the gradual decline sparked by the Roman conquest. Off Viale Teocrito just west of Villa Landolina you can see the most important of the city's early Christian monuments, the ruined church of **San Giovanni**. The church occupies the west portion of a Byzantine basilica, once the cathedral of Syracuse, which was reconstructed by the Normans in 1200 and toppled by earthquake in 1673. Its façade is preceded by an arched portico incorporating medieval fragments salvaged from other buildings and showing Catalan influence. Remnants of the earlier churches include a delightful 14th-century doorway and rose window, and the 7th-century apse, visible from the garden.

San Giovanni is famous for its extensive **catacombs**, dating from the 3rd to the 6th century. Their regular grid structure was made by enlarging a disused Greek aqueduct, traces of which can still be seen in the ceiling of the 'decumanus maximus', or principal gallery. Smaller passages lead to five circular chapels known as 'rotonde'; the Rotonda d'Adelfia takes its name from the beautiful sarcophagus now in the archaeological museum. Next to the catacombs is the evocative **crypt** of San Marciano, first bishop of Syracuse, who was martyred on this spot in AD254. It is a Greek cross with three apses; the sanctuary was transformed in the Byzantine era (late 6th–early 7th century) into a basilica, which was probably destroyed by the Arabs in 878. The four piers incorporating four capitals with representations of Evangelists date from a Norman reconstruction of c 1200.

An old tale tells that the church of **Santa Lucia** was built on the spot where St Lucy, patron saint of Syracuse, was martyred in AD304. It was founded in Byzantine times and appears today as a three-aisled basilica with semicircular apses. The oldest part (the doorway, apses and base of the campanile) are Norman works of the 12th century; the rose window dates from the 14th century. The recently restored façade was begun in 1629 on a plan by the Spanish architect Giovanni Vermexio and completed in the 18th century, possibly by Rosario Gagliardi. Outside the church and connected to it by an underground passage is the octagonal Cappella del Sepolcro, built by Giovanni Vermexio in 1630 to host the tomb of the saint, whose remains were swept off to Venice long ago and have never been returned. A famous painting of the *Burial of St Lucy* by Caravaggio, formerly

View of Ortygia

in the apse of the church, is now in the Galleria Regionale at Palazzo Bellomo. Beneath the church are Sicily's oldest Christian catacombs and the most extensive in existence after those in Rome (now closed).

The part of the city on the mainland nearest Ortygia corresponds to the ancient Achradina. Here, in the big, busy square known as the **Foro Siracusano** (Map 6) are some remains of the ancient Agora.

The Island of Ortygia

For Syracusans Ortygia is *Lo Scoglio*, 'The Rock': its entire surface amounts to less than one square kilometre. Approaching it from the mainland is one of the special experiences of Syracuse. Leaving behind the anonymous

139

buildings of the modern quarter, as soon as you cross the Ponte Nuovo you are immediately immersed in a world of discovery, where the imprints of many ages work together to give the city a surprisingly unitary and harmonious aspect. Every neighbourhood around the two main axes, Via Dione-Via Roma and Via Amalfitania-Via della Mestranza, has its own distinctive character. Everything, in short, tells a story.

Surrounded by lawns, papyrus plants and palm trees in Piazza Pancali, the remains of the **Tempio di Apollo** (Ortygia Map 3) greet visitors arriving from the mainland. This Doric peripteral hexastyle temple is one of the earliest religious edifices built by the Greeks in Sicily (c 575BC); its design is ascribed to the architect Epicles. Although the dedication to Apollo is confirmed by an inscription on the stylobate, some scholars identify it with the Artemision recorded by the Roman author and statesman Cicero. Due to its strategic position, it was used as a church by the Byzantines, a mosque by the Arabs, a church again by the Normans, and barracks by the Spanish. Its two monolithic columns and fragmentary cella walls were freed of later accretions in 1938.

South of the Temple of Apollo is the waterfront overlooking the **Porto Grande**, guarded by an old Spanish gate. The 19th-century promenade of the **Passeggio Adorno**, above the wooded seaside quay, is an ideal place from which to admire this vast bay, more like a lake in terms of its size and shape, where the Syracusans trapped and destroyed the

Athenian fleet of Demosthenes in 414BC. The promenade is reached by Via Savoia and Via Ruggero Settimo. The neighbourhood on the left faithfully reflects the layout of ancient Ortygia, with buildings arranged in blocks called strigas. From a terrace above the trees, Via del Collegio leads away from the sea, skirting one side of the Jesuit Chiesa del Collegio, built in the 17th century and always closed.

To the right lies **Piazza del Duomo** (Ortygia Map 5), one of the most charming Baroque squares in Italy. The **Palazzo Municipale**, on the left, occupies the former Palazzo Senatoriale, designed in 1628 by Giovanni Vermexio. Excavations beneath the building have brought to light foundations of a 6th-century Ionic temple dedicated to Artemis but never completed, the construction of which is documented in a small display within; here too are remains of various periods of habitation, including a dwelling of the 8th century BC, the oldest Greek structure in Syracuse. Across the way is the **Palazzo Beneventano del Bosco**, a medieval palace with a late Baroque façade and courtyard.

The **Cathedral** of Santa Maria del Piliero or delle Colonne stands at the highest point of Ortygia, on ground that has been sacred since the city's earliest history. It incorporates remains of a Doric Temple of Athena erected in the early 5th century BC; beneath this are traces of an Archaic temple and of Siculan huts dating from the 8th century. The cathedral was begun in the 7th century and extensively rebuilt in the 18th. The graceful Baroque façade, erected in 1728–54, was designed by Andrea Palma. The statues are by Ignazio Marabitti. The perimeter of the church was formed by closing up the spaces between the columns of the temple (12 of which are still visible along the medieval north wall) and the nave was obtained by piercing the walls of the cella with 16 arches, eight on each side.

Cicero mentions that the cella's interior was painted with scenes of Agathocles' triumphs over the Carthaginians, and later sources tell that the Byzantine church was once covered with mosaics, lost long ago. The present **interior** was stripped of its Baroque decoration in the early 20th century. On the west wall are two columns from the opisthodomos of the cella. Nineteen columns of the peristyle are incorporated in the aisles, those on the north side being engaged. The holy-water stoups by Gaetano Puglisi date from the beginning of the 19th century; the stained-glass windows, by Eugenio Cisterna, from the early 20th century.

The first chapel of the south aisle is the baptistery; it contains an antique marble font with a Greek inscription resting on 13th-century bronze lions and, on the wall, mosaic fragments from the medieval church. Next to this is the Cappella di Santa Lucia, housing a processional statue of Syracuse's patron saint on a coffer ascribed to Nibilio and Giuseppe Gagini. The third chapel was probably designed by Giovanni Vermexio (1550); its altar has a beautiful relief of the *Last Supper* by Filippo della Valle (1762). A painting attributed to Antonello da Messina of St Zosimus, bishop of Syracuse, which once hung in the chapel at the end of the aisle, was removed after an attempted theft in 1973. There are some 16th-century bronze candelabra in the chancel, and a *Madonna della Neve* by Antonello Gagini in the Byzantine apse of the north aisle. In the north aisle are statues of *St Lucy* by Antonello Gagini; t*he Madonna and Child* by Domenico Gagini; and *St Catherine of Alexandria* by the Gagini workshop.

From the south end of the square Via Picherale leads to the seafront and the **Fonte Aretusa** (Ortygia Map 5), one of the most delightful spots in Syracuse. This beautiful freshwater spring, once surrounded by walls, now flows into a duck pond planted with papyrus. The myth of its namesake is told by the ancient poets Pindar, Virgil and Ovid. The nymph Arethusa, it seems, was an attendant of Diana, goddess of the hunt. Pursued by the amorous river-god Alpheus, she called upon her mistress to save her. Diana changed her into a spring and whisked her from her native Elis, in Greece, to Ortygia, in Sicily. Alpheus followed her closely, returning to the surface just offshore (where, in fact, there is another freshwater spring). A modern legend tells that British Admiral Horatio Nelson replenished his fleet at the fountain before the battle of the Nile. A small tropical aquarium has been set up in the garden near the fountain, and artisans in the area use the papyrus that grows wild around Syracuse (especially along the River Cyane, west of the city) to make fine paper. Signs around the fountain point you to their shops.

On the southernmost tip of Ortygia rises the **Castello Maniace** – still a military installation today and so, off limits. It is named after the Byzantine general

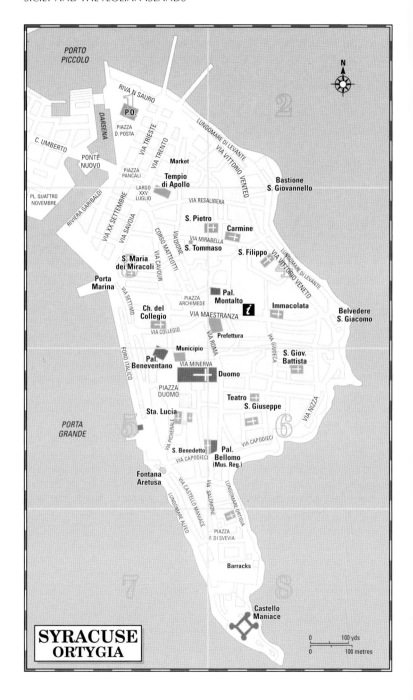

SYRACUSE
ORTYGIA

George Maniakes, who recaptured the city from the Arabs. The castle, some 52m square with massive cylindrical corner towers, was designed by Holy Roman Emperor Frederick II in 1239 but later altered at least four times – by the Spanish (the gate of the drawbridge was designed by Vermexio); after the 1693 earthquake; when the powder magazine blew up in 1704; and most recently for use first as a prison and then as a barracks.

The Story of Arethusa

Arethusa tells her story to Ceres in Ovid's *Metamorphoses* (V, 572–641). Wearied with the chase, the beautiful nymph was returning one day from the Stymphalian wood; the heat was great and her toil had made it insufferable. At a certain point she chanced upon a clear, silent stream shaded by silvery willows and poplars. After testing its coolness she removed her garments and plunged naked into the waters. While she swam, gliding in a thousand turns and tossing her arms, she heard a kind of murmur deep in the pool. In terror she leaped onto the nearer bank.

As she stood by, Alpheus called from his waters: 'Whither in haste, Arethusa? Whither in such haste?' As she was without her robes (she had left them on the other bank), she fled; but he pressed after her. She was just as swift-footed as he, but he had greater endurance. As she ran she saw her pursuer's long shadow stretch out ahead of her, heard the terrifying sound of his feet and felt his deep-panting breath fan her hair. Exhausted by the toil of flight, she cried aloud to Diana for help. The goddess heard, and threw an impene-trable cloud of mist about her. The river-god circled around her, wrapped in the darkness, and vainly searched through the hollow mist. Twice he went round the place where the goddess had hidden her, unknowing, and twice he called her name.

Arethusa felt as the lamb when it hears the wolves howling around the fold; and Alpheus remained close by, for he saw no traces of her feet further on. He watched the cloud and the place. The beleaguered Arethusa broke out in a cold sweat, and the dark drops rained down from her whole body. Wherever she put her foot a pool trickled out, and sooner than she could tell the tale she was changed to a stream of water. But sure enough Alpheus recognised in the waters the maid he loved: and laying aside the form of a man which he had assumed, he changed back to his own watery shape to mingle with her. Just when all seemed lost, Diana cleft the earth, and Arethusa, plunging down into the dark depths, was borne away to Ortygia, where she returned safely to the upper air.

Via Salomone and Via San Martino return past the 6th-century Byzantine church of San Martino to another building from Frederick's time, the **Palazzo Bellomo**, displaying Swabian architectural influence in its doorway, embrasure-like windows, and ground-floor walls, and Catalan-Gothic influences on the floor above. With the adjacent 14th-century Palazzo Parisi, it houses the **Galleria Regionale di Arte Medievale e Moderna**. The collection includes architectural fragments and sculpture on the ground floor, and paintings, drawings and applied arts (silver, gold, ivory, coral, majolica, church furnishings, illuminated manuscripts and furniture) on the first floor. The key works here are the fine Renaissance tomb of nobleman Giovanni Cardinas, ascribed to Antonello Gagini; Antonello da Messina's damaged *Annunciation* of 1474; and Caravaggio's 1609 masterpiece, *The Burial of St Lucy*.

Via Roma, with delightful overhanging balconies, leads away from the seafront to **Piazza Archimede**, with a fountain of Diana by Giulio Moschetti. It is overlooked by fine patrician palaces: Palazzo Lanza on the south side preserves elegant two-light windows, and Palazzo dell'Orologio (now the Banca d'Italia) on the west has a Catalan-Gothic staircase in its courtyard. A few paces away on Via Montalto is Palazzo Montalto, with a fine Chiaramonte-style façade displaying delicate two- and three-light windows and an elegant niche with a Latin inscription commemorating the year of its construction, 1397. North of Piazza Archimede begins Corso Matteotti, the former Via del Littorio, lined with square-cut Fascist-period buildings that seem to march through the medieval town fabric.

Westward from Piazza Archimede stretches one of the town's most magnificent streets, **Via della Maestranza**. It is lined with Baroque palaces, their rich golden façades adorned by magnificent wrought-iron balconies carried by sumptuously carved corbels. Via della Giudecca diverges right to the former ghetto, though nothing remains of its original architecture. Via Vittorio Veneto, which links Via Maestranza to the Porto Piccolo, is lined with palaces of the Spanish period.

The Environs of Syracuse

The areas north, west and south of Syracuse have a common natural and cultural history. The eastern offshoots of the Hyblæan Hills here form a low, flat plateau scored by *cave*, deep gorges in the limestone abounding in luxuriant vegetation. The coast is everywhere flat and marshy, with sandy beaches. The region's common cultural heritage begins with the Castelluccio Culture, a Bronze Age civilisation taking its name from a village near Noto, which spread throughout southeast Sicily in the 18th–15th centuries BC. A second unifying influence is Syracuse itself, which held sway over the area from the 8th century BC right up to the Middle Ages. A third is the vast reconstruction programme that followed the disastrous earthquake of 1693, when traditional farming and grazing activities were tailored to fit 'modern' market needs (for instance, by introducing almond plantations around Avola and Noto, and wine growing around Pachino), and the cities were rebuilt in accordance with the latest theories of architecture and town planning.

Just south of Syracuse, in an area that can still be considered suburban, are two sights that are interesting in a quiet, unobtrusive way. The first of these is the **Olympieion**, the scant but picturesque ruins of a Doric temple of Olympian Zeus. It can be reached by car from the Noto road, which crosses first the River Anapo and then the Cyane c 3km (1 3/4 miles) from Syracuse. Two columns and part of the stylobate of this peripteral hexastyle temple, built in the 6th century BC in a position of great strategic importance on the right bank of the Cyane, are still standing. The suburban temple, fortified during the war with Athens, played a key role in the fighting as the base of the Syracusan cavalry.

From here you can walk to the source of the **Cyane**, in a grove of eucalyptus and cypress trees overgrown with reeds and thick clumps of Egyptian papyrus. This exotic plant, which grows wild nowhere else outside North Africa, is traditionally thought to have found its way here as a gift to Syracuse from the Hellenistic ruler Ptolomy Philadelphus of Egypt, although it may have been introduced later by the Arabs. The name of the spring ('blue' in Greek) describes the azure colour of its waters, but a myth relates how the nymph Cyane, who tried to prevent Dis from carrying off Proserpina, was changed into a spring and condemned to weep forever. A leisurely way to visit the Olympieion and the Cyane is by boat – from Ortygia or from the confluence of the Anapo and Cyane rivers (inquire at the Tourist Office in Syracuse).

Highway 115, the main artery of the southeast, continues along the uninteresting coastal plain, touching upon the dull, sprawling towns of Cassibile and Avola. From the latter a scenic mountain road winds its way up to Avola Vecchia and the Belvedere, overlooking the grandest of all southeastern Sicily's limestone canyons, the **Cava Grande del Cassibile**. From the Belvedere you can make the 250m descent to the canyon floor and wander among its lush vegetation, which includes groves of rare Eastern plane trees (*Platinus orientalis australis*), willows, poplars, oleanders and *macchia*, pausing from time to time for a refreshing dip in the cool emerald waters of the River Cassibile, which here forms a series of stepped cascades and pools. If you're lucky you'll glimpse one of the canyon's most famous inhabitants, the 'wandering hawk' (*Falco peregrinus*). Dug into the rock are dozens of prehistoric tombs (11th–9th century BC), where material now in the archaeological museum in Syracuse was found.

Noto

Noto lies 33km (20 miles) from Syracuse, 152m above sea level on the hill of Meti, overlooking the valley of the Asìnaro and the plain of the Tellàro river. Though famous the world over, it is a relatively small town, of 22,000 inhabitants. The Sicilian writer Leonardo Sciascia called it a 'garden of stone, a city of gold, a theatrical city, a Baroque city'.

Noto arose in 1703, on the left bank of the Asìnaro, a few kilometres southeast of Noto Antica (see below), which was destroyed in the earthquake of 1693. In antiquity it was a Greek subject ally of Syracuse (*Néeton*) and then a Roman colony (*Neetum*). During the Arab domination it became the capital of a province, the *Val di Noto*, which encompassed the entire southeastern part of the island. After the demographic and economic collapse that followed the 1693 earthquake, the city was rebuilt in accordance with the period's most advanced ideas in city planning – a move which increased its cultural status as well as its economic well-being and its population. Nevertheless, in 1817 Noto lost its role as provincial capital to Syracuse and was gradually forgotten. Here, as elsewhere in Sicily, the old city centre was largely abandoned after World War II in favour of modern apartment blocks on the outskirts. This trend has recently been reversed, however, and as more people move back into the old centre its lovely old palaces are gradually returning to their original splendour. Unfortunately restoration has not always kept apace of decay: in 1995, as a team of experts was preparing to confront the huge task of consolidating and restoring the cathedral, the dome collapsed (fortunately without causing injury), bringing about a loss that will never fully be repaired. Although its greatest church will remain closed for some years (as though in compensation, the *Netini* have begun working furiously on just about every other building), the city still merits special attention. Laid out by Giovanni Battista Landolina, it is truly unique for the uniformity of its architectural heritage, most buildings having been built at the same time, in the same style (by the master of Sicilian Baroque, Rosario Gagliardi, and his followers), and using the same wonderful golden-brown stone. It has recently come under the tutelage of UNESCO.

The main gateway to the historic centre is the imposing Porta Reale (1843), adjoining the pleasant public gardens on the east. Beyond the gate begins Noto's 1km-long main street, Corso Vittorio Emanuele, along which its most monumental buildings are arranged. Steep side streets, often stepped, lead up and down the hillside to the right and left, offering fine views of the town and the surrounding countryside.

Along the Corso lie three squares, each overlooked by a great Baroque church. The first on the east is Piazza Immacolata, with the conventual church of **San Francesco** (also called the Immacolata), designed by Gagliardi's best pupil, Vincenzo Sinatra. It has a fine façade and a lovely white stucco interior. Across the square, wooden scaffolding holds up the crumbling walls of the Benedictine monastery of the Santissimo Salvatore, with two storeys of twin pilasters, fine windows, and a massive tower. On the other side of the Corso, on the left, rise the convent and church of **Santa Chiara**, designed by Gagliardi. The church has a beautiful elliptical interior with more stuccoes and a *Madonna and Child* attributed to Antonello Gagini, brought from the abandoned city of Noto Antica. When restoration work is completed these two convents will hold the small Museo Civico, with prehistoric, Greek and medieval archaeological finds from Noto Antica and the Norman abbey of Santa Lucia del Mendolo (at Santissimo Salvatore), and a small collection of modern art (at Santa Chiara).

The second square, Piazza del Municipio, is dominated by the broad façade of the **Cathedral** (San Nicolò di Mira) at the top of a grand staircase now sadly blocked, half-way up, by a wooden fence. Construction of the church took most of the 18th century and involved the talents of both Gagliardi and Sinatra. The cathedral is flanked by the 18th-century **Palazzo Landolina** (left) and the 19th-century **Bishop's Palace** (right), next to which rises the main façade of the **Santissimo Salvatore** (1791). This was designed by Andrea Gigante and probably built by Antonio Mazza, who was also responsible for the ceiling painting in the interior (usually closed). The south side of the square is fronted by the lovely **Palazzo Ducezio**, now the town hall. Its ground floor, with a harmonious Classical colonnade, was designed by Vincenzo Sinatra in 1776 as the meeting place of the Senato, or town council; the upper floor was added in 1951.

Ahead on the left rises the three-storeyed concave façade of the **Chiesa del Collegio** (also called San Carlo), designed by Gagliardi in 1730 and restored by Sinatra in 1776. It has a handsome white stucco interior. Next to the church rises the former Jesuit college, which extends all the way to the final square on the Corso, Piazza San Domenico. Here, behind a little garden with a 17th-century fountain surmounted by a statue of Hercules from Noto Antica, stands Rosario Gagliardi's church of **San Domenico**. Its bold, convex façade, with two orders of Classical columns and a particularly exuberant roofline, is considered the architect's crowning achievement. The interesting interior has a central plan with five domes. Across the square is the 19th-century Teatro Vittorio Emanuele.

The side streets of Noto, especially between the Corso and the parallel Via Cavour, where many of the town's leading families had their palaces, are full of small Baroque treasures. Next to San Domenico, Via Bovio leads up to the former **Convento dei Crociferi**, begun by Paolo Labisi and completed by Vincenzo Sinatra. Across the Corso from the Chiesa del Collegio, Via Nicolaci climbs past the delightful Baroque balconies of **Palazzo Nicolaci Villadorata** to the handsome church of Monte Vergine on Via Cavour. To the right, beyond the end of the fine **Palazzo Astuto**, steps ascend to Via Sallicano and the upper part of the town, known as **Noto Alta**, passing the palace of the Impellizzeri family and the former

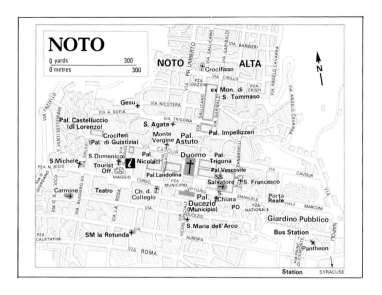

monastery of San Tommaso, now a prison. Simpler and less monumental than the lower town, this area lies around the small Piazza Mazzini. Here is Gagliardi's church of the **Crocifisso**, with a splendid central portal and a statue by Francesco Laurana of the *Madonna della Neve* (1471) in its stuccoed interior.

A lovely winding road runs past the little suburb of San Corrado di Fuori, with pleasant early 20th-century villas, to the romantic ruins of **Noto Antica**, abandoned since the earthquake of 1693 and now completely overgrown. The original Noto dates from prehistoric times and achieved particular splendour in the Greek period. It was one of the richest Arab strongholds on Sicily, giving its name to the *Val di Noto*, one of the three 'provinces' into which the Arabs divided the island. It fell to the Normans in 1091, and most of the ruins belong to the medieval city.

Another byroad leads south from Noto to the **Oasi Naturale di Vendìcari**, a complex of coastal marshes where splendid Mediterranean *macchia* provides a protected home for large populations of migratory birds. From the entrance to the reserve, footpaths lead through the saltfields of the Pantano Grande to the medieval watchtower known as the Torre di Vendìcari, flanked by a ruined tuna fishery. From here the view embraces the entire reserve, from the splendid isle of Vendìcari to that of Capo Pàssero, in the distance. Two footpaths lead off from the tower – one northwards, the other southwards. The northern path runs along the low rocky coast amid windswept *gariga* – low groves of lentisk, thyme, and dwarf palm. Beyond the little bay of Calamosche is the mouth of the Tellaro, the northern limit of the reserve; here on a golden-sand beach, unfortunately near the hotels of Noto Marina, lie the scant ruins of **Eloro**, a Syracusan colony of the late 8th century BC. The southern trail skirts the Pantano Grande and the Pantano Roveto, sheltered from the sea by low dunes. The latter dries up in the summer to become the natural habitat of a curious red cactus known as *salicornia*. In summer you can ford the outlet of the marshes and continue along the beach to the fishing village of **Marzamemi**, in whose shallow bay archaeologists have found 14 ancient shipwrecks (four Greek, five Roman and five Byzantine).

Pantalica, Palazzolo Acreide and Megara Hyblæa

West of Syracuse, reached by a beautiful country road (Highway 124), are two of the southeast's most interesting archaeological sites. Surrounded by splendid uncontaminated nature, **Pantalica** possesses a particular charm. The site is a rocky terrace set between steep walls carved over thousands of years by the waters of the River Anapo and of its affluent, the Calcinara. Its configuration made it a safe place in antiquity, and some archaeological remains – one building, the *anaktoron* or palace, and some traces of walls – make archaeologists think this was the site of the legendary Sikel town of Hybla, which flourished between the 13th and the 8th centuries BC. Tradition recalls the Sikels as the Bee People, and by an evocative coincidence the necropolis of Pantalica closely resembles a large honeycomb cut in the rock, with over 5000 artificial-cave tombs and multiple inhumation tombs perforating the canyon's sheer walls. The site, abandoned for reasons unknown after the 8th century BC, was occupied again in the early Middle Ages, when its almost total inaccessibility offered refuge from the Arab incursions. From this period date a cave-village with rudimentary houses and churches (the so-called Villaggio Bizantino), some with traces of frescoes. To explore the necropolis today, especially out of season when the silence is broken only by birdsong, represents an authentic return to the dawn of history. Access to the top of the plateau is by a byroad (signposted) from the little Baroque village of **Ferla**. The adventurous can descend to the canyon floor and follow, on foot or in Forest Service vans, the dirt bed of an abandoned railway which connected Ferla to Sortino along the banks of the Anapo. The landscape here is among the most dramatic in the Mediterranean, with fragrant *macchia*, dark pine and ilex forests, and brilliant white limestone cliffs all crowned, usually, by a deep blue sky. The road from Syracuse to Ferla passes a car park at the entrance to the Valle dell'Anapo, where a map of footpaths in the area is available, and there is another entrance to the site on the road from Solarino to Sortino.

Highway 124 climbs steeply out of the Anapo valley to the sleepy village of Cassaro, then winds westwards through verdant farmland to **Palazzolo Acreide**. This pleasant 18th-century town is a direct descendent of the Greek city of *Akrai* (Roman *Acræ*), founded by the Syracusans in 663BC on

North aisle of the Cathedral at Syracuse, with Statues by Gagini (p 141)

the watershed between the Anapo and Tellaro. The town flourished particularly under Hieron I (3rd century BC) and again in Byzantine times before
being destroyed, presumably by the Arabs, in the 9th century. The present
town arose in the 12th century as *Placeolum*. It was partly destroyed by the
earthquake of 1693 and rebuilt in the 18th century, which accounts for its
predominantly Baroque appearance.

Before going up to the ruins of Akrai, take a quick look at the Baroque
buildings along the two main streets of the post-1693 town, Corso Vittorio
Emanuele and the nearly parallel Via Carlo Alberto. Along the latter is the
17th-century **Casa Museo** of local ethnographer Antonino Uccello, with
charming displays of farm tools, household objects, puppets, and other
material from the provinces of Ragusa and Syracuse. The streets meet in
Piazza del Popolo, in front of the magnificent, tall façade of **San
Sebastiano**, an 18th-century church designed by Paolo Labisi. At the other
(west) end of the Corso the contemporary **Annunziata** has a sumptuous
Baroque doorway adorned with spiral columns, festoons and vines, and a
splendid inlaid-marble altar within. **San Paolo**, nearby, has a portico reminiscent of that of Palazzo Ducezio in Noto; some scholars attribute it to the
same architect, Vincenzo Sinatra.

The ruins of the ancient city – the earliest of the Syracusan sub-colonies
in Sicily – lie in a beautiful, romantic position on the hill known as the
Serra Palazzia or Acremonte, above the modern town. To get there, follow
Corso Vittorio Emanuele to its west end. The Greek **theatre** dates from the
3rd century BC but was altered in Roman times. It is a small, well-propor-

Panorama of Cava Grande del Cassibile (p 145)

tioned building preserving traces of the orchestra and scena and a nine-wedge cavea with 12 tiers of seats. There is a marvellous view from the top. Slightly to the west are remains of a **bouleuterion**, with more seats arranged in a semicircle. Near here begin the new excavations, which have brought to light some 200m of the ancient street plan.

Behind the theatre, to the south, extend two Greek **latomie**, or stone quarries, which the city's Byzantine Christians transformed into tenements and cemeteries – you can still make out some of the lattice-work tomb fronts. The narrower and deeper of the two quarries, the Intagliatella, preserves a rock carving with scenes of heroes banqueting and making sacrifices, and numerous niches in the walls designed to contain *pinakes* for the cult of the heroes. Nearby is the recently excavated stylobate of a 6th-century **Temple of Aphrodite**; in the little hollow north of here extended the agora.

A custodian accompanies visitors to the **Templi Ferali**, a second quarry in the southeast flank of the hill, and to the remote but remarkable **Santoni**, 12 rough sculptures of the 3rd century BC, connected with the cult of Cybele as *Magna Mater* (Great Mother), hewn out of the rock. The surrounding territory is full of Siculan, Greek and Christian burial grounds, visible from the circular Strada Panorama.

Megara Hyblæa lies along the coast just north of Syracuse. In a way, this is the quintessentially Sicilian archaeological site and an eloquent sign of the times. Surrounded by the industrial centre of Augusta, it offers a stunning vision of antiquity accompanied from beginning to end by views of Europe's largest concentration of oil refineries and chemical plants, and of their huge tankers anchored offshore. Wild flowers grow among the rocks, but the pollution in the area is so bad that the inhabitants of nearby Marina de Melilli had to be relocated in 1979 and the town bulldozed under.

Megara Hyblæa (Greek *Megára Yblaia*) was founded in 728BC by settlers from Megara in Greece, and it lasted until 482BC when Gelon destroyed it and moved the inhabitants to Syracuse; a second city, founded by Timoleon in 340BC, was razed by the Romans in 214. The ruins include the central areas of the Archaic and Hellenistic cities, some Archaic fortifications, including the original **west gate** to the city; the considerably less extensive Hellenistic fortifications, including the **north** and **south gates** and a small **west gate**, parts of the **agora, temples, sanctuaries** and **thermae**. A small **museum**, near the custodian's house, contains finds from the excavations and helpful plans of the site.

Enna and the Interior

Enna stands at the centre of Sicily's great highland plateau, which gradually descends from the Nebrodi Mountains on the island's north shore to the low southern coast. It is an immense expanse of rolling hills and shallow valleys that interlace to create the impression of a single vast plain. The marked effects of light and shadow typical of the steep north and east coasts are here completely absent: the sun bathes the landscape in a uniform light, dwelling only in a few folds of the bare hills. The colours of the landscape are the grey of the clay-rich earth in winter, the all-over green of the young grain in spring and the deep gold of the mature wheat in summer and autumn.

Goethe travelled through this fertile desert in April 1787, and his description is exact enough, still, to fit the area today. 'There are no great level areas,' he observed, 'but the gently rolling uplands were completely covered with wheat and barley in one great unbroken mass. Wherever the soil is suitable to their growth, it is so well tended and exploited that not a tree is to be seen. Even the small hamlets and other dwellings are confined to the ridges, where the limestone rocks make the ground untillable.... The dwarf palms and all the flowers and shrubs of the southwestern zone had disappeared and I did not see much red clover. Thistles are allowed to take possession only of the roads, but all the rest is Ceres' domain.' There is a subtle warning in the poet's words; you'll find the sunbaked hills of Sicily's vast interior intolerable if you are in a hurry to get beyond them ('we soon came to long for the winged chariot of Triptolemus to bear us away out of this monotony'); but if you pause to observe them, you'll discover they are beautiful and exciting, fascinating and absorbing.

The whole region has been inhabited since prehistory, but the greatest evidence has been found in the green and hospitable valleys of the Platini and Salso Rivers. In these areas – which in recent years have undergone successful reafforestation programmes – lie the two main archaeological sites of the interior, the Greek city of Morgantina and the Roman villa of Piazza Armerina. That most towns have preserved Arabic traces in their names demonstrates the enormous impact the Arabs had on the region's economic and social development, thanks to their rationalisation of the road and irrigation systems. Another relic of the Arab domination is the labyrinthine layout of the older centres, which can be distinguished on the basis of their street-plans from the gridlike 'new' cities established in the 16th–18th centuries as part of the Spanish agricultural improvement plan.

Urban organisation in the interior revolves around two cities, Enna and Caltanissetta. The former, an impregnable fortress of very ancient origins, has played a key role in the island's political history. The latter, devoid of natural defences, has rarely influenced the course of events. Today this situation is slowly being overturned: with the decline of its military importance, the development of Enna has ground to a halt, while Caltanissetta has grown and prospered. The smaller towns, which are distributed in a balanced way in the two provinces, are all farming centres. Those that gravitate around Enna are this and nothing else; those situated in the sulphur-rich region west of Caltanissetta preserve clear traces of an intense mining activity, which in the 19th century represented one of the island's chief economic resources.

The Cathedral at Noto before the collapse of the dome (p 146)

Enna

Enna stands on a high, flat eminence amid fertile rolling hills, at the exact centre of the island. At 931m above sea level it is the *Belvedere della Sicilia*, enjoying wonderful views in all directions – when it's not lost in the clouds. It was long the most impregnable stronghold in Sicily, and for centuries it was the only town in the interior. Today it is a provincial capital and undoubtedly the island's most interesting inland city.

Enna is heir to the Siculan *Henna*, a very ancient settlement known to the Greeks as *Enna*, to the Romans as *Castrum Hennæ*, to the Arabs as *Kasr Janna* and to Italians as *Castrogiovanni* until 1927, when Mussolini restored its Greek name. The mythical scene of the rape of Persephone (or Kore, the Roman Proserpina), throughout antiquity it was the centre of the cult of her mother Demeter (the Roman Ceres), goddess of the harvest. Although the city was gradually Hellenised by its Greek neighbours, it remained independent until 397BC, when it fell by treachery to Dionysius the Elder of Syracuse. For a while it was under Carthaginian rule, but in 258 it fell to Rome. The Romans had to fight hard to keep it: the First Servile War broke out in Enna under the slave Eunus in 135BC.

Afterwards an important Byzantine fortress, in 859 Enna was taken by the Arabs, who were compelled to scale the cliffs and crawl in one by one through a sewer by night, so effective were its defences. The Normans reclaimed it in 1087, built a stronger castle and replaced the Islamic population with a Lombard colony. The city flourished anew under the Hohenstaufen and Aragonese, but the 17th-century programme of the

Rock tombs of the Filiporto Necropolis, Pantalica (p 149)

Spanish crown to found new villages in the immense fiefs of the interior, with a view to boosting agricultural production, caused a depopulation of the city and a consequent arrest of its growth, which has only recently been reversed.

Enna's historic centre speaks a sober medieval language little contaminated by Baroque flourishes. The focus of town life is the tree-filled Piazza Vittorio Emanuele, on whose north side is the imposing flank of **San Francesco d'Assisi**. A 13th-century church much altered over the centuries, it stands on a tall stone base with sloping walls like those of a fortress. The powerful 15th-century campanile has attached arches and two orders of Gothic single-light windows. Behind San Francesco opens Piazza Crispi, with a magnificent view across the valley to Enna's near twin, the medieval hill town of Calascibetta, from which the Normans launched their 11th-century siege of Enna. On the clearest days, the view ranges all the way to Ætna. Over the fountain stands a bronze copy of Bernini's *Rape of Persephone.*

Via Roma, Enna's main street since the 14th century, rises gently to the top of the town, touching upon one square after another. In Piazza Colajanni stands the church of **Santa Chiara**, a 17th-century foundation renovated in the 18th century and today a war memorial. The aisleless interior has a 19th-century majolica pavement with two pictures celebrating unusual themes – the advent of steam navigation and the triumph of Christianity over Islam.

The 14th-century **Cathedral** was founded by Eleonora of Aragon. It was rebuilt in the 16th century after a fire, but traces of the old structure can be seen in the apses (visible from the Museo Alessi, see below) and in the ogival-arched portal of the south transept. The main façade is characterised by an unusual 17th-century campanile above the vault of the portico. On the side facing Piazza Mazzini is a beautiful 16th-century portal with a low relief telling the story of St Martin and the pauper.

The Latin-cross **interior** is divided into three aisles by ogival arches on stout grey basalt columns with finely decorated bases and capitals; Gian Domenico Gagini carved the symbols of the Evangelists on those at the west end. The nave ceiling, with octagonal coffers, is a work of the 17th century; it has curious wooden corbels in the form of buxom winged griffins. The altarpieces on the south side are by Willem Borremans, and Filippo Paladino painted the five beautiful New Testament scenes in the presbytery (1613). In the Cappella della Visitazione two magnificent tarsiated spiral columns frame a painting of the *Visitation of Mary* which conceals the *Nava d'Oro*, a sumptuous platform on which a 15th-century statue of the Madonna is carried in procession on 2 July.

The **Museo Alessi**, behind the east end of the Duomo, takes its name from its principal collection, assembled by Canon Giuseppe Alessi (1774–1837), a native of Enna. Among its main attractions are rare

---

The Story of Demeter and Kore

In Ovid's *Metamorphoses* (V, 345–571), Calliope tells the touching tale of the rape of Proserpina (the Greek *Persephone*, often simply called *Kore*, 'the girl') by the king of the lower world, Dis or Tartarus, and of the desperate efforts of her mother, Ceres (*Demeter* in Greek), to win her back. Ceres finds her daughter, but Jupiter rules that the young girl must spend half the year with her captor, and half with her mother. The girl's absence from her earthly homeland, and her mother's sorrow (Ceres is goddess of the harvest) account for the changing of the seasons. Here is Calliope's story, in an abridged version of the beautiful translation of Frank Justus Miller (1915):

The king of the lower world had left his gloomy realm and, in his chariot was traversing the land of Sicily, carefully inspecting its foundations. After he had examined all to his satisfaction and found that no points were giving way, he put aside his fears. But Venus Erycina from her mountaintop saw him wandering to and fro and ordered Cupid to pierce his heart with an arrow of love. For he was the last of the three sons of Saturn to remain unmarried. Already Pallas and Diana had revolted against her, choosing to remain virgin, and Ceres' daughter, too, would follow suit if she, Venus, should suffer it; for she aspired to be like them. 'Go,' she entreated, 'and join the goddess to her uncle in the bonds of love.' The god of love loosed his quiver at his mother's bidding and selected from his thousand shafts the sharpest and the surest and the most obedient to the bow. With this barbed arrow he smote Dis through the heart.

Not far from Henna's walls is a deep pool of water called Pergus. A wood crowns the heights around its shores, and the cool, shady ground bears bright-coloured flowers. There spring is everlasting. Within this grove Proserpina was playing and gathering violets or white lilies. While with girlish eagerness she was filling her basket and her bosom and striving to surpass her friends in gathering, almost in one act Dis saw and loved and carried her away: so strong was his passion, fired by Cupid's arrows. The terrified girl called plaintively on her mother and her companions; but her captor urged on his horses, shaking the dark reins on their necks and manes. Through deep lakes and over high mountains they sped until, near Arethusa, they reached the pool of Cyane.

Here, the most famous of the Sicilian water-nymphs, recognising the goddess, stood forth from her waters and blocked the way, crying to Dis: 'No further shall you go! Thou canst not be the son-in-law of Ceres against her will. The maiden should have been wooed, not ravished.' Dis, urging on his terrible steeds, whirled his royal sceptre and smote the pool to its bottom. The stricken earth opened up a road to Tartarus and received the down-plunging chariot in its cavernous depths. Cyane, grieving for the rape of the goddess and for her fountain's rights thus offended, nursed an incurable wound in her heart and dissolved all away in tears. Into those very waters whose divinity she had been but now, she was melted, her body vanishing into thin streams, her living blood into clear water.

Meanwhile the frightened mother sought her daughter in every land and on every deep. Not Aurora, rising with dewy tresses, not Hesperus saw her pause in the search. Over what lands and what seas the goddess roamed it would take long to tell. When there was no more a place to search in, she came back to Sicily, and in the course of her wanderings here she came to Cyane. Having no means of speech, the nymph showed on the surface of her pool Proserpina's girdle, which had chanced to fall upon the waters. As soon as she saw the garment, as if she had for the first time learned that her daughter had been stolen, Ceres tore her hair and beat her breast. As she did not know as yet where her child was, she reproached all lands, but especially Sicily, where she had found traces of her loss. There with angry hand she broke the ploughs that turn the soil, and in her rage she gave to destruction farmers and cattle alike and bade the ploughed fields to betray their trust and blighted the seed. The fertility of this land, famous throughout the world, lay false to its good name: the crops died in early blade, now too much heat, now too much rain destroying them. Stars and winds were baleful, greedy birds ate up the seed as soon as it was sown, and stubborn grasses choked the wheat.

At this juncture Arethusa lifted her head from her pool and prayed the goddess of fruits to cease her boundless search and stop punishing the land, which had been true to her. Imploring the goddess's mercy, she explained that she herself had seen Proserpina in the earth's lowest depths. The maiden had seemed sad and her face had been perturbed with fear; but yet she was a queen, 'the great queen of that world of darkness, the mighty consort of the tyrant of the underworld'. The mother, upon hearing these words, stood as if turned to stone and was for a long time like one bereft of reason. But when her overwhelming frenzy had given way to over-whelming pain, she set forth in her chariot to heaven. There, with clouded countenance, she appeared before Jove, her brother, father of her daughter and brother of the girl's abductor. 'My daughter, sought so long, has at last been found,' she said, 'if you call it finding more certainly to lose her, or if you call it finding merely to know where she is. That she has been stolen, I will bear, if only he will bring her back; for your daughter does not deserve to have a robber for a husband – if now she is not mine.' And Jove replied: 'She is, indeed, our daughter, yours and mine, our common pledge and care. But if only we are willing to give right names to things, this is no harm that has been done, but only love.' If Ceres wished to separate them, Jove remarked, Proserpina would be allowed to return to heaven on one condition only: if in the lower-world no food had yet touched her lips – for so had the fates decreed.

Ceres was resolved to have her daughter back. Not so the fates; for the girl had already broken her fast. Simple child that she was, while she wandered in the trim gardens, she had plucked a pome-granate hanging from a bending bough and eaten seven of the seeds. But Jove, seeking to balance the claims of his brother and his grieving sister, divided the revolving year into two equal parts and ruled that the goddess, the common divinity of two realms, should spend half the months with her mother, and with her husband half. Proserpina's expression and bearing changed straightaway: she who but lately had seemed sad even to Dis, donned a joyful countenance – like the sun which, long concealed behind dark and misty clouds, disperses the clouds and reveals its face.

Byzantine icons on the ground floor; Renaissance gold and silver from the cathedral treasury – notably the enamelled and gem-studded *Crown of the*

Virgin crafted in 1653 by Leonardo and Giuseppe Montalbano and Michele Castellani, and a beautiful 16th-century brooch in the shape of a pelican pecking its breast (symbolising the sacrifice of Christ) – on the first floor; and Alessi's extraordinary coin collection on the top floor, outstanding both for the number of its coins, which give a broad picture of the economic history of Sicily since antiquity, and for the presence of rare Greek, Roman and Byzantine specimens.

Across Piazza Mazzini, **the Museo Archeologico Regionale** occupies the handsome Palazzo Varisano. Opened in 1985, it has beautifully displayed finds from archaeological sites throughout Enna province, notably a large quantity of burial treasures, some dating from the 3rd and 2nd millennia BC. The most interesting objects are from a Copper Age settlement and Greek centre of the 5th–4th century BC at Cozzo Matrice, where there was a fortified sanctuary of Demeter and Kore.

At the top of the town, on the site of an Arabic fortification strengthened by the Normans, Frederick II built the **Castello di Lombardia** in the 12th century. It still has six of its 20 original towers and a complex system of sequentially arranged inner courtyards, the first of which is used for open-air theatre in summer. From the third courtyard, where there are remains of a small church and some tombs carved in the rock, a modern stair climbs to the top of the tall **Torre Pisana**. The view from the terrace (fog permitting) is stupendous, ranging from Centuripe and Ætna on one side, to Lake Pergusa and Calascibetta on the other.

Just beyond the castle, on a rocky spur, you can make out traces of what may be the Archaic **Temple of Ceres**, which Cicero says was still full of statues of the goddess in the 1st century BC. More steps climb to the summit of the hill, where there is yet another breathtaking view.

In the lower town, near the southwest end of Via Roma, stands the **Torre di Federico II**, an octagonal prism rising 24m over a small hill at the centre of a park. Built in the 13th century, it exhibits the simplicity of volume and almost total absence of decoration that were the hallmarks of Frederick's military architecture. The interior (not always open) has three storeys, the first of which, occupied by a single large room, has a fine vaulted ceiling with stone arches. A spiral staircase set in the 3m-thick wall leads to the rooms of the upper floors. From here, it is said, all three corners of the island can be seen on a clear day. Frederick is believed to have constructed the tower to mark the exact centre of the island (*Umbilicus Sicilæ*, Sicily's navel) as well as the intersection of its three main thoroughfares.

Morgantina

The excavations in the lonely countryside near Aidone can very likely be identified with the Hellenised Siculan city of **Morgantina** (Greek *Morgantíne, Morgántion*). The site, which appears to have been inhabited since the Bronze Age, was colonised by the Greeks in the early 6th century BC and seems to have flourished particularly during the 4th and 3rd centuries. Having sided with Carthage in the Second Punic War, it was destroyed in 211BC by mercenary hordes in the service of the Romans, who kept it in a state of subjection until the 1st century of the Christian era.

Today the ruins lie along a minor road, but at the height of its development Morgantina was an important market centre on the main highway between the island's north and south coasts. Surrounded by hills with sheer cliffs on the north and south sides, the easily defended site dominated a vast agricultural region.

The spot retains a certain bucolic beauty, thanks to the complete lack of modern buildings in the vicinity. Excavations begun in 1955 have revealed the rectangular Greek **agora**, from the time of Agathocles (4th century BC). On two levels joined by a monumental flight of steps, it probably doubled as an ekklesiasterion. The upper level is occupied, at the centre, by the rectangular Roman **macellum**, a covered market with shops, and is delimited on the north and east sides, respectively, by the Roman **gymnasium** and **stoa**, in whose surfaces you can still see column bases. Behind the agora was a **Sanctuary of Demeter and Kore**, where numerous terracotta votive objects have been found.

At a lower level is a **theatre** of the 4th century BC, its seats and scena in an excellent state of preservation. The large oblong building behind the scena was probably a public granary, with kilns for the manufacture of pottery and tiles at the ends. Behind the east stoa, a paved street climbs up the east hill, which hosts one of the residential quarters on terraces sloping down toward the agora. The houses here – the **Casa del Capitello Dorico** and the **Casa di Ganimede** – date from the Greek period (3rd century BC) and were probably inhabited by the town's more affluent citizens, judging from the refinement of the wall decorations and floor mosaic. Substantial remains of another patrician neighbourhood are behind the theatre, on the west hill; here are the so-called **Case del Magistrato**, **del Capitello Tuscanico**, **Pappalardo and della Cisterna ad Arco**, all equally luxurious.

Around the site are remnants of late 4th-century **walls** and, on the separately fortified hill of the **cittadella** (3km/1¾ miles away by a country lane), vestiges of a Bronze and Iron Age village and of the earliest Greek settlement. Excavations here have brought to light rock-hewn tombs containing large stores of Siceliot pottery, and Archaic antefixes dating from the 6th century BC.

Morgantina was in the headlines a few years ago for the theft of a statue of Aphrodite that was brought to light during the excavations. The statue has never been recovered. Other finds from the digs are in the excellent **Museo Archeologico Regionale** in the Capuchin convent of Aidone, which offers a thorough overview of settlements in the area from prehistory to the Greek period.

Piazza Armerina

Piazza Armerina spans three hills in the midst of some of the more beautiful, fertile countryside in central Sicily. Settled in the 8th or 7th century BC, it was inhabited by the Romans, Byzantines, Arabs and Normans. The town is not particularly interesting in itself, but nearby, at Casale (5km/3 miles southwest off Highway 191), excavations have brought to light a magnificent **Roman villa**, Sicily's finest Roman site and one of the island's foremost attractions. To get there, take the highway towards Barrafranca, which descends westwards through the cool Gela valley; after 4km (2 1/2 miles) a turning leads south in just over 1km to the entrance, with a car park and café.

Scholars generally hold that this luxurious country mansion was built in the 3rd or early 4th century after Christ as a summer retreat for a member of the imperial family – possibly Diocletian's co-emperor Maximian (Maximianus Herculeus), who ruled from 286 to 305. Then as now it lay in a secluded spot, 5km (3 miles) from the nearest Roman town, *Philosophiana* (Soffiana). Similar in size and aspect to other imperial residences – Nero's Domus Aurea in Rome, Hadrian's Villa at Tivoli and Diocletian's Palace at Split – it consists of four distinct though connected groups of buildings on different levels. The buildings seem to have been inhabited until they were obliterated by a landslide in the 12th century. The buried ruins remained unnoticed until 1761 and it was not until 1881 that excavations were begun. So far only the main structure of the villa has been exposed; the slaves' quarters and the outbuildings still remain to be explored.

Though enough of the walls have been unearthed to give an idea of the elevation, the villa is famous chiefly for its polychrome **mosaic pavements**. They cover almost the entire floor space (3500 sq m) and are considered unique for the range of their subjects and the variety of their colours. In style the mosaics recall those of Roman villas in North Africa, showing the romantic influence of Hellenistic art and using colour to suggest modelling and foreshortening. They were extensively restored after damage from a flood in 1991.

Most of the site lies beneath a clear plastic shelter (shaded, for clarity, on the plan) following the original design of the villa. Elevated walkways protect the mosaics from the thousands of visitors who troop through each year, but they also lock you into an obligatory itinerary that allows little room for improvisation. On crowded days your pace, too, will be set for you.

While excavations are in progress the present entrance is through an aediculum. The monumental **main entrance**, which probably resembled a Roman triumphal arch with three doorways flanked by columns and fountains, is on the right. It led to the **atrium**, a polygonal court with a square

Mosaic at the Roman villa of Casale, Piazza Armerina

fountain at the centre, surrounded by a portico on Ionic marble columns. New arrivals found themselves facing the thermae, where they could freshen up after a long journey, if necessary; on their right was the entrance to the villa proper; on their left, an exedra with remains of what is known today as the **great latrine**.

The aediculum and vestibule of the **thermae** gave access to the long apsidal narthex, where newcomers would have mingled with villa 'insiders' entering from the far end of the room. From here a doorway on the left led into the first of the bathing rooms, the octagonal frigidarium, with plunge baths in the larger of the radiating apses (the others served as dressing rooms). Marine and bathing scenes adorn its floor. Beyond this was an aleipterion, where bathers could be massaged by slaves before passing to the tepidarium and the calidaria. If you look closely at the latter you can see remains of the hipocaustum, or hot-water plumbing, which passed beneath the raised floor.

From the atrium you enter the villa as ancient visitors did, through the **tablinum**, a reception room paved with representations of servants welcoming guests. This gave access to what for all intents and purposes was a great open lobby: the rectangular **peristyle**, surrounded by beautiful Corinthian marble columns and adorned by mosaic medallions with animal heads wreathed in laurel. It was planted as a garden, with a large fountain at the centre. The little aedicula opposite the entrance was the shrine of the patron deity of the house.

Off the west walk opened a small court giving access to the small latrine, whose brick drain, marble hand-basin and pictorial decoration are still in place. From here it is possible to look down into the narthex of the thermae, whose pavement bears a beautiful representation of a chariot race at the Circus Maximus in Rome. Adjacent is the inner entrance to the thermae. Its mosaic, showing a mother with a boy and girl and two slave-girls carrying bathing necessities and clean clothing, may represent the imperial family. On the north side of the peristyle are numerous rooms with geometric and figurative mosaics, notably two chambers decorated with representations of the seasons and cupids fishing, and a slightly larger room with scenes of a local hunting expedition and the hunters' subsequent feast.

Steps ascend from the east walk to a passage running the width of the building and closed at either end by an exedra. This is an **ambulacrum**, a wide corridor where Roman patricians were in the habit of walking up and down and discussing business matters – in a word, it is an office, and its decoration has recently led some scholars to speculate that the villa's proprietor (whose portrait probably appears at the centre) might have been a wealthy merchant who made his fortune by procuring wild animals for Rome's circuses and gladiatorial games, and not Maximian. In fact, the detailed and intertwined narrative depicts tigers, ostriches, elephants and rhinos being captured, caged and shipped across the sea. The scenes are remarkable not only for the number of species of wild animals shown (some of which, like the North African lion, the Romans hunted into extinction), but for the meticulous naturalism with which they are portrayed. In the exedrae are personifications of the Middle East (left) and Africa (right), the two principal sources of the exotic animals.

In the southeast corner of the peristyle, beyond an anteroom is a famous mosaic of 10 scantily clad young women performing gymnastic exercises; the large apsidal chamber opening on the peristyle on this side, decorated with a representation of Orpheus charming the animals with his lyre, was a summer living room.

To visit the south wing and the private apartments, you must leave the villa and follow an external footpath around the triclinium (see below). The **xystus** is a large elliptical court surrounded on three sides by a portico. The rooms to the north are adorned with mosaics of cupids harvesting and pressing grapes, and fishing. From the east end the walkway ascends to the **triclinium**, a large banqueting hall with deep apses on three sides. The central pavement bears a powerful mosaic representing 10 of the 12 Labours of Hercules (the missing episodes are the *Stymphalian Birds* and the *Girdle of Hippolyte*). In the apses are the *Glorification of Hercules* (on the north side), the *Conquered Giants* (east), and *Lycurgus and Ambrosia* (south).

A path leads round the back of the villa along the line of the aqueduct to the **private apartments**. On the south, around a semicircular porticoed atrium are a living room with an unusually detailed representation of the myth of Arion; a vestibule decorated with nursery scenes; a bedchamber with theatrical scenes, musical instruments and Greek musical notation; another vestibule with a stylised tableau of Eros and Pan, and yet another bedchamber with delightful scenes of children chasing (and being chased by) rabbits and ducks.

Outside the building, beyond a small latrine, is the large **basilica**, where guests were officially received, with an inlaid-marble apse. The north group of apartments consists of a chamber with a decorative mosaic of fruit, and an antechamber with a large portrayal of Ulysses and Polyphemus. The adjoining chamber has a mildly erotic scene (consisting of a kiss and a bare bottom) in its centre panel. The exit leads around the outside of the buildings back to the entrance.

Caltagirone

Caltagirone spreads out like a great eagle (which not coincidentally is the town emblem) on a rolling highland 608m above the sea. One of the most affluent inland towns of the island, it has been known since the Middle Ages as the *Regina dei Monti*, 'Queen of the Hills'. It gained is present appearance, marked by narrow streets, irregular squares and steep stairways, in the Baroque period, after the disastrous earthquake of 1693. Caltagirone has been famous since Arab times for its brilliantly coloured ceramics, and the traditional use of majolica in the decoration of churches and secular buildings makes it one of the most striking towns in Sicily.

Although archaeological evidence suggests the site was inhabited as early as the Bronze Age, Caltagirone made its historical debut with the Arabs (the name is a combination of the Arabic *kal'at*, castle and *ghiran*, caves), under whom it was important enough to attract a colony of Genoese merchants. The Normans took the city in 1090, and Caltagirone grew steadily until the 17th century, only to be razed by the notorious earthquake. It was damaged again by a World War II bombardment, which claimed the lives of 700 *Calatini*.

Caltagirone is not a city of great monuments. The **Cathedral** of San Giuliano, originally a Norman church, was destroyed by the 1963 quake and rebuilt in the early 18th century; when it's façade began to crack it was demolished and replaced with the present Art Nouveau one, completed in 1909; the campanile was added in 1954. Nearby, in the Piazza del Municipio, is the former seat of the Bourbon governors, the **Corte Capitanale,** a charming small Baroque edifice decorated by Antonuzzo and Gian Domenico Gagini.

This square stands at the lower end of Caltagirone's splendid **Scala di Santa Maria del Monte,** which has linked the city centre with the upper part of the town since 1606. In 1953 the staircase was rebuilt in lava and embellished with majolica tiles reproducing the traditional colours and motifs for which Caltagirone is famous. On the Feast of St. James, 24–25 July, it is lit by the flames of over 4000 oil lamps. At the top of the Baroque church of **Sante Maria del Monte**, built as the cathedral over a norman original. Although it is usually locked, its interior holds a 13th-century Tuscan *Madonna* (over the high altar) and precious gold and silverwork (in the treasury). All around are picturesque medieval streets.

From near the foot of the steps, Via Luigi Sturzo (named after Father Luigi Sturzo, 1871–1959, one of the founders of the Italian Republic and a native of Caltagirone) climbs past some interesting palaces to the churches of San Domenico (left; closed) and **San Salvatore** (right), with a façade by Natale Bonaiuto (1794). The latter has a pretty octagonal interior with a Gagini-school *Madonna* and Don Sturzo's tomb, in a modern chapel. Via Sturzo ends at **San Giorgio** (1699), where there is a beautiful little painting of the *Trinity* attributed to Roger van der Weyden. Tradition attributes the church's foundation to the Genoese merchants who settled here in 1030, and traces of the original ogival doorway and narrow splayed embrasures can still be seen. The terrace affords good views of the countryside.

Other interesting churches are the small **Santa Chiara**, designed in 1743 by Rosario Gagliardi (with a fine majolica pavement) and **San Giacomo**, a Norman foundation rebuilt in its present form in 1694–1708 (incorporating the Portale delle Reliquie, by Antonuzzo Gagini, with bronze doors by Agostino Sarzana). Near the broad Piazza Umberto I, a former Bourbon prison of 1782 houses the **Museo Civico**, with modest collections of antiquities, paintings and ceramics.

Along Via Roma, where the old town meets the new, extend the beautiful **public gardens**, laid out in 1846 by Giovanni Battista Basile. They are planted with exotic trees and adorned with great decorated vases, sumptuous Art Nouveau balustrades and a 16th-century fountain. The adjacent **teatrino**, a panoramic viewpoint designed in 1792 by Natale Bonaiuto, gives access to the fascinating **Museo Regionale della Ceramica**. Second only to that of Faenza in size, the museum holds a fine collection of Sicilian ceramics from the prehistoric era to the 19th century. The displays document the evolution of styles and techniques in all the island's principal ceramics centres, especially Caltagirone, which is the oldest and largest on the island.

The kilns of Caltagirone began working in Arab times, thanks to the local presence of high-quality clay and to the city's then prime location, at the junction of the old roads linking Enna, Catania and Syracuse. In the 17th and 18th centuries an extraordinary variety of objects – including ornamental vases, wine and water jugs, braziers, oil lamps, amphoras and pots – was made here. In Caltagirone ceramics the detailing is in azure, often associated with green and yellow, on a compact white background. A distinctive decorative motif is the *reticella*, or fishnet design.

Caltanissetta

Caltanissetta is a pleasant provincial capital standing on the gentle slope of a hill. The name is Arabic and was probably formed by combining the ancient Sikel place name of *Nissa* with the Arabic prefix *Kal'at* (castle). Although the spot seems to have been inhabited as long ago as the 7th–6th century BC, it was later abandoned and the present town was established in the 9th century AD. Formerly a centre of sulphur mining, today Caltanissetta is known principally for its Holy Week celebrations, with processions and religious plays that begin on Palm Sunday and end on Easter Sunday.

Churches in Caltanissetta all seem to have two names. The **Cathedral**, commonly known as Santa Maria la Nuova, is also dedicated to St Michael Archangel, one-time patron of the city. Built in the late 16th and early 17th centuries in a very late Renaissance style, it was altered in the 19th century with the reconstruction of the transept and dome. Within, on the nave ceiling, are the masterpieces of the 18th-century painter Willem Borremans, representing the *Immaculate Conception* and *Crowning of the Virgin*. Borremans was also responsible for the altarpiece. Across from the cathedral in the central Piazza Garibaldi is the 16th-century church of San Sebastiano, with a Neoclassical façade.

The main Corso Umberto I leads away to the north and south in a wide arc, lined with the town's most magnificent palaces. The finest of these is the **Palazzo Moncada**, across the street from the town hall and actually set one block in from the Corso. It was begun in 1625 and never completed.

Sant'Agata, also called Sant'Ignazio, adjoins the former Jesuit College, now the town library. Built in the early 17th century, it has a deep orange Baroque façade theatrically set on a bend in the Corso. The Greek-cross interior is richly decorated with stuccoes and coloured marbles.

The **Museo Civico**, on Via Napoleone Colaianni (near the train station), houses antiquities from Caltanissetta and its province. It is especially well known for two extraordinary items: a 6th-century terracotta votive model of a Greek temple, from Sabucina, and a group of Early Bronze Age votive figurines from Monte San Giuliano, the earliest representation of the human figure so far discovered in Sicily. There are also beautiful black- and red-figure vases and some interesting Arabic finds.

Near Caltanissetta on the Palermo road is the **Abbazia di Santo Spirito**, founded by Roger and his wife Adelasia to commemorate the Norman conquest of Caltanissetta (1086) and consecrated in the mid-12th century. The Romanesque design features three semicircular apses with vertical pilaster strips surmounted by blind arches and framing ogival-arch apertures. Inside are some detached 15th-century frescoes, a large baptismal font and, in the north apse, an inscription bearing the date of consecration.

Practical Information

Getting There

BY AIR
Southeastern Sicily is served by **Catania Fontanarossa Airport**, which lies c 5km (3 miles) south of the city. Autostrada A18/E90 and Highway S114 connect the airport to Syracuse in about 50min. There are direct flights from Bari, Bologna, Cagliari, Florence, Lampedusa, Milan, Naples, Rome, Turin, Verona and Venice; most international flights connect through Rome. For information or reservations free-phone *Alitalia* tel. 1478 65643, *Meridiana* tel. 530 006, or *Alpi Eagles* tel. 167 555 777.

BY RAIL
Intercity trains run from **Messina to Syracuse** several times daily, covering the 182km (113 miles) in c 2hr 40min. They stop at Taormina-Giardini Naxos, Giarre-Riposto, Acireale, Catania (1hr 30min) and Lentini. There is a **local service** between **Catania** and **Palermo** (243km/150 miles in c 3hr 20min, stopping at Enna and Caltanisetta) and, less frequently, one between **Syracuse** and **Agrigento** (307km/190 miles in c 6hr; a change is necessary at Canicattì).

BY ROAD

The motorway from **Messina to Syracuse**, like that from Messina to Palermo, has yet to be completed. At the time of writing you have to take Autostrada A18/E45 to Catania, then switch to Highway S114, most of which is now four-lane expressway. The total journey of approximately 230km (143 miles) takes c 2hr.

Here are some of the fastest routes from point to point in southeastern Sicily: **Messina–Syracuse**, 160km (100 miles) in 2hr by A18/E45 and S114; **Syracuse–Piazza Armerina**, 145km (90 miles) in 2hr via Catania by S417, A19, S192, S117b and local roads, or 126km (78 miles) in 2hr 20min via Palazzolo Acreide and Caltagirone by S287, S124 and local roads; **Syracuse–Noto**, 30km (18 miles) in 30min by S115/E45 and local roads; **Noto–Ragusa**, 54km (33 miles) in 1hr by S287, S115/E45 and local roads; **Ragusa–Agrigento**, 135km (84 miles) in 2hr 10min by S115/E45 and local roads; **Agrigento–Enna**, 90km (56 miles) in 1hr 20min by S189, S640, A19, S192 and local roads.

The southeastern portion of the Great Sicilian Loop looks like this: **Agrigento–Enna**, 86km (53 miles) in 1hr 20min; **Enna–Piazza Armerina**, 29km (18 miles) in 40min; **Piazza Armerina–Ragusa**, 92km (57 miles) in 1hr 30min. **Ragusa–Noto**, 54km (33 miles) in 50min; **Noto–Syracuse**, 35km (22 miles) in 30min. **Syracuse–Catania**, 60km (37 miles) in 1hr.

Tourist Information

CALTAGIRONE Palazzo Libertini di San Marco
(tel. 0933 53809, fax 0933 54610).

ENNA Via Roma 413 (tel. 0935 500 544, fax 0935 500 720); Piazza Napoleone 6 (tel. 0935 26119).

NOTO Piazza XVI Maggio (tel. 0931 836744).

PIAZZA ARMERINA Via Cavour 15 (tel. 0935 680 201, fax 0935 684 565).

RAGUSA Via Capitano Bocchieri 33, Ibla
(tel. 0932 621 421, fax 0932 622 288).

SYRACUSE Largo Paradiso (tel. 0931 60510); Via San Sebastiano 45
(tel. 0931 67710, fax 0931 67803); Via Maestranza 33
(tel. 0931 65201, fax 0931 60204).

Hotels

CALTAGIRONE
Villa San Mauro, Via Portosalvo 10 (tel. 0933 26500, fax 0933 31661). Modern, with good views over the old town; moderate.

CALTANISSETTA
San Michele, Via Fasci Siciliani (tel. 0934 553 750, fax 0934 598 791). Outside the city centre, comfortable, with an excellent restaurant; moderate.
Plaza, Via Berengario Gaetani 5 (tel./fax 0934 583 877). Modern and functional; moderate.

ENNA
Grande Albergo Sicilia, Piazza Colaianni 7 (tel. 0935 500 850, fax 0935 500 488). Centrally located and inexpensive.

MODICA
Motel di Modica, Corso Umberto I (tel. 0932 941 022, fax 0932 941 077). On the outskirts of town, comfortable and inexpensive.

NOTO
Club Helios, Viale Lido, Località Pizzuta,(tel. 0931 812 366, fax 0931 812 378). In Noto Marina. Seasonal; large and modern, on the beach; moderate.

PIAZZA ARMERINA
Pomara, San Michele di Ganzaria (tel. 0933 977 090, fax 0933 976 976). Modern and comfortable; restaurant known for its Sicilian cuisine, especially fish; inexpensive.

RAGUSA
Montreal, Via San Giuseppe 6 (tel./fax 0932 621 13). A comfortable hotel in the city centre; inexpensive.
Rafael, Corso Italia 40 (tel. 0932 654 080, fax 0932 653 418). A renovated 19th-century building in the old city centre; moderate.

SYRACUSE
Jolly, Corso Gelon 45 (tel. 0931 461 111, fax 0931 461 126). In the new town, modern and functional; expensive.
Panorama, Via Necropoli Grotticelle 33 (tel./fax 0931 412 188). Near the archaeological area; inexpensive.
Villa Politi, Via M. Politi 2 (tel. 0931 412 121, fax 0931 36061). A former patrician villa surrounded by gardens, near the Latomia dei Cappuccini; moderate.

At Fontane Bianche, 15km (9 miles) south of Syracuse:
Fontane Bianche, (tel. 0931 790 611, fax 0931)790 571). Seasonal; modern and comfortable; moderate.
Villa Lucia (tel. 0931 721007). A lovely country house within walking distance of a private beach; moderate.

Restaurants

CALTANISSETTA
Cortese, Viale Sicilia 166 (tel. 0934 591 686; closed Mon). Friendly atmosphere and good food; inexpensive.

ENNA
Centrale, Piazza 6 Dicembre 9 (tel. 0935 500 963; closed Sat). Traditional Sicilian cuisine (*crostini all'ennese, cavatelli alla siciliana, lacerato abbutunato, torte di mandorle*) served in rooms decorated with local ceramics; inexpensive.

MODICA
Fattoria delle Torri, Modica Alta, Via Nativo 30 (tel. 0932 751 286; closed Mon and Jul). Simple and rustic, in an 18th-century palace; specialities include *tortino di sardine con patate e lattuga, ravioli di fave verdi con ricotta, arrosto in salsa negra* and *budino di latte di mandorle*; inexpensive.

PALAZZOLO ACREIDE
La Trota (tel. 0931 96010, fax 0931 875 694). Trout-stocked fishing pond and fresh trout in tanks; moderate.

PIAZZA ARMERINA
Da Battiato (with rooms), Contrada Casale (tel./fax 0935 685 453). Known for its grilled and roast meats; 3km (1 3/4 miles) west of town, close to the Roman Villa; inexpensive.

RAGUSA
Orfeo, Via Sant'Anna 117 (tel. 0932 621 035; closed Sat evening, Sun and two weeks in Aug). Simple and pleasant, near the cathedral; inexpensive.
U' Saracinu, Via del Convento 9, Ibla (tel. 0932 246 976; closed Wed and Jul). A maze of small rooms; known for its regional cooking, especially *sorbetto al mandarino*; inexpensive.
Villa Fortugno (tel. 0932 667 134; closed Mon and Aug). In a renovated patrician palace on the road to Marina di Ragusa, 5km (3 miles) southwest of the city; moderate.

SYRACUSE

Archimede, Via Gemellaro 8 (tel. 0931 69701; closed Mon). Seafood, notably *acciughe fresche marinate, riso al nero di seppia e ricotta, spaghetti col neonato, pesce alla griglia e all'acqua di mare*; inexpensive.

Arlecchino, Via del Tolomei 5 (tel 0931 66386; closed Mon). Traditional Sicilian cuisine, including *risotto ai ricci, pasta con le sarde, pesce gratinato and pesce al cartoccio, semifreddi di mandorle e miele; moderate.*

Darsena-da Ianuzzo, Riva Garibaldi 6 (tel./fax 0931 66104; closed Mon). Sicilian specialities, summer veranda; moderate.

Jonico-a Rutta 'e Ciauli, Riviera Dionysius il Grande 194 (tel. 0931 65540; closed Tue, Christmas, New Year's Day, Easter and 15 Aug). Sicilian cuisine in a villa with large fireplace, small ethnographical collection and summer seating on a terrace overlooking the sea and coast; moderate.

Minosse, Via Mirabella 6 (tel. 0931 66366; closed Mon and Oct–Nov). Traditional Sicilian cuisine in the heart of the old town; try the *paste siracusane alla mollica, pesci alla marinara, capretto and cassata*; moderate.

At Fontane Bianche, 15km (9 miles) south of Syracuse:
La Spiaggetta, Viale dei Lidi 473 (tel. 0931 790 334, fax 0931 790 317; closed Tue in winter). Large and often busy with celebrations, but generally good, with broad sea views; moderate.

Museums and Monuments

CALTANISSETTA
Museo Civico: Mon–Sat 9.00–13.30.
Museo del Folklore: Mon–Sat 9.00–12.00.

CALTAGIRONE
Museo Civico: Tue–Fri 9.00–13.00, Sat 9.00–13.00, Sun 10.00–12.00.
Museo Luigi Sturzo: Mon–Fri 9.30–13.30, 16.00–19.00; Sat–Sun 9.30–13.30.
Museo Regionale della Ceramica: daily 9.00–14.00.

CAMARINA
Museo Regionale Camarina: daily 9.00–12.00, 16.00–18.00
Parco Archeologico di Caucana: Mon–Sat 9.00–14.00, 15.00-18.00; Sun and hols 9.00-13.00, 15.00-18.00.
Zona Archeologica: Mon–Sat 9.0014.00, 15.0018.00; Sun and hols 9.00–13.00, 15.00–18.00.

ENNA
Castello di Lombardia: daily 8.00–18.00.
Museo Alessi: Tue–Sun 9.00–13.00, 16.00–19.00.
Museo Archeologico Varisano, daily 9.30–13, 15.30–18.30.

MEGARA HYBLAEA
Antiquarium: Mon–Sat 9.00–14.00, Sun and hols 9.00–13.00.
Zona Archeologica: daily 9–dusk.

MODICA
Museo Ibleo delle Arti e Tradizioni Popolari: daily 9.00–13.00.
Parco Archeologico della Forza: Oct–Mar 8.30–12.00, 14.30–16.30; Apr–Sep 9.00–12.00, 15.00–19.00.

NOTO
Museo Civico: closed indefinitely.

PIAZZA ARMERINA
Villa Romana del Casale: daily 9.00–dusk.

RAGUSA
Museo Archeologico Ibleo: Mon–Sat 9.00–14.00, 15.00–18.00; Sun and hols 9.00–13.00, 15.00–18.00.
SYRACUSE
Castello Eurialo: 9.00–dusk.
Galleria Regionale di Arte Medievale e Moderna di Palazzo Bellomo: daily 9.00–14.00.
Museo Archeologico Regionale Paolo Orsi: Tue–Sat 9.00–13.00, 15.00–18.30.
Parco Archeologico: daily 9.00–16.00.
Teatro Greco: summer 9.00–19.00, winter 9.00–17.00.

7. NORTHEASTERN SICILY

South of the Strait of Messina, Italy's Apennine spine emerges as the Peloritani, Nebrodi and Madonie Mountains. To the east, the Ionian coast is steep and precipitous, leaving little room for farming, industry, or residential building. To the north, on the Tyrrhenian coast, the passage from sea level to the mountain crests is more gradual, the slopes of the Peloritani lending themselves to terraced cultivation. The bleak, arid appearance of the east coast is due to its exposure to the *scirocco*, the warm south wind that burns the vegetation in the bud. The north slopes, swept by the cool north wind, *tramontana*, has tall forests in the hills and fruit orchards and vineyards at the lower levels. Off the coast of Milazzo, the volcanic archipelago of the Æolian Islands rises majestically from the deep, blue sea.

This is the area of Sicily that appears most modern at first glance (it is served by two major motorways, A20 for Palermo and A18 for Catania) and the one where the sense of insularity is least evident. Nevertheless, its influence over the island's history has been strong and continuous. From the time of Dionysius the Elder of Syracuse (late 5th–early 4th century BC), up to the 19th century, Messina, Taormina, Milazzo and Lipari controlled the strategic region at the meeting of the Tyrrhenian and Ionian Seas, an important crossroads for maritime traffic between the Eastern and Western Mediterranean. In recent decades, Catania has been the centre of the island's most promising economic development.

Catania and Mt Ætna

Sicily's east coast is dominated by **Mt Ætna**, the largest active volcano in Europe. Regardless of whether you approach it by land, sea or air, its broad, conical mass, rising to an altitude of over 3000m and dusted with snow in all but the warmest months, is an unforgettable sight.

Ætna has always been the great fear and glory of **Catania**, which spreads out at the foot of its southern slopes. More than once the mountain's hot, flaming magma has invaded the city's streets; but Ætna's snowy heights have also been a major resource for the *Catanesi*. Of course, its fertile soil yields abundant crops ('Cacti and vines give evidence of meticulous cultivation.... The beans grow in tall bushes,' Goethe tells us); but Ætna has also provided less ordinary harvests, as Patrick Brydone relates:

'The bishop's revinues are considerable, and arise principally from the sale of snow, the snow on mount Ætna. One small portion of which, lying on the north of the mountain, is said to bring him in upwards of 1000.l. a year; for Ætna furnishes snow and ice, not only to the whole island of Sicily, but likewise to Malta, and a great part of Italy, and makes a very considerable branch of commerce; for even the peasants in these hot countries regale themselves with ices during the summer heats; and there is no entertainment given by the nobility, of which these do not always make a principal part: a famine of snow, they themselves say, would be more grievous, than a famine of either corn or wine. It is a common observation amongst them, that without the snows of mount Ætna, their island could not be inhabited; so essential has this article of luxury become to them.'

For a quintessentially Catanian breakfast, try the fruit ices (*granite*: the *moro di gelso*, or mulberry, for purists) topped with whipped cream and served with a soft roll. For ice cream, no place in Sicily can match the *gelaterie* of Acireale. Ætna also produces one of Sicily's finest wines, *Ætna rosso*.

Catania

Catania is Sicily's economic powerhouse, a busy provincial capital, the seat of a bishop and a university. It is a large, lively city (380,000 inhab.), with all the problems of any large metropolis – including traffic, pollution and petty crime. It is also home to several fine galleries of contemporary art and to one of Italy's best opera houses, named after native composer Vincenzo Bellini. To the delight of gourmets, every day except Sunday the area between the cathedral and the waterfront hosts a beautiful and colourful **fish market**, one of the largest in the Mediterranean.

The Greek *Katane* was colonised by Chalcidians from Naxos in the 8th century BC and taken by the Romans, who called it *Catina* or *Catana*, in 263BC. It flourished under the Roman Empire and again in the Middle Ages, but its development came to an abrupt halt in 1693, when earthquake destroyed its medieval fabric and claimed the lives of well over half its inhabitants.

The new city employed state-of-the-art anti-seismic measures: the meandering courses of the old main thoroughfares were freed of rubble and made straight and wide (today they form Via Etnea and the central part of Via Vittorio Emanuele); the other streets were likewise widened and their length was punctuated by broad squares expressly designed to allow the populace to escape from collapsing buildings and reassemble in the case of new tremors. A controversial role in the reconstruction was played by the

Panorama of the interior of Sicily, with Mt Ætna in the background

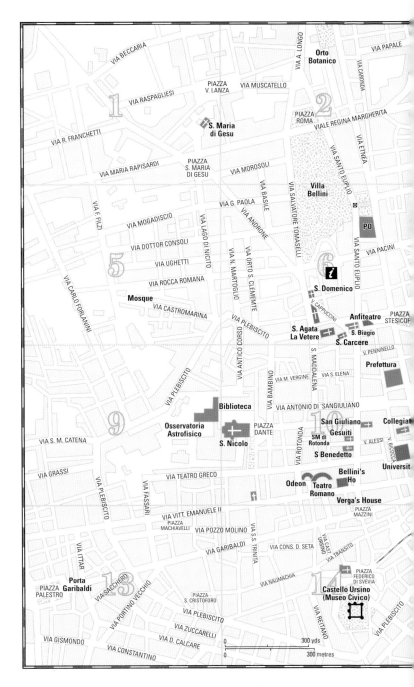

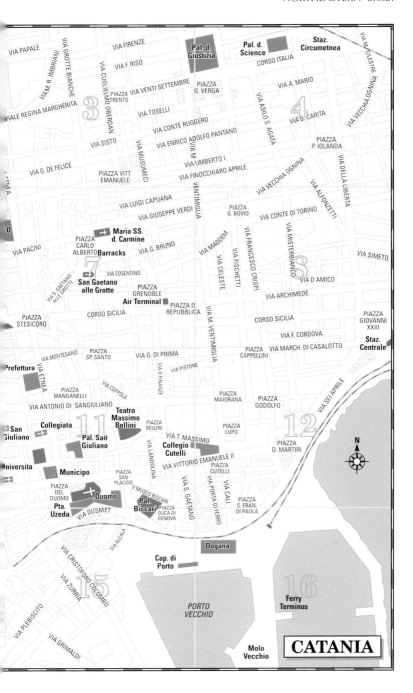

CATANIA

Benedictine Order, which took advantage of the authority deriving from its immense possessions to enlarge its old buildings and construct new ones, notwithstanding the restrictions that governed ecclesiastical building within the city limits (the space was needed for residential building, of which there was an acute shortage).

The chief architect of the reconstruction was Giovanni Battista Vaccarini, official city planner after 1730. Today Vaccarini's fascinating Baroque scheme still sets the tone in Catania, despite the 19th- and 20th-century growth that has sent the city sprawling up the southern slopes of Ætna and over the fertile plain of the River Simeto.

Piazza del Duomo (Map 11) is the traditional centre of Catania. Laid out immediately after the 1693 earthquake on the site of the medieval *platea magna*, it was designed to be the seat of civic and ecclesiastic authority and the meeting point of the city's main thoroughfares. The centrepiece of the square is the delightful **Elephant Fountain**, designed by Vaccarini in 1736 incorporating an antique Roman lava elephant, commonly called *u liotru*, and an Egyptian obelisk with hieroglyphics dealing with the cult of the goddess Isis – all surmounted by the device of St Agatha, Catania's saintly patroness. Architecturally the square is defined on the east by the lively front of the cathedral, with its marble enclosure, and by the dome of the Badia di Sant'Agata. On the north rises the handsome **Municipio**, with pilaster strips and rustication on the ground floor and beautiful balconied windows above. It was designed by Vaccarini in 1741. Across the square stands the former **Seminario dei Chierici**, an elaborate building dating from the early 18th century.

Catania's **Cathedral** is dedicated to St Agatha. It was founded by Count Roger in 1078 and rebuilt after the earthquakes of 1169 and 1693. The main façade, another Vaccarini creation, has three tiers of columns (the ones on the bottom are antique) and a statue of the patron saint on the second storey. Vaccarini also designed the lovely north flank, which incorporates a 1577 marble doorway attributed to Gian Domenico Mazzola. Around the back (visible from the courtyard of the Archbishop's Palace) are the mighty black-lava apses of the medieval church, carved with arches and surmounted by battlements.

The Latin-cross **interior**, with its tall dome and triple apse, makes quite an impression. The pavement is modern; the side altars with their gilded carved frames date from the 18th century. The apses and transept have been restored to their original Norman state. In the second bay of the south aisle is the simple tomb of composer Vincenzo Bellini (1801–34), by Giovanni Battista Tassara, inscribed with a phrase from his opera, *La Sonnambula*. A 16th-century doorway in the south transept, adorned with low reliefs illustrating scenes from the life of the Virgin (by G.B. Mazzola) gives access to the Norman Cappella della Madonna, with two sarcophagi; the larger one (on the left) is Roman and holds the remains of six Aragonese kings and princes; the other (right) is medieval and is the tomb of Constance of Aragon (died 1222), wife of Holy Roman Emperor Frederick II. In the south apse, an ornate wrought-iron gate marks the Cappella di Sant'Agata; within are the relics and part of the substantial treasure of the saint (shown only during religious festivities), including a gilded silver bust of 1373–76 and a large Gothic reliquary chest containing her limbs. The choir has beautiful stalls carved in 1588 with scenes from the life of St Agatha, by Scipione di Guido. A marble doorway by Gian Domenico Mazzola (1563) with scenes from the Passion leads from the north transept to the Cappella del Crocifisso, which occupies one of the Norman towers. Nearby is the sacristy, with 18th-century cabinets and a fascinating painting of 1675 showing the destruction of Catania in the eruption of Ætna in 1669. The adjoining Sacrario Capitolare holds a collection of precious vellums. Grates in the floor provide ventilation for the Roman 'Terme Achilliane' (closed to visitors), which extend under the church, seminary and piazza.

Between the cathedral and the seminary stands the **Porta Uzeda**, a city gate built in 1696 at the end of the long, straight Via Etnea. Outside, Via Dusmet leads left to **Palazzo Biscari** (Map 11/15), an ornate 18th-century palace with caryatid-pilasters and balconies formed by cartouches and putti, designed by Francesco Battaglia and his son Antonino. Here, in 1758, Prince Ignazio Paternò Castello assembled his private museum, which Goethe and other Grand Tourists considered the city's finest attraction; its contents are now in the Museo Comunale (see below). Classical music concerts are sometimes held in the palace's sumptuous interior.

One block north is Via Vittorio Emanuele II, locally known as the 'Strada del Corso'. Perpendicular to Via Etnea, it crosses the city from east to west, lined with Baroque palaces and churches. If you turn left here you soon return to the Piazza del Duomo, passing the cathedral (left) and the abbey church of **Sant'Agata**, designed by Vaccarini in 1735 (right). From the opposite corner of the piazza the long, straight Via Garibaldi runs westwards amid more 18th-century mansions to Piazza Mazzini, a beautiful square surrounded by a peristyle of 32 antique marble columns. Here you again turn left.

The **Castello Ursino** (Map 14) stands on a spot that was surrounded on three sides by the sea before the lava flow of 1669. The huge square fortress, with large cylindrical towers at the corners and smaller towers midway along the north and west walls, was built for Emperor Frederick II by Riccardo Lentini in 1239–50 and repeatedly altered in subsequent centuries. Once the residence of Aragonese princes, today it is home to the **Museo Civico**, based on the collections assembled by the Prince Paternò Castello, Catania's Benedictine monks, and the powerful Zappalà Asmundo family. It includes antiquities, medieval and Renaissance sculpture, paintings, decorative arts, coins and arms and armour. The most outstanding holdings are a *Torso of an Emperor*, from the basilica of Roman Catania, a 6th- or 5th-century Attic *Head of an Ephebe* (possibly belonging to the torso in the archaeological museum in Syracuse) from Lentini and a 5th-century terracotta *Kore*. In the decorative arts section you can see some fine examples of Catania's unique **amber jewellery**. This is made from *ambra del Simeto* or *simetite*, found in the Miocene molasse, sand and marl that collects along the banks and at the mouth of the River Simeto, just south of the city. Popular legend tells that it is born of the river's foaming waters in winter. Simetite owes its particular value to its rare, transparent veining: as a rule ambers range in colour from pale to reddish yellow; the Catanian ambers are streaked with brown, green or blue. Simeto amber is made into earrings and brooches: those shaped like small bunches of grapes are the most traditional. The quantity of amber gathered every year is relatively small. Its commerce is therefore limited to Sicily.

Mother-of-pearl inlay is another skill that has been practised in Catania for centuries, especially by the workshops that make the finely crafted guitars and jewellery boxes for which the city is famous.

One block north of Piazza Mazzini, on the corner of Via Vittorio Emanuele II and Piazza San Francesco, is the **Museo Belliniano** (Map 10), birthplace of Vincenzo Bellini, with a small collection of autograph scores and other memorabilia of the composer. Down the block, at Via Vittorio Emanuele 266, is Catania's partially excavated **Roman Theatre**, which was 86m in diameter and could hold 7000 spectators. The cavea, divided into nine wedges and two main tiers, was ringed by three corridors at different heights. Nearby stood a smaller, 1500-seat odeon, used for the rehearsals of the chorus and for music competitions.

Backtrack past Bellini's house to Piazza Francesco to pick up **Via dei Crociferi** (left), one of Catania's loveliest Baroque streets. The beginning of the street is spanned by the **Arco di San Benedetto**, said to have been built in a single night in 1704 by the powerful Benedictines – in defiance of the city council, which opposed the project on the grounds that it posed an earthquake hazard. The church of San Benedetto, with a monumental atrium and sumptuous interior, stands across the street from the former **Collegio dei Gesuiti**, still a school, whose splendid courtyards are attributed to G.B. Vaccarini (1742). The church of **San Giuliano** (1760), with a convex façade and domed interior, is also by Vaccarini; it has a 15th-century painted *Crucifix* over the high altar.

Opposite San Giuliano, Via dei Gesuiti leads west (left) to the crescent-shaped Piazza Dante and the church of **San Nicolò** (Map 10). This is the largest church in Sicily, measuring 105 x 42m, with a soaring 62m dome. Begun in 1687, its construction was halted first by the 1693 earthquake, then by technical difficulties due to its size. The present building was rebuilt in 1735 by Francesco Battaglia, probably to a design by Antonino Amato. The powerful façade with its immense columns was left unfinished in 1798. The vast three-aisled interior is simple and well proportioned. A 19th-century meridian traverses the transept floor. The beautiful 3000-pipe organ, with its carved and gilded wooden cabinet, stands over the grave of its builder, Donato del Piano (died 1775). The wooden cabinets in the Rococo sacristy, though only a pale reflection of their past splendour, repay a glance.

The adjacent **monastery**, the largest in Europe after that of Mafra in Portugal, today is home to the University Faculty of Letters and Philosophy. It was rebuilt after 1693 to a plan by Antonino Amato and his son Andrea. Its rich ornamentation and relatively simple lines bear eloquent witness to the expertise of Catania's early 18th-century stonecutters. It encloses two harmonious courtyards, in one of which excavations have brought to light remains of an Archaic Greek edifice.

From the north end of Piazza Dante, Via Antonino di Sangiuliano returns towards the city centre. At the intersection with Via dei Crociferi are some fragments of Roman streets and mosaics. The street continues to **Via Etnea**, the long, straight high street of Catania which climbs slowly towards Ætna, visible at the end. Turning right, you return past Piazza dell'Università, surrounded by a fine ensemble of 18th-century palaces by Vaccarini; turning left, you come shortly to Piazza Stesicoro, with a monument to Bellini. Here is the partially excavated Roman **amphitheatre**, a once-magnificent structure that had a circumference of 389m and could seat 16,000; its arena was surpassed in size only by that of the Colosseum. It is thought to date from the 2nd century AD. Further north are the beautiful public gardens of **Villa Bellini** and the **Orto Botanico**, famous for its cacti plants.

Ætna in Myth and Legend

Of the many ancient myths associated with Mt Ætna, the best known are those of Typhœus and Polyphemus.

Typhoeus is one of the Giants, sons of Earth who put the heavenly gods to flight. Struck with lightning by Zeus and buried under Sicily, he struggles and strives often to rise again; but his right hand is held down by Peloros and his left by Pachynos. Lilybæon rests on his legs, and Ætna's weight is on his head. Flung on his back beneath this mountain, the fierce Giant spouts forth ashes and vomits flames from his mouth. Often he puts forth all his strength to push off the weight of the earth and to roll the cities and great mountains from his body: then the ground shakes, and even Poseidon (Neptune in Roman mythology) is afraid that the crust of the earth might split open in wide seams and the light of day be let in and frighten the trembling shades, or souls of the underworld.

Polyphemus is one of the Cyclopes, sons of Poseidon, a race of fierce and barbarous one-eyed Giants who despise Olympus and its gods and whom no stranger has ever seen save to his own harm, given their quenchless thirst for blood. Having lost the art of smithcraft known to their ancestors who worked for Zeus, they live as ignorant and lawless shepherds, dwelling sullenly apart from one another in caverns hollowed in Sicily's eastern hills.

In the *Odyssey* Homer tells how Odysseus (Ulysses to the Romans) and his companions, having landed at the foot of Ætna, made themselves at home in such a cavern and, unaware of the danger they were in, feasted cheerfully on the Giant's provisions. When Polyphemus returned at the end of the day and closed the entrance behind him with a slab of stone so huge that 20 teams of oxen could not have moved it, they knew they were trapped. They appealed to the Giant for mercy, but in response he simply grabbed two by the feet, dashed out their brains, and devoured them raw. Aware that the Cyclops alone was strong enough to shift the stone from the entrance, the Greeks were compelled to wait for the right moment to make their escape.

The next night, as Polyphemus slept, Odysseus and his remaining companions heated a stake in the embers of the fire and drove it into the Giant's eye. Raging with pain, the blinded Polyphemus swore vengeance on the surviving Greeks. But Odysseus tied each of his comrades under the belly of a ram, and when Polyphemus let his flock out to pasture the next morning, gently stroking their backs to make sure that no one was astride them, the Greeks managed to slip by. As they seized their oars and began to row off, Odysseus shouted an ironical goodbye. For answer, Polyphemus hurled a large rock, then another into the sea after the ship: these rocks remain today as the *Faraglioni dei Ciclopi*.

Mt Ætna

Dominating eastern Sicily between Taormina and Catania, Mt Ætna (3350m) is Europe's largest live volcano and one of the world's most active. Its immense size (it is larger than metropolitan New York and visible from the moon) makes the other mountains around it seem small in comparison. Eruptions occur frequently, both from the four live craters at the summit and from those that litter the slopes. The unpredictability of the volcano's activity makes it unsafe for visitors to climb to the craters. However, the villages on Ætna's slopes, as well as its tall forests and eerie lava flows, may be explored without peril.

Known since antiquity as the forge of Hephæstus and of the Cyclopes, or as the 'column of heaven' beneath which dwelled the enemy of the gods, the Giant Typhœus whose twistings and turnings translated into eruptions and earthquakes, Ætna is the most distinctive feature of the Sicilian landscape. Visible from every part of the island, *a Muntagna* (the Mountain) as it is simply called by its inhabitants has fascinated and frightened travellers through the ages. Every season is good for discovering its natural treasures – in the warmer months you can walk for days along tranquil cart roads and through dark forests without encountering a soul. In winter, you can glide on cross-country skis over the trails of La Galvarina, Monte Scavo and Monte Maletto.

The **geography** of the mountain is not as simple as it may look at first glance. Nearly circular in shape, Ætna rises above the island's east coast in solemn isolation. Long ago the area on which it stands was an immense gulf: the volcano assumed its present appearance over some 600,000 years. Embraced by the sea, the Alcantara and Simeto valleys and the Plain of Catania, it covers an area of 210 sq km (81 sq miles) and, at the time of writing, rises to an altitude of 3324m. (Its height, like that of all active volcanoes, is variable: 3274m in 1900, 3263m in 1934, 3290m in 1956, 3340m in 1964 and 3323m in 1971.) It presents a striking contrast between the proportions of its base, which rises gradually to c 1500m, and those of its peak, which mounts steeply to nearly 3300m. This contrast is underscored by the layering of human settlements and cultivation on its lower slopes, black lava flows and green forests in the area above, and the lava desert at the top.

Ætna isn't shaped like a regular cone: at 2900m it levels off to form a broad elliptical plateau, the residue of an ancient crater, above which rises the terminal cone. Here is the great **Central Crater**, which was joined in 1911 by the large **Northeast Subterminal Crater**, in 1968 by the **Bocca Nuova**, and in 1971 by the **Southeast Crater**. The mountain's contours are made even more irregular by the countless cones, dents and temporary craters formed by its lateral eruptions; and by the crags, cliffs and gorges of the spectacular Valle del Bove – an immense high-altitude basin 5km (3 miles) wide and 8km (5 miles) long, lying between steep walls more than 1000m high. Scored by countless lava flows, the **Valle del Bove** hosts some of Ætna's more fascinating rock formations – mighty banks of composite rock made up of *scoriae* (cellular lava) and *lapilli* (ejected stone fragments) and huge dykes formed by infiltrations of liquid magma in pre-existent structures. Another special feature of Ætna is its many lava-flow caverns, the only formations of their kind in Europe. There are more than 180 of them, the most impressive being the Grotta del Gelo.

Needless to say, Ætna represents a unique **natural environment** whose abundant plant life varies considerably from the lower to the higher altitudes. From sea level to c 500m the rich volcanic soil sustains extensive citrus orchards which, over time, have replaced the olives and carobs, prickly pear and agave which in turn replaced the natural Mediterranean *macchia*. Below 100m the original ilex groves have been almost entirely replaced by vineyards and olive, almond, pistachio and hazel orchards. From 1000 to 1500m junipers, oaks and Turkey oaks alternate with chestnut groves and apple orchards. At this level grows Ætna's single most famous tree, the *Castagno dei Cento Cavalli*, a chestnut whose perimeter measures 60m.

Above the chestnut groves, especially around Linguaglossa, grows the *pino larìcio*, a native pine that thrives on the rocky volcanic soil. Higher up this gives way to forests of Ætnean beech and birch, similar to those of Northern Europe and the Alps. The tree line runs at about 2000m; above, the vegetation is dominated by low *astragalus siculus* (which grows only on Ætna), violets and groundsel, and by a few pioneer species that struggle to adapt to the difficult conditions of high-altitude life. Above 3000m begins the volcanic desert.

The human presence on the volcano's lower slopes has spelled extinction for the fallow deer, roe deer, boar, wolves, vultures and griffons which populated the area as late as the 19th century. Today you are likely to see the odd fox, wildcat, weasel, ferret, marten, dormouse, field mouse, porcupine, hare, rabbit or hedgehog. Birds include kites, buzzards, sparrow hawks, peregrines, kestrels, royal eagles, Sicilian partridge, imperial ravens and owls. Common reptiles are the *vipera hugyi* and colubrids (non-venomous snakes), including the leopard colubrid.

Ætna's upper slopes are now under the protection of the **Parco Regionale dell'Etna**, established in 1981. Europe's most important volcanic park and the first large nature reserve in Sicily, it affords an endless number of excursions, especially if you don't mind scrambling up, down and across the rugged lava flows. For those drawn inexorably to the summit, a word of caution is in order. As a famous guide pointed out two centuries ago: 'Most foreign visitors are too apt to consider the ascent a trifling affair ... we, who are near neighbours of the mountain, are content if we have reached the summit twice or three times in a lifetime, for we never attempt it except under ideal conditions.' Alternately, you can make a partial circuit of the volcano on well-marked trails maintained by the Ætna Park Authority, headquartered in Nicolosi.

If you're not athletically inclined, a small-gauge railway makes a scenic loop around Ætna in half a day, running more or less parallel to the 141km (87-mile) road circuit. For those with an instinctive fear of volcanoes, the most attractive feature of Ætna is the seafront of its eastern slopes, the famous **Riviera dei Ciclopi** whose seven cities include the beautiful resorts of Aci Castello, Acireale and Aci Trezza. The origin of the prefix 'aci' is linked to the presence in antiquity of a stream, cancelled by later eruptions, which legend associates with the tender love story of Acis and Galatea.

A Circuit of Ætna

This circuit, or *giro*, of the volcano begins and ends in Catania.

Aci Castello, as the name suggests, grew up around its Norman fortress. Now a suburb of Catania, it hosts many of the city's more luxurious hotels. Built in 1076 entirely of lava on a splendid basalt spur, the **Castle** seems to

The Story of Acis and Galatea

Ovid tells the unhappy love story of the handsome youth Acis and the graceful Nereid Galatea in the Metamorphoses (XIII, 750–897). Galatea, he says, loved Acis as intensely as she despised the dreadful Polyphemus – the savage Cyclops whom the very woods shuddered to look upon, who scorned Olympus and its gods, yet who burned with desire for her and vexed her with endless wooing. When the seer Telemus came to Ætna and told Polyphemus that Odysseus would take from him his one eye, the giant mocked and answered, 'You are wrong; another has already taken it.'

One day, as Acis and Galatea were making love by the sea, the Cyclops came stalking with huge, heavy tread along the shore. Spying the young lovers, the fierce giant cried: 'I see you, and I'll make that union of your loves the last.' Ætna trembled with the din of his voice, and the frightened Galatea dived into the nearby sea. Her hero fled on foot, but the Cyclops ran after him and hurled a boulder wrenched from the mountainside at the youth. Although the merest edge of the rock reached Acis, it was enough to bury him. Galatea, who witnessed the scene in horror, did the only thing that fate allowed her to do – she transformed Acis to save him from death. The crimson blood that trickled from beneath the mass presently became the colour of a stream swollen by the early rains, and in a little while it cleared entirely. Then the mass that had been thrown cracked wide open and a tall, green reed sprang up through the crack. The hollow opening in the rock resounded with leaping waters, and suddenly a youth stood forth waist-deep from the water. The youth was Acis, changed to a river god. To this day, his waters flow from Ætna to the sea.

form a single block with the natural eruptive mass on which it stands. Covered by lava in 1169, it was rebuilt in the late 13th century by Roger of Lauria, the rebel admiral of Frederick III of Aragon. Frederick took it back in 1297 by building a tower of equal height next to it. Today the castle houses a small **museum** with mineralogical, palaeontological, and archaeological collections. From the square in front of the fortress, where the black-and-white, lava-and-plaster Chiesa Madre also stands, you can admire a superb panorama of the Riviera dei Ciclopi with the tall Faraglioni (see below) in the background.

Until quite recently **Aci Trezza** was just a fishing village. It was immortalised in Giovanni Verga's novel *I Malavoglia*. Now a wealthy suburb as well as a resort, it nevertheless preserves strong ties with its past, fishing still being the main occupation. There are a number of good restaurants around the small harbour, as well as a strangely silent fish market, where quick deals are made with pure body language. Out to sea rise the large basalt rocks known as the **Faraglioni dei Ciclopi**, which myth identifies as the rocks hurled by the blinded Polyphemus to sink the fleeing ship of Ulysses; the largest, Isola d'Aci, hosts an oceanographic and marine biological study centre of the University of Catania.

Acireale is a city of obscure origins. It may stand on the site of the Greek *Akis*, and remains of a Republican Roman temple and thermae have been found at nearby Capo Molini. Long visited as a spa, it spreads over a great stream of lava at the seaward end of a pleasant valley planted with citrus groves. The city was built on the present site in 1326, after the Roman and Byzantine settlement (*Akis* was *Aquilia* to the Byzantines) was destroyed by an earthquake and by Robert of Anjou's navy. After being a feudal dominion for several centuries, in 1642 it was brought under the direct control of Philip IV of Spain, whence the name *Aci Reale*, the 'Royal Aci'. Again severely damaged by earthquake in 1693, the 'new' city was rebuilt in the 18th century.

The central Piazza del Duomo is lined with Baroque buildings, some of which, like the 17th-century church of Santi Pietro e Paolo and the Palazzo Comunale, pre-date the 1693 earthquake. The **Cathedral** (1597–1618) has a Gothic Revival façade by Giovanni Battista Basile incorporating a 17th-century marble portal and flanked by two campanili with coloured-tile roofs; within are frescoes by Pietro Vasta (1737) and Antonio Filocamo (1711). At the pavement tables of the elegant *gelaterie* that line the square you can taste Acireale's famous ice cream; if you come in February, you can also see the most beautiful carnival celebration in Sicily.

South of the cathedral the Corso leads past the 17th-century church of **San Sebastiano**, its ornate façade, completed in 1705, preceded by a balustrade bearing 10 statues of Old Testament figures. Pietro Vasta frescoed the dome, chapels and transept. **Palazzo Pennisi di Floristella**, across the little square to the north, contains a collection of Greek coins; more of these, together with antiquities and paintings, may be seen in the **Pinacoteca dell'Accademia Zelantea**, reached from the cathedral square by Via Cavour and Via Marchese di San Giuliano.

At the south end of the town, in a large park, are the **Terme di Santa Venera**. The baths use the same sulphuric spring waters that fed the ancient Terme Xiphonie, possibly of Greek origin and certainly frequented from the Roman age onwards. North of Piazza del Duomo the main Corso Umberto I is lined with shops and cafés. At its end is the public garden of the **Villa Belvedere**, from which there are stunning views of the little port of Santa Maria La Scala, the Ionian Sea, and Ætna.

The towns in the hinterland of Ætna are less commercial, hence more authentic but also poorer than those on the coast. **Linguaglossa** ('Glowing Tongue' in dialect) probably takes its name from a lava flow of 1634, commemorated by a plaque on the town hall. It stands at the foot of a large, beautiful pine forest, the **Pineta di Linguaglossa**, and is a good starting point for excursions to the summit or around the north flank of the volcano.

Randazzo, built largely of black lava, is a harsh, unfriendly place. Although it is the closest town to the main crater of Ætna, it has always been spared by the volcano's devastating lava flows. It became important in the Middle Ages as a market centre, its urban structure evolving around the churches of its three ethnic communities – the Latin **Santa Maria** (founded in the early 13th century and subsequently remodelled), the Greek **San Nicolò** (dating from the 14th century but rebuilt after 1583), and the Lombard **San Martino** (13th–14th century, subsequently remodelled). For centuries community harmony was preserved by making each of these churches the cathedral for a short time – only after 1916 was Santa Maria given the honour *in perpetuam*. A number of factors led to the town's decline beginning in the 16th century: the establishment of nearby Bronte (1535), the lava flows that severely damaged the surrounding cultivations, and the plagues of 1575 and 1580, which were so severe that entire neighbourhoods had to be abandoned and destroyed. Although a partial recovery took place in the 17th century, today Randazzo is a dreary backwater. A small museum in **Palazzo Vagliasindi**, on Piazza Rabatà, houses artefacts of the 5th–2nd centuries BC, from a Greek necropolis at Sant'Anastasia, and a small but interesting collection of Byzantine antiquities. A square tower of black lava is all that remains of the Aragonese castle.

Just outside the town, on the road to Cesarò, is the Benedictine **Abbey of Maniace**, also known as the 'Castello'. It stands near the site where the Byzantine general George Maniakes defeated the Saracens in 1040. Founded in 1174 by Margaret, mother of William I, it was given, together with the duchy of Bronte, to Admiral Horatio Nelson in 1799 in recognition of his services to the Bourbon Kingdom of Naples. Nelson's descendants lived there until 1981, transforming the abbey into a luxurious country manor with a marvellous garden of exotic plants.

Adrano, on the southwestern slopes of Ætna, occupies the site of a Siculan religious sanctuary. It was known to the Greeks as *Adranón*, to the Romans as *Hadranum*, and to Italians as *Adernò* until 1929. It preserves sections of cyclopean walls from the Greek period in Contrada Mendolito, near which there is a Saracen bridge over the River Simeto.

The most important monument is the rectangular Norman **Castle,** erected by Count Roger in the 11th century, altered in the 14th century and recently restored. Today it houses the **Museo Archeologico**, with finds ranging from the Neolithic to the Greek period, notably ceramics and utensils of the Castelluccio Culture and a clay bust of a Siculan god. The church of the **Assunta** (or Chiesa Madre) is likewise a Norman foundation, rebuilt in the 17th and 19th centuries. Legend has it that the 16 columns of the interior come from the ancient temple of Adranón. The former monastery of **Santa Lucia** (1158) was given its present form in the 15th and 16th centuries. The church has an elliptical interior and a façade flanked by two bell towers. The

Museo Petronio Russo has a modest collection of local antiquities. A Siculan town unearthed in the Mendolito district yielded the bronzes known as the Mendolito Hoard (8th century BC), now in the archaeological museum in Syracuse.

Paternò is a large town whose economy revolves around its orange plantations. Founded by the Normans, it grew up at the foot of the basalt rock of its **Castle**, built by Count Roger (1073) but rebuilt in the 14th century. There are plans to make this powerful lava cube a museum. Across the square from the castle stands the church of **Santa Maria dell'Alto** (or Chiesa Madre), rebuilt in 1342 over a Norman church. The piazza enjoys good views over the town, the plain of Catania, the Simeto valley and, of course, the incomparable spectacle of Ætna.

A popular summer resort, **Nicolosi** is the chief gateway to the summit of Mt Ætna from the south. It is also the headquarters of the **Parco dell'Etna**, where you can pick up books, maps and pointers on the volcano's nature trails. A particularly impressive road leads up through oak, chestnut and pine woods and over bare lava flows to the Rifugio Sapienza, from which a cable car ascends to the Montagnola, at 2600m; during summer you can continue from here in big jeeps, to within a few metres of the summit.

Taormina

In *Travels in the Two Sicilies in 1777–1780* (1785), Henry Swinburne writes: 'Were I to name a place that possesses every grand and beauteous qualification for the forming of a picture; a place in which I should wish to employ the powers of a Salvator or a Poussin, Taormina should be the object of my choice. – Every thing belonging to it is drawn in a large sublime style; the mountains tower to the very clouds, the castles and ruins rise on mighty masses of perpendicular rock, and seem to defy the attacks of mortal enemies; Etna with all its snowy and woody sweeps fills half the horizon; the sea is stretched out upon an immense scale and occupies the remainder of the prospect.'

Spectacularly located on a terrace of Monte Tauro, dominating the sea and with views westwards to Mt Ætna, **Taormina** is easily Sicily's most picturesque town. It is also one of the island's oldest and best-loved resorts, known for its luxuriant vegetation, old-time charm, breathtaking vistas and secluded beaches. Unfortunately all these attractions are now endangered by over-ambitious commercial exploitation: in the words of novelist D.H. Lawrence: 'Capri is an unhatched egg compared to this serpent.'

The site was settled in the Archaic period by Sikels and by the inhabitants of Greek Zancle (Messina). It was resettled from nearby Naxos in 403BC, when Dionysius the Elder of Syracuse destroyed that city, allowing the fugitives to occupy the terrace of Monte Taura which thenceforth would be called *Tauromenion*. The residential area of the Greek city was probably located near the church of San Pancrazio (where remains of some 3rd-

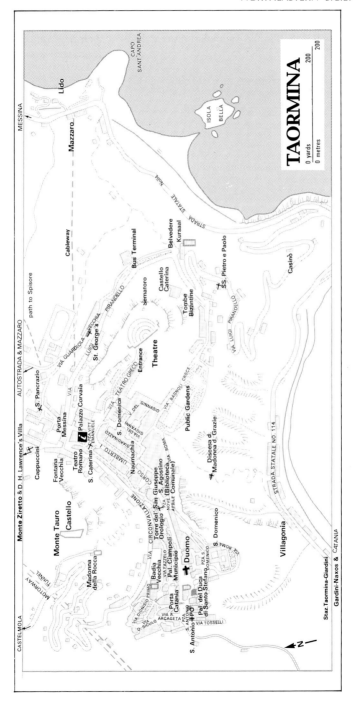

TAORMINA

0 yards   200
0 metres   200

CAPO
SANT'ANDREA

Lido

MESSINA

Mazzaro

ISOLA
BELLA

STRADA STATALE NON

Cableway

Bus Terminal

Belvedere
Kursaal

path to Spisone

Castello
Caterina

SS. Pietro e Paolo

AUTOSTRADA & MAZZARO

S. Pancrazio

VIA GUARDIOLA VECCHIA

LUIGI

VIA LUIGI PIRANDELLO

Sematoro

Tombe
Bizantine

Casinò

VIA LUIGI PIRANDELLO

Cappuccini

Porta
Messina

VIA

Palazzo Corvaia

St. George's

VIA PIRANDELLO

Theatre

Entrance

VIA TEATRO GRECO

VIA BAGNOLI CROCE

Monte Ziretto & D. H. Lawrence's Villa

Fontana
Vecchia

Teatro
Romano

S. Caterina

S. Domenica

VIA DEL GINNASIO

Public Gardens

VIA PENNAVITT

VIA EMANUELE

UMBERTO

S. Domenica TEATRO GRECO

VIA DEL GIOVANNI

Naumachia

VIA GUARDIAZZO

Discesa d.
Madonna d. Grazie

VIA ROMA

STRADA STATALE NO. 114

Monte Tauro

Castello

Madonna
della Rocca

CORSO

VILLAGIONE

CIRCONVALLAZIONE

S. Giuseppe

Torre del
Orologio

S. Agostino

PZA.
NOVE

PIAZZA
APRILE

(Biblioteca
Comunale)

S. Domenico

Villagonia

Staz. Taormina-Giardini

CASTELMOLA

MOTORWAY
TUNNEL

VIA DIONISIO PRIMO

Badia
Vecchia

Pal. Ciampoli

Municipio

VIA FAZZELO

Duomo

PZA. S.
DOMENICO

VIA
ARCAGETA

Pal. del Duca
di Santo Stefano

Porta
Catania

S. Antonio

S. Antonio

VIA TOSSELLI

VIA
SICULO

Gardini-Naxos & CATANIA

N

189

The lava flow on Mt AEtna in 1981

century houses survive), and the acropolis was on the hilltop where the medieval castle stands today. Further south stood the *polis* proper, with its market place and agora surrounded by public and religious buildings – a bouleuterion, some temples and the famous theatre – all of which underwent variations in form and use in Imperial Roman times.

Taormina flourished during the Byzantine period, becoming first the seat of an archbishop and later the capital of Byzantine Sicily. The Arabs, who held it from 962 until 1079, rationalised the city's water system, permitting the cultivation of the surrounding hills, and shifted the city centre to better accommodate its increasing population. New residential quarters grew up near the Porta Saracena, and a tower controlling the entrance to the city from the Via Valeria was built on the site of the old Roman forum.

Following the Norman conquest Taormina again flourished in the 12th–14th centuries; during this period the present cathedral was built, the landed aristocracy constructed their elegant townhouses, and the mendicant religious orders established the first large convents outside the city walls. In the 16th and 17th centuries Taormina gained increasing importance as a stage on the road from Messina to Syracuse. In the following century, however, the coast road was opened, reducing the city to what it is today – a resort. In the 20th century the construction of new roads up to Castelmola and down to the coast accelerated the town's growth and prepared the way for its blessing and its bane, coach tours.

The Sights

Regardless of whether you arrive by road or rail (there is a funicular from the station, by the sea), you'll probably reach Taormina at its east end, near the **Porta Messina**, a medieval gate rebuilt in 1808. Taormina's lovely main street, Corso Umberto I, follows the course of the ancient Via Valeria, crossing the historic city centre from east to west. This was also the main axis of the Greek settlement. The first building of note inside the gate is (right) **Palazzo Corvaja**, a 15th-century patrician palace built around the 11th-century Arab guard tower. The Tourist Board has its offices inside, and if the wooden doors are open you can glance into the pleasant courtyard. Across the street on the same side of the Corso is the 17th-century church of **Santa Caterina d'Alessandria**. This was built over the Roman odeon, which in turn was constructed by transforming a bouleuterion (or, by another interpretation, a Doric temple) of the Greek period. Behind the church can be seen five wedges with brick steps – the cavea of the odeon – and part of the original stonework of the scena.

The famous **Theatre** is reached by a street lined with shops selling Caltagirone ceramics and other souvenirs, opposite Palazzo Corvaja. It is a beautiful, imposing construction built into the natural slope of the hill. The largest antique theatre in Sicily after that of Syracuse (it measures 109m in diameter), it is known as much for its magnificent position as for its imposing architectural forms. It moved Goethe to remark in 1787: 'No audience in any other theatre ever beheld such a view.' The original theatre dates from the Hellenistic period, but the building you see today is mainly the product of a Roman reconstruction and enlargement. The cavea, divided into nine wedges of seats, was crowned by two porticoes – an inner one and a somewhat grander outer one. The scena is remarkably well preserved, though the marble facing of its inner wall has been lost. Still visible are the foundations of the stage, the wings, and traces of the porticoes at the back. A large cleft in the scena affords what is no doubt the most famous of all views of Ætna.

Returning to Corso Umberto I, you turn left to reach the handsome Piazza IX Aprile, with a terrace overlooking the sea and Ætna, and several pavement cafés. On the left is the former church of Sant'Agostino (1486), now the public library; on the right, at the top of a staircase, the small church of **San Giuseppe**, with a Rococo stucco interior. The Corso narrows as you enter the so-called Borgo Medievale, beyond the 12th-century **Torre dell'Orologio**; the street here is lined with fine old palaces, some showing Norman-Saracenic and Catalan-Gothic details.

Just before the 15th-century Porta Catania, Piazza del Duomo, with a curious fountain topped by a female centaur, opens on the left. The **Cathedral** of San Nicolò was erected in the 13th century. Its façade has a small rose window and a 17th-century doorway. Two other fine doorways, dating respectively from the 15th and 16th centuries, adorn the north and south flanks. The interior preserves its Romanesque basilican design, with six pink antique marble columns; over the second altar in the south aisle is a beautifully executed and magnificently framed polyptych by Antonello de Saliba (1504).

Across the square on the south rises the **Palazzo dei Duchi di Santo Stefano**, a Norman-period building with two splended double-light windows and a crowning frieze with geometric motifs of Islamic inspiration. The interior is now used as an exhibition space, as is the small **Badia Vecchia**, a crenellated tower on the Circonvallazione above.

There are a number of interesting walks in the immediate environs of Taormina. From the Circonvallazione, a road and stepped footpath leads to the supposed site of the acropolis of Tauromenion, now occupied by the Arabic **Castle**, which is still in a good state of preservation. The walk to the castle will take you about 45 minutes and it is straight uphill – but the stunning view over the ramparts to Taormina and the sea is worth the effort. From the castle, the road and a footpath (marked) continue up to **Castelmola**, a picturesque medieval village known for its (sweet!) almond wine.

On Cape Schisò, at the south end of the bay now occupied by the modern resort of Giardini Naxos, excavations have brought to light the ancient Chalcidian colony of **Naxos**. Thucydides claims that Naxos was established in 735BC. If this is so, it is the earliest of all Greek colonies in Sicily, antedating Syracuse by one year. It is known with certainty that the city was razed to the ground in 403BC by Dionysius the Elder, who considered its alliance with Athens a thorn in his side. The **ruins** – which include extensive traces of 5th- and 6th-century walls, remains of houses and streets and a religious sanctuary with vestiges of sacrificial altars and a temenos of Aphrodite – lie in a beautiful position among fruit and shade trees, bougainvillea and jasmine. Finds from the excavations are preserved in the excellent small **museum**, in an old Bourbon fort at the tip of the cape.

You need a car to visit the **Gole dell'Alcantara** near Motta Camastra, 25km (15miles) southwest. This extraordinarily deep gorge cut in the basalt at the foot of Mt Ætna by the River Alcantara can be followed upstream for several hundred metres. When not crowded with visitors (as it is for much of the summer), it is quite impressive, its carved basalt prisms assuming spectacular sculptural shapes. If you left your waders at home, you can rent some on the spot.

The Peloritan Peninsula

The Peloritan Peninsula is not a particularly attractive place. Although the hills are, in places, covered with dark pine forests, on the whole unchecked building has reduced Sicily's northeast tip to a strip suburb running from Messina to Milazzo. Regardless of whether you travel by rail or by road, you'll find it hard to resist the urge to move on to better things. Nevertheless, a half-day devoted to this region is well spent. Messina has a couple of interesting sights, Milazzo isn't as bad as it looks from a distance, and the beach at Tindari is rightly considered one of the most photogenic in Sicily.

Messina

Messina, the port of entry to Sicily for those arriving by car or train, is a busy provincial capital on the strait bearing its name, here just 8km (5 miles) wide. With 270,000 inhabitants, it is Sicily's third largest city (after Palermo and Catania). It was established before the first wave of Greek colonisation – that is, before the 8th century BC – by Siculans who called it *Zancle* (sickle) in reference to the hooked promontory which protects its beautiful, deep harbour. Occupied by Greeks from Cumæ and Chalcis, in the 5th century BC it came under Anaxilas, tyrant of Rhegion (Reggio Calabria). He changed its name to *Messána*, in honour of his native Messenia in the Peloponnesus. The city struck an early alliance with Rome, and between the 3rd century BC and 5th century of the Christian era it flourished thanks to the construction of two Roman consular roads along the coasts to the south and west – the Via Valeria to Catania, and the Via Pompea to Palermo. In the Middle Ages Messina was important as a centre of monastic learning and a crusader port. Known for its silk, wool and furs, it continued to prosper until the 17th century, when it lost its privileges by rebelling against Spanish viceregal rule.

Most of the building of these early periods was destroyed in the disastrous earthquakes of 1783, 1894 and 1908. The latter was felt as far away as Malta; nearly 85,000 of its 100,000 victims lost their lives in Messina and its environs. The recovery plan of 1911 designed a city of exceptionally wide streets and sturdy, low buildings laid out on a rigidly orthogonal grid. Though much criticised, this scheme faithfully reflected the urgent needs of the moment and minimised the danger of future catastrophes. Bombed to bits in 1943 (when 5000 of its inhabitants lost their lives), modern Messina offers little in terms of monuments and sites, though on the whole it is a discreetly pleasant place. Antonello da Messina, the Renaissance painter who brought the Flemish technique of oil painting to Italy, was a native; his works can be seen in the museum.

Near the waterfront at the centre of the city is Piazza del Duomo, with the beautiful Orion Fountain by Fra Giovanni Angelo Montorsoli (1547). The **Cathedral** was commissioned by Roger II and consecrated in 1197 in the presence of Holy Roman Emperor Henry VI. It was destroyed by the 1783 earthquake, rebuilt, toppled by the 1908 earthquake, rebuilt again and damaged in the 1943 bombings. It nevertheless retains a great deal of its original medieval appearance. The lower part of the façade is adorned with 15th-century carvings of farming and domestic life, and the great portal has been reconstructed from original fragments. On the south flank is a 16th-century doorway designed by Polidoro da Caravaggio. Its counterpart on the north flank now gives access to the baptistery.

The campanile, reconstructed after 1908, holds a large astronomical clock made in Strasbourg in 1933. Its mechanism powers a delightful series

Street scene, Taormina

of mechanical figures representing allegories of the days of the week and the ages of man, the sanctuary of Montalto, Gospel scenes, the Madonna's letter delivered to the ambassadors of Messina (this story is told below) and, at the top, figures from the Sicilian Vespers. Come at noon to see them in action.

The grey-and-pink basilican **interior** has three aisles divided by columns and ogival arches and covered by a painted trussed ceiling. Most of the things you will see here are modern reconstructions, painstakingly assembled from fragments salvaged after the 1943 bombing. The side-altars are copies of the 16th-century originals by Montorsoli. In the south aisle is a 16th-century statue of St John the Baptist attributed to Antonello Gagini; further on, a coeval surround marks the entrance to the treasury (usually closed). Another doorway of similar design can be seen on the other side of the church. At the end of the aisle are two fine 14th-century tombs holding the remains of archbishops. Over the majestic high altar is a copy of the Byzantine *Madonna della Lettera*, destroyed in 1943. The Cappella del Sacramento, in the north apse, was designed in the late 16th century by Jacopo del Duca, a pupil of Michelangelo. Miraculously spared from catastrophe, it holds the cathedral's only original 14th-century mosaic, showing

The Theatre at Taormina with Ætna in the backgound

the enthroned *Madonna* with archangels, saints and queens.

Just two blocks south of the cathedral is Messina's other noteworthy church, **Santissima Annunziata dei Catalani**. Now the University Chapel, it is open only during services. The exterior is as fine as any Norman church in Sicily, with beautiful 12th-century arcading on its apse, transepts and dome, and three 13th-century doors in its west façade. The interior, in red, white and yellow stone, has tall Corinthian columns and a lovely dome.

The **Museo Regionale** was set up in 1914 in a former silk mill reached by Viale Annunziata (off map, c 3km/1¾ miles north of the cathedral); its core collection is made up of works salvaged from the 1908 earthquake.

In the atrium is a composition that is particularly meaningful to the *Messinesi*: 12 18th-century gilded bronze panels narrating the Legend of the Holy Letter. The story tells of a long, severe famine, which came to an end when the Madonna, moved to compassion, sent Messina a ship filled with wheat and other food (but devoid of crew), together with a letter containing a lock of her hair and a blessing for the city and its inhabitants.

In the other rooms are works ranging from the early Middle Ages to the late Baroque period. Highlights include a lovely little mosaic of the Madonna and Child, called 'La Ciambretta' (13th century) and fragments of trusses from the cathedral roof (12th–13th century), painted with Old and New Testament scenes; several fine 15th-century works, including a splendid wood *Crucifix*, a majolica tondo of the *Madonna and Child* by the Della Robbia workshop, a marble low relief of *St George and the Dragon* attributed to Domenico Gagini, a painted marble *Madonna and Child*

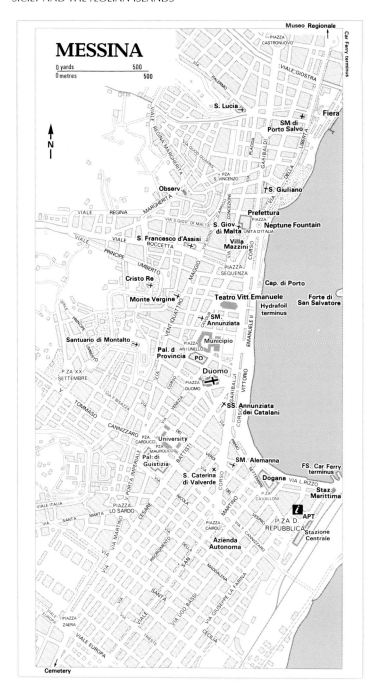

MESSINA

0 yards 500
0 metres 500

N

Museo Regionale
Car Ferry terminus
PIAZZA CASTRONUOVO
VIA PALERMO
VIALE GIOSTRA
S. Lucia
Fiera
SM di Porto Salvo
VIALE REGINA MARGHERITA
VIA QUOD QUAERIS
PIAZZA S. VINCENZO
PIAZZA
GARIBALDI
VIA LIBERTÀ
VIA DELLA
Observ.
VIA CONCEZIONE
S. Giuliano
VIALE REGINA MARGHERITA
Prefettura
PIAZZA UNITA D'ITALIA
VIA S.GIOV. DI MALTA
S. Giov. di Malta
Neptune Fountain
VIALE REGINA
VIA S. MONS
VIA CONCEZIONE
S. Francesco d'Assisi
BOCCETTA
Villa Mazzini
VIALE PRINCIPE UMBERTO
VIA MAGGIO
PIAZZA SEQUENZA
CORSO
Cristo Re
Cap. di Porto
Monte Vergine
Teatro Vitt. Emanuele
Forte di San Salvatore
VIALE PRINCIPE
VIA VENTIQUATTRO
SM. Annunziata
Hydrafoil terminus
Santuario di Montalto
VIA COLOMBO
PIAZZA ANTONELLO
Municipio
EMANUELE II
UMBERTO
Pal. d Provincia
PO
CORSO VITTORIO
Duomo
P.ZA XX SETTEMBRE
VIA CORSO
PIAZZA DUOMO
VIA VENEZIA
V. TOMMASO
VIA F.BIGAZZA
SGARIBALDI
SS. Annunziata dei Catalani
CANNIZZARO
PZA. CARDUCCI
University
CORSO GARIBALDI
VIA DEL
PORTA IMPERIALE
Pal. di Giustizia
PZA. MAUROLICO
VIA BATTISTI
VIA VERDI
SM. Alemanna
FS. Car Ferry terminus
VIALE ITALIA
S. Caterina di Valverde
VIA NICOLA
VIA SETTE FARINE
Dogana
VIA L. RIZZO
Staz. Marittima
PIAZZA LO SARDO
MARTA
VIA SANTA
VIA MARTINO
VIA CESARE
VIA MARTINO
PIAZZA CAIROLI
VIA T. CANNIZZARO
VESPRO
P.ZA CAVALLONI
APT
P.ZA D. REPUBBLICA
Stazione Centrale
VIA RESORGIMENTO
VIA DELLA
VIA SAN
Azienda Autonoma
VIA MADDALENA
VIA GIUSEPPE LA FARINA
VIALE EUROPA
PIAZZA ZAERA
SANTA
VIA UGO BASSI
VIA TRESTE
CECILIA
VIALE EUROPA
Cemetery

attributed to Francesco Laurana, Antonello da Messina's lovely polyptych of the *Madonna with St Gregory and St Benedict and the Annunciation* (1473), another panel painting, of the *Pietà and Symbols of the Passion* attributed to the Flemish 'Master of the St Lucy Legend'; a statue of *Scylla* from the Neptune Fountain in Piazza Unità d'Italia, by Giovanni Angelo Montorsoli (1557); and two large canvases painted by Caravaggio during his brief stay in Messina (1608–09), representing the *Nativity* and the *Raising of Lazzarus*. These late works inspired numerous imitations, some of which are displayed in the same room. The new garden pavilion displays Greek and Roman antiquities.

Milazzo

Milazzo is successor to the Greek *Myláí* and the Roman *Mylæ*. Its promontory was the site of important protohistoric settlements between the 14th and 8th centuries BC, and a colony of Greek Zancle was established here in 716BC. After falling to Dionysius the Elder in 392BC, it was one of the northernmost possessions of Syracuse. Romanised after the time of Hieron II, the town was made the seat of a bishop by the Byzantines. Its fame as a port came in the 9th and 10th centuries, under the Arabs. It was reclaimed by the Normans in 1061 and fortified by Frederick II, Alfonso of Aragon and Charles V.

Driving into Milazzo, past the huge refineries and power plants on the outskirts and the solid curtain of new building around the harbour, one has the impression that Messina is a wholly modern city. In reality, although it has been compromised by urban sprawl, it has a lovely old historic centre. The 18th-century lower town, on the waterfront, begins after the hyrdrofoil and ferry landings; the *borgo*, at the foot of the castle, dates from the 16th–17th century and has pleasant winding streets and old houses still enclosed by 15th-century fortifications.

The **Castle**, with its 14th-century doorway set between two 15th-century towers, rises on the site of the acropolis. It was built by Holy Roman Emperor Frederick II in the 13th century and later enlarged. Inside is an imposing keep, as well as the **Old Cathedral**, dedicated to the Assumption. This is one of the few extant examples of 17th-century Sicilian Baroque architecture (the others were toppled by the 1693 earthquake). In recent years the castle has been used for summer theatre – a point to remember if you're stranded in Milazzo overnight waiting for passage to the Æolian Islands.

In the lower town, at a fork on the Lungomare Garibaldi, is the church of **San Giacomo Apostolo**, erected in 1432 and altered in later centuries; it contains the high altar of the old cathedral, a fine example of 17th-century marble inlay. The street leading inland passes the New Cathedral (1937–52), of little interest. The church and convent of the **Carmine**, whose 18th-century façades face Piazza Caio Duilio, were founded in the 16th century. One wing of the convent is now the town hall.

The environs of Milazzo afford several pleasant excursions. On the unspoilt promontory of **Cape Milazzo** are a lighthouse and the cave sanctuary of Sant'Antonio da Padova; olives, palms and prickly pear grow wild, and trails wind down to the water. **Tindari**, 30km (19 miles) west, takes its name from the Greek *Tyndarís*, founded by Dionysius the Elder in 396BC and abandoned after a landslide in the 1st century of the Christian era. The

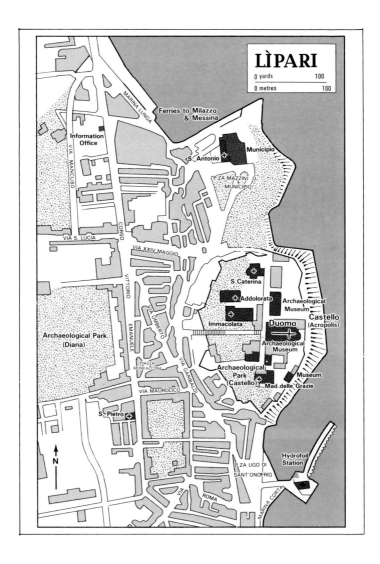

site is planted with olives, pines, prickly pear and bougainvillea, and enjoys good views over the sea and the Æolian Islands. There are remains of Græco-Roman walls, a Greek theatre remodelled by the Romans for glad-iatorial spectacles, a basilica, thermæ, houses and tabernae. Traces of a Byzantine settlement on this spot, destroyed by the Arabs, also survive. Below the headland the beautiful beach is shaped by the flow of the tides into constantly changing curved forms. The modern sanctuary of the Madonna di Tindari is a place of pilgrimage.

The Æolian Islands

These seven volcanic islands dotting the sea off Sicily's north coast are among the more attractive and interesting in the Western Mediterranean. Famous for their natural beauty as well as for their unique history, they offer a variety of attractions, from the green hills and precipitous coasts of **Lipari** and of **Panarea**, to the spectacular active volcanoes of **Vulcano** and **Stromboli**, the fertile vineyards of **Salina**, and the solitude of outlying **Alicudi** and **Filicudi**. Also known as the Lipari Islands, the archipelago has been inhabited since the Neolithic era, when people came here for the valuable volcanic glass, obsidian – harder than flint and better suited to making sharp tools. The ancient Greeks made the islands the home of King Æolus, the god of the winds, and Homer wrote of them in the *Odyssey*. All the islands are worth exploring, and frequent hydrofoils make island-hopping easy.

Lipari

Although it measures just 38 sq km (14^1/$_2$ sq miles), **Lipari** is the largest of the seven Æolian Islands and the capital of the archipelago. It was settled in the 4th millennium BC, the earliest communities making their homes on the rugged west coast and on the rock where the castle now stands. The latter site was also chosen by Greeks from Rhodes and Cnidus when they came to set up their colony in 580BC. Called *Meligunis* or *Lìpara* after its mythical first king, this important western outpost flourished under the Greeks until 252BC, when the archipelago was taken by the Romans. The Greek acropolis became the centre of the Roman city, and on the same site the Normans later founded the Benedictine church and cathedral of San Bartolomeo. After a prosperous period based on the export of sulphur, alum and pumice, Lipari was attacked and destroyed in 1544 by the Tunisian pirate Kaireddin Barbarossa. Some years later the Spanish made the island safe for resettlement, and the villages of Cannetto, Acquacalda, Quattropani and Pianoconte grew up outside the town walls. The modern town developed in the 18th century, along the high street now known as Corso Vittorio Emanuele.

Today Lipari is a charming place, famous in Italy and abroad for its beautiful sea- and landscape and for its local vernacular architecture – consisting of simple whitewashed houses with broad porches shaded by grapevines or flowering bougainvillea. The town of Lipari, spread out around its two marvellous harbours, has a vaguely Spanish air. The narrow side streets repay exploration, and few experiences are as pleasurable as sipping cappuccino in the little piazza fronting the Small Harbour, where the hydrofoils come in.

Rising above the town, and reached both by a cobbled street and by a staircase carved in the 16th-century town wall, is Lipari's chief attraction, the **Citadel**. It stands on the site of the Greek acropolis and contains the **Cathedral**, a Norman foundation destroyed in 1544 by Barbarossa and reconstructed in its present (rather uninteresting) Baroque form; a small **archaeological park**, with remains ranging from the Neolithic to the Roman period (colour-coded plaques help you distinguish and date the individual structures) and the excellent **Museo Archeologico Eoliano**.

The latter holds one of the most fascinating and carefully designed displays of antiquities in Italy. The **prehistoric section** (Rooms 1–11) is housed in the former Bishop's Palace, adjoining the cathedral on the south. The palace in its present form was built in the 18th century over the Benedictine monastery founded by the Normans in 1083. Here is a vast and beautiful collection of material, traceable to the island's first inhabitants (who settled on the fertile plateau of Castellaro Vecchio) and to a second population that supplanted them and took over their obsidian trade (based on the more defensible rock of the citadel).

Lipari's First Inhabitants

During the early 4th millennium BC both groups of Lipari's early settlers exported the precious sharp stone and imported goods from trading partners on the Italian mainland, as the presence of Italic ceramics attests. The later culture also produced distinctive ceramics of its own, painted with three colours and characterised by bands with red flames edged with black on a light background, or by incised meanders and spirals.

After the mid-4th millennium, complex, refined vases of the Serra d'Alto Culture (from a village near Matera, in present-day Basilicata) were imported. Towards the end of the millennium, the threat of attack having ceased, the settlement spread from the castle rock to the surrounding plain. The obsidian trade was at its peak, and the city produced a new, autochtonous pottery (called the Diana style from the name of the plain) with simple monochromatic volumes and tubular or spool-shaped handles.

In the initial phases of the Æneolithic (early 3rd millennium) the population moved back to the castle, and the production of local ceramics suffered a slight decline. The appearance of unprecedented techniques and decorative motifs suggests the presence of a new culture, which may have come to Lipari from the Eastern Mediterranean. From the same period excavations have yielded dross from copper smelting.

The progressive introduction of metalworking in the mid- and late Æneolithic period threw the obsidian trade into crisis and initiated a phase of economic and demographic decline in the islands; Æolian culture began to gravitate toward Sicilian models.

The early Bronze Age (3rd millennium BC) marked a reawakening of activity connected with the arrival of new peoples – possibly from mainland Greece, as their ceramics and other objects suggest. These would have been the fierce Æolians of Greek myth, 'men of bronze' feared throughout the Mediterranean, the race whose king, Æolus, gave hospitality to Odysseus. Large villages of round huts grew up on all the islands, the most important being those at Lipari, at Capo Graziano on Filicudi, and at Capo Milazzese on Panarea. Whether or not their inhabitants were as fierce as they were reputed to be, it is certain that the islands' new importance, after the decline of the obsidian trade, derived from their strategic position, dominating one of the most important east-west trade routes of the Mediterranean. The presence, after the 16th century BC, of elegant painted ceramics from Mycenæ demonstrates the ties maintained between the Æolian islands and the Ægean.

For reasons unknown, around 1270BC a new culture from peninsular Italy seems to have settled in the islands. Diodorus Siculus suggests they may have been Ausonians, from Central Italy, and their culture is consequently referred to as Ausonian I (1270–1125BC). A second wave of invaders, hostile to the first, is referred to as Ausonian II (11th–9th centuryBC). During the Ausonian I phase bronze items were used as objects of exchange – a sort of primitive currency, pre-dating coins. Before the end of the 12th century the Ausonian I settlement on Lipari was violently destroyed (leaving its public treasury, 80kg of bronze, buried in the ground). It was replaced by the Ausonian II culture, whose necropolis of Piazzetta Monfalcone has been reconstructed in the Classical section of the museum.

Around 900 BC a second wave of destruction brought an end to the Ausonian II settlement, whose wood huts collapsed in flames burying everything they contained – one has yielded fragments of over 200 vases. After this cataclysm the settlement was not reconstructed and Lipari lay deserted (or almost) until the arrival, three centuries later, of the Greeks.

The earliest Greek colony was founded between 580 and 576BC by Doric Greeks from Cnydos, in Asia Minor. Their shrine of Æolus on the acropolis has yielded ritually fragmented ceramics, including a large vase by the Antimenes Painter (c 540–530BC) with ships and the Labours of Hercules and Theseus painted on the brim.

The **prehistory of the lesser islands** (Rooms 12–15) is documented by finds in the small building opposite the Bishop's Palace. Material from Panarea, Filicudi, Alicudi, Salina and Stromboli traces the history of settlement on these islands from the late 5th millennium BC to c 1270, when the first Ausonian invasion caused the islands to be abandoned. They seem to have been deserted for many centuries, perhaps until the 5th century BC.

In a building on the north side of the cathedral is the **Classical Section**, preceded by finds from the necropolises of Milazzo (Rooms 16–18) and Lipari (Rooms 19–25). In the Milazzo rooms are both inhumation sepulchres (with *pithoi*, large jugs in which corpses were huddled and buried), and incineration sepulchres (where the cremated remains of the deceased were collected in clay urns and deposited in shallow wells or covered with stones). Room 19 is entirely taken up by a reconstruction of the Bronze Age necropolis at Piazza Monfalcone on Lipari. The remaining rooms of this section display tomb accessories from the Greek and Roman necropolis in the Diana district on Lipari, where excavations have been underway since 1950. The 2500 tombs unearthed thus far have yielded a vast amount of material documenting life in Greek Lipàra from its foundation (c 580BC) to its conquest by the Romans during the First Punic War (252–251BC), and in the subsequent Roman town until the late Imperial age.

The remarkable burial treasures range from the 6th century BC (late-Corinthian and Attic black-figure ceramics, local black-glazed and striped ceramics) through the 5th century (beautiful vases with decorations linked to the cult of Dionysus), to the 4th century (including four kraters considered youthful works of the painter Asteas of Pæstum). To the latter century belong the numerous sacred theatrical masks and statuettes, linked to works of Sophocles, Euripides, Aristophanes and Menander, and used as votive offerings to Dionysus, god both of the theatre and of other-worldly blessings. There is also a group of miniature clay portraits of illustrious figures: Euripides, Menander, Homer, Socrates, Lysias, Alexander the Great, and so on. The innovative works of the Lipari Painter date from the 3rd century BC, and more than 100 vases by his hand have been preserved. In the Roman period began the custom of recycling material from earlier tombs – a trend that, in the Imperial age, actually arrived at the reuse of Greek sarcophagi. The ground floor of the new east wing houses objects recovered during underwater archaeological campaigns.

The 31km (19-mile) **circuit of the island** can be made in half an hour by taxi. The road leaves Lipari via the Marina Lunga, touches upon the little fishing village of **Cannetto**, then reaches the **pumice quarries** of the island's

The Archaeological Park on the acropolis, Lipari

northwest shore. Lipari's pumice is composed mainly of silica and alumina and is valued by builders as a lightweight thermoacoustic insulator, by the textile industry for its abrasive qualities (stone-washed jeans) and in the manufacture of cosmetics. The village of **Acquacalda**, on the island's north shore, is situated at the foot of the *rocce rosse*, the volcanic hills where obsidian was quarried in prehistoric times. The Chiesa Vecchia of **Quattropani** stands alone on a hilltop enjoying stunning views across the water to Salina, Filicudi and Alicudi. From here the road crosses the fertile Castellaro plateau, where Malvasia wine is made, to Pianoconte and the little park and viewpoint of **Quattrocchi**, from which the descent is made to Lipari.

If you prefer walking, a beautiful cross-country hike (4hr, unmarked; ascent/descent c 300m, challenging) takes you through stunning landscape along the clifftops on the island's uninhabited west side. From the white-washed village of **Pianoconte**, an old Roman road (which joins the modern highway at the tabernacle known as La Madonazza) leads to the **Terme di San Calogero**, the oldest thermal complex in the Mediterranean; ruins of Roman, Greek and Mycenæan thermae can be seen to the right of the 19th-century thermal establishment, now closed but due to reopen when restoration work is completed. From here you set out downhill towards the sea, bearing north on a dirt track through vast meadows dotted with Mediterranean *macchia* and finally climbing by a footpath to the village of **Quattropani**, overlooking the island's north shore. All the time you enjoy magnificent views over the sea to **Salina** with its two extinct volcanoes,

Monte dei Porri and Monte Fossa delle Felci, and its high coastal cliffs topped with vineyards where Malvasia wine is produced. Local buses connect Quattropani and Pianoconte with Lipari.

Vulcano

A narrow channel separates Lipari from **Vulcano**, known for its natural mud baths and hot springs, of which you should take due advantage, weather permitting (they're outside, just up to the right from the dock). Of the island's three volcanoes, the only active one is the **Gran Cratere**. The 400m ascent (marked) winds up the volcano's dramatic north flank, in a lunar landscape of black and red rock and volcanic dust; at the summit you can make a full circuit of the deep crater, walking over bright yellow sulphuric steam vents and enjoying magnificent views over the volcano, the neighbouring islands, and the Sicilian coast. The circular walk, starting and ending at Vulcano harbour, will take you roughly 3hr and is about the only thing to do on Vulcano, as most of the island's 21 sq km (8 sq miles) have been taken over by hotels and summer houses, with environmental consequences that are easy to imagine.

Panarea

The smallest and easily the most picturesque of the islands (actually, a bit *too* picturesque), tiny **Panarea** is 3km (1¾ miles) long and just over 1km (half a mile) wide. Boats dock at the only village of any size, **San Pietro**, where most of the cafés and shops are. At **Punta Milazzese**, about half-an-hour's walk to the south (signposted) is a Bronze Age village (c 1600BC) discovered in 1948. Pottery found at the site is now in the museum at Lipari; on either side of the headland are good, secluded beaches. Another pleasant walk leads northwards, in view of several of the islets that surround Panarea (Basiluzzo, Spinazzola, Lisca Bianca, Dattilo, Bottaro, Lisca Nera, I Panarelli and Le Formiche), to the Spiaggia della Calcara, where a few small steam vents can be seen. For some years San Pietro and the lesser villages of Ditella and Drauto have been the summer headquarters of the Italian film and fashion set.

Stromboli

At the northeastern tip of the archipelago, **Stromboli** hosts the Æolian Islands' only permanently active volcano, immortalised by Rossolini in his film of the same name. It will take you most of a leisurely afternoon to walk through the picturesque villages of **Scari**, **San Vincenzo**, **Ficogrande** and **Piscità**, then climb one-third of the way to the volcano's summit (by footpath: follow the red flashes), up the beautiful north flank to the **Osservatorio** (273m), from which there are splendid views of the craters and of the lava flow known as the *Sciara del Fuoco* (Trail of Fire). Volcanic activity permitting, the adventurous may wish to continue onward with one of the special guides who (armed with two-way radios permitting constant contact with the volcano's monitoring station) take visitors to the top (918m). The climb is tough, but rewarding.

Brydone (in *A Tour through Sicily and Malta*, 1773) observed that 'Stromboli is ever at work, and for ages past has been looked upon as the great light-house of these seas'. Stromboli's almost perpetual eruptions of fiery molten rock are an unforgettable spectacle at night. Lava flows down the Sciara del Fuoco on the volcano's northwest flank, leaving the four villages to the east and lovely **Ginostra** to the south quite safe. You can hire a boat at the dockside – or on the other islands – and linger just offshore to enjoy the spectacle.

Salina

Salina, the Greek Dydime (twin), is the second largest of the islands and the most luxuriant in vegetation. The latter feature makes it a favourite stopping place of migratory birds (and birders). The chief towns are **Santa Marina** and **Rinella** (where the hydrofoils dock), **Leni**, **Malfa** and **Pollara**. Massimo Troisi's last film, *The Postman*, was made at Pollara.

These villages are quite simple, and except for the characteristic Æolian architecture of their houses and the great natural beauty of their settings, they hold little of interest. Salina's principal attraction is the newly established nature reserve of **Monte Fossa delle Felci**, the highest peak in the archipelago (962m) and the larger of the twin volcanoes that gave the island its Greek name (the other is Monte dei Porri, 860m). The many fine walks in the reserve draw visitors year round. All are interesting, thanks to the Mediterranean *macchia* and huge ferns that cover the mountain's slopes, and the wild rabbits, peregrine falcons and kestrels that live among its rocks. From Santa Marina you can make the 4hr ascent via **Serra Favaloro** (marked with red flashes) or take an hour longer via **Monte Rivi** (green flashes); another trail leads up from the little square of Lingua (brown flashes). Monte Rivi can be reached from Malfa in 3hr (light green flashes), and the summit in 1hr more (ochre flashes). If you don't want to go down the same way you came up, the descent can be made to Leni and Rinella in c 2hr (yellow flashes). Hydrofoils ply from Rinella to Lipari; be sure to check schedules before you set out.

Filicudi and Alicudi

Filicudi and Alicudi are the westernmost islands of the archipelago. They are also the least visited by tourists, and with good reason: their out-of-the-way location makes them difficult to reach, and they are notoriously short on hotels.

Lipari's uninhabited west shore

Filicudi is the larger of the two: it reaches an altitude of 774m and has an area of 10 sq km (3³/4 sq miles). Its attractions include the **Grotta del Bue Marino** (Grotto of the Monk Seal) and the rock pinnacle known as **La Canna** (The Chimney, 71m tall). On **Capo Graziano** are remains of a prehistoric village dating from c 1800BC (reached in 2hr from the harbour; follow the blue flashes). A walk famous for its stunning views (green flashes) leads in 3hr from the harbour to the eminence of **Zucco Grande**, which rises 228m straight out of the sea.

If you're looking for a holiday far from the crowds and don't miss modern creature comforts, **Alicudi** is the place for you. It is the furthest island from Lipari and the least developed. Its 5 sq km (2 sq miles) rise steeply from sea level to the crater of its extinct volcano, the **Montagnola**, at 675m. From the harbour you can climb to the summit (marked with green flashes) in c 3hr. Hire a boat to see the **Timpone delle Femmine**, huge fissures where women are said to have taken refuge during pirate raids.

A panoramic view of Stromboli

Cefalù

Cefalù is an attractive beachside town backing onto a dramatic spur of the Madonie Mountains. The Greek *Kefaloídion* and Roman *Cephaloedium*, it was founded in the 5th century BC on a site inhabited since prehistory, and is first mentioned in 396BC, when it signed a treaty with Carthage. It was conquered by Dionysius the Elder of Syracuse, and then by Agathocles in 307BC; the Romans seized it in 254 BC. Cefalù was an important Byzantine town until the 9th century, and one of the chief Islamic strongholds in Sicily after that. The Normans took it from the Arabs in 1064, altering its original appearance (as they would do in Palermo) to make it a shining symbol of their presence in Sicily. In the 13th and 14th centuries the powerful Ventimiglia family held sway; their sumptuous palace remains the town's chief secular monument. The 16th and 17th centuries witnessed a flurry of monastic building, and in the 18th century the feudal lords of the fertile hinterland constructed handsome townhouses along its main streets. The abolition of feudalism in the 19th century reduced Cefalù to a sleepy backwater, and only recently it has found new fortune as a resort.

The central Corso Ruggero divides the old town into two parts: one with winding, stepped alleys ending against the steep cliff; the other with straight streets leading down towards the beach and the curtain of houses that makes up the seafront of the walled city. A curious common denominator – iron balcony corbels, attached to medieval and modern buildings alike – gives the street a certain architectural unity. At the corner of Via Amendola stands the **Ostério Magno**, the former palace of the Ventimiglia, built over an earlier, Norman residence.

At the centre of town the Corso enters the terraced Piazza del Duomo with, rising at its high end, the splendid **Cathedral**. Legend says Roger II erected this great church in fulfilment of a vow after escaping a violent storm off Cefalù. Begun in 1131, the building is noticeably grander than its surroundings, and the discrepancy has led some historians to suggest it was intended to be the first step in the creation of a new city equal in dignity to Messina and perhaps even Palermo. The façade, added in 1240 by Giovanni Panettera, rises between two tall towers whose massiveness is relieved by beautiful single- and double-arched windows. The central section is surmounted by two orders of blind arcades, the lower one with interlacing arches, and is preceded by a triple-arched porch by Ambrogio da Como (1471) which may have served as an example for the portico of the cathedral of Monreale. Beneath this opens the sumptuously ornamented west doorway.

The austere **interior** follows a Latin-cross plan, with shallow transepts and a raised presbytery and 16 antique columns carrying stilted ogival arches. The central apse and the adjoining walls are decorated with brilliant gold-ground mosaics, the best preserved and perhaps the earliest of their kind in Sicily. The focal point of the composition is the enormous figure of *Christ Pantocrator* in the central apse. Quintessentially Sicilian in appearance, with blonde Norman hair, a dark Arabic beard, and a straight Greek nose and lips, the Son of God displays a verse from John (8:12, 'I am the Light of the world, he who follows me will not walk in darkness') that gives special significance to the brilliant gold background against which He is framed. The *Virgin, Archangels* and *Apostles* adorn the lower part of the apse; *Angels* and *Seraphim* populate the vault. The composition continues on the south wall of the presbytery with handsome figures of *Prophets, Warrior Saints* and *Greek Patriarchs and Theologians*; and on the north wall with *Prophets, Martyrs,* and *Bishop Saints*. The mosaics are thought to have been executed in the 12th century by Byzantine mosaicists, perhaps assisted by local craftsmen. Restorers are gradually freeing the nave and aisles of their Baroque marbles and stuccoes; the modern stained-glass windows are by Michele Canzoneri.

On the Piazza del Duomo are several late Baroque palaces – the Seminary and Bishop's Palace, Palazzo Maria and Palazzo Piraino at the south corner of Corso Ruggero II. From here Via Mandralisca leads down to the **Museo Mandralisca**, founded by Enrico Piraino, Baron Mandralisca, who lived in Cefalù in the mid-19th century. A man of many interests, Mandralisca collected antiquities, coins and paintings, as well as the seashells which constituted the principal object of his studies. The highlight of the collection (in Room 3) is Antonello da Messina's beautiful *Portrait of an Unknown Man* of 1465.

Leaving Piazza del Duomo on the right, Corso Ruggero leads north to Via Carlo Ortolano di Bordonaro, which follows the coast westwards. Steps on the right descend to the **Bastione di Marchiafava**, with splendid views over the coast and traces of archaic megalithic fortifications. Remains of a pre-Hellenic sanctuary (the so-called Temple of Diana) and of a Byzantine fortress can be seen on the **Rocca di Cefalù** – although the climb up is strenuous, the views over the city, the cathedral and the sea make it well worth while.

Cefalù is a good base for exploring the Madonie and Nebrodi Mountains, and there are a number of things to see on the neighbouring coast. At **Castel di Tusa**, 23km (14 miles) east, is an extraordinary hotel, **Atelier sul Mare**, with rooms built to the audacious designs of internationally known contemporary artists; the same patron has sponsored the site-specific open-air sculpture project, Fiumara d'Arte (see box). A very different kind of art is produced 10km (6 miles) further on at **Santo Stefano di Camastra**, whose traditional ceramics industry is linked to the presence of excellent clay in the environs. The distinguishing features of Santo Stefano ceramics are a certain rustic character and a meticulous attention to glazes, which as a rule are bright and hard. Located 18km (11 miles) west of Cefalù are the scant ruins of **Himera**, a colony of Greek Zancle destroyed by the Carthaginians in a famous battle of 409BC; although the excavations are not open to the public, a small museum displays some of the more important finds.

Fiumara d'Arte, Atelier sul Mare and the Cottage Museum at Pettineo

Fiumara d'Arte, the Hotel Atelier sul Mare and the Cottage Museum at Pettineo would be extraordinary anywhere, but they are especially so in Sicily, which is commonly thought to be cut off from the modern world.

Fiumara d'Arte is an open-air museum of contemporary sculpture occupying the banks of the River Tusa. It was conceived and produced by a young Sicilian entrepreneur, Antonio Presti, who opened it to the public while still in his twenties. The project is still under way today and includes works by Pietro Consagra (*Matter Might Not Have Been*) Tano Festa (*Monument to a Dead Poet*), Hidetoshi Nagasawa (*Room of the Golden Boat*), Italo Lanfredini (*Ariadne's Labyrinth*), Piero Dorazio and Graziano Marini (*Arethusa*), Paolo Schiavocampo (*A Curve Left Behind by Time*), Antonio Di Palma (*Mediterranean Energy*) and others.

Atelier sul Mare, at Castel di Tusa, is an anonymous modern hotel which Presti is slowly but surely transforming into one of the more remarkable museum environments in Europe. To date, 14 of the 40 rooms have been completely redesigned and reconstructed by internationally known artists. According to the catalogue, 'You can enjoy the unique experience of living and relaxing in a symbiosis with a work of art created for aesthetic enjoyment and enhancing the pleasure of your visit. And only by entering and living in a room will the work of art be fully realised; your presence, your using the room, will be an integral and functional part of the work.' One of the invited artists, Japanese sculptor Hidetoshi Nagasawa, envisions a stay at the hotel in these terms: 'I can imagine the hypothetical visitor who comes into the Atelier, goes to the reception desk, takes his key, goes up to his room and shuts the door. From that moment the space becomes his to enjoy, a living museum. Not a hotel with the works of art well exhibited, but a museum in which people can live and where all the art works are made to human scale.... Whoever wants to, can live in the work of art for an hour, a day, a week: I think that is something unique.'

Not content with these two ambitious projects, each year Presti invites artists from around the world to Pettineo, an old village nestled in the Nebrodi Mountains, to paint a kilometre of canvas laid out along the village streets. At the end of the event the works produced are entrusted to the inhabitants, who keep them in their houses where they can be seen by visitors, thus giving rise to the **Cottage Museum at Pettineo**. For more information, call the Atelier sul Mare (tel. 0921 334 295).

The Nebrodi and Madonie Mountains

The rugged **Nebrodi** and **Madonie Mountains**, whose peaks rise to nearly 2000m above Sicily's north coast, are among the wilder and more scenic areas of the island. The two ranges closely resemble each other in terms of flora and fauna. Planted with vines and grain at the lower altitudes, their slopes are covered by a thick mantle of oaks and by Europe's southernmost beech forests above. The fauna is that typical of the Apennines: foxes, weasels and wildcats inhabit the forests, and golden eagles, peregrine falcons, kites and sparrowhawks nest on the rocky ridges. To preserve this precious environmental heritage, part of the area has been declared a nature reserve. The rolling pastures of the Nebrodi are home to a special breed of horses – *Sanfratellini* – obtained by crossing Arabian horses with a Norman breed imported to the island in the 11th century. They are valued both as riding and as work horses.

The towns of the region, preserved by their relative isolation from money-driven development, are among the most fascinating in Sicily. Here life is still conducted as it has been for centuries – with simplicity, pride and integrity.

Caccamo

A Carthaginian stronghold in the 5th century BC, **Caccamo** was an important market town in the Middle Ages. It stands on a steeply inclined rock overlooking a valley – a site that has favoured the preservation of its architectural heritage (there is practically nowhere to build). The homes, public buildings and 20-odd churches of the town date mainly from the 12th to the 18th centuries. The **Cathedral** is a Norman foundation renovated in 1614; inside are a font and bas-relief of the *Madonna with Angels and Saints*, by Domenico Gagini and his school. The 17th-century **Santissima Annunziata** holds a beautiful altarpiece by Willem Borremans (*Annunciation*, 1725); **Santa Maria degli Angeli** (1497) has a *Madonna* by Antonello Gagini; and **San Benedetto** (1615) boasts a splendid Sicilian majolica pavement and stuccoes by Giacomo and Procopio Serpotta. Caccamo's most noteworthy monument, however, is its immense 12th-century **Castle**, built as an extension of the rock wall overlooking the valley. The fortress has two claims to fame: its curious spiral plan and the baronial conspiracy against the Norman king William the Bad, hatched here in 1160. The latter is narrated in all its gruesome details by naive murals around the town.

Collesano

This well-preserved old town has a medieval network of narrow streets connected by steps and alleys and a formidable Norman **Castle**. The oldest churches are San Giacomo (1451), San Sebastiano (1371) and **Santa Maria la Vecchia**. The latter, founded in the 12th century and rebuilt in the 15th century, holds a marble *Madonna* by Antonello Gagini (1516). The Chiesa Madre, or **Santa Maria la Nuova**, was built in the late 15th century (there is a Catalan-Gothic portal in the south flank), though the façade was completed in the 20th century. It has a 15th-century tabernacle carved by Donatello Gagini, a 16th-century painted *Crucifix*, and a painting of the *Virgin and Angels* by Giuseppe Salerno, the area's leading local painter, who worked under the name, 'Lo Zoppo di Ganci' (The Lame Man of Gangi).

Collesano is a renowned centre of pottery production. It seems to have taken over the pottery trade of nearby Polizzi, whose vases are mentioned in documents of the 15th century. The Collesano workshops flourished especially in the 18th century, when they surpassed in fame those of Palermo, from which they took their forms, colours and decorative schemes. Some beautiful examples of Collesano decorated ceramics are preserved in the Museo Pitrè in Palermo; but the town is perhaps best known for something quite different, the severe 'rustic' ceramics designed for everyday use. Singular objects of this sort are the 19th-century figurative oil lamps (of which there is an extraordinary collection in the Museo Pitrè); also unique, and still in production, are the circular water bottles known as *bucciaddati*.

Scacciapensieri and Zufoli

The *scacciapensieri* or *marranzanu* (jew's harp) is a small, lyre-shaped musical instrument which, when placed between the teeth, gives tones from a metal tongue struck by the finger. It is emblematic of an Arcadian and bucolic Sicily, today largely lost or abandoned. The writer, painter and musician Alberto Savinio said that this simple instrument 'allows the human voice to say things it does not dare say alone'. The origin of the instrument can be traced to the pastoral tradition, which also gave rise to *fricaletti* or *zufoli*, fipple flutes made from carved and sometimes painted rushes.

The Petralìe

Located on the old highway from Catania to Palermo, Petralìa Soprana and Petralìa Sottana have ancient origins. The site was settled long ago, probably because of its elevated position. It enjoys broad views over the hills to Ætna, and its cool microclimate makes it one of more wooded areas of the interior. The arrest of urban development due to emigration, in the 17th century, has kept both centres almost intact.

Ancient *Petra*, the present-day **Petralìa Soprana**, is mentioned in documents of the 3rd century BC but achieved administrative and strategic importance only with the Arabs. It was fortified by the Normans, who valued it for its rock-salt mines, in the 11th century. Petralìa Soprana is a town of lovely medieval houses whose rough stone walls – like those of neighbouring Gangi – have not been prettified with plaster. Its favourite son, the sculptor Fra' Umile da Petralìa, is commemorated by a bust in one of the central squares. He was known for his naturalistic carved wooden crucifixes. The **Cathedral** is a 15th-century church with an 18th-century porch and vernacular statues of St Peter and St Paul at the top of its campanile. The 19th-century stucco interior holds Fra' Umile's first *Crucifix* (c 1624), in the sanctuary, and a fine *Deposition* attributed to Pietro Novelli, over the fifth south altar. Of the other churches, the most noteworthy is **Santa Maria di Loreto**, which overlooks its pleasant piazza from behind a wrought-iron gate. Built on the ground once occupied by the Norman castle, it has a beautiful façade of 1750 by two local sculptors named Serpotta and two little spires topped with coloured terracotta.

Within, the high altarpiece has been attributed to Gian Domenico Gagini; the *Madonna* is probably by Giacomo Mancini. Via Belvedere, on the right of the church, leads to a little terrace by the apse from which you can see Ætna on a clear day.

Petralìa Sottana originated as an advanced bastion of the Norman castle on the hilltop, and no distinction was made between the two towns until the 15th century. That both were domains of aristocratic families is demonstrated by the relative sophistication of their monumental buildings. At Petralìa Sottana are an interesting 17th-century **Chiesa Madre** incorporating an earlier church (of which a late Gothic portal remains on the south flank) and the **Santissima Trinità**, preserving a marble ancona with 23 low reliefs of the life of Christ by Gian Domenico Gagini.

Gangi

Bundles of wheat tied with red ribbons are hung in the streets of **Gangi** in August to celebrate the *Sagra della Spiga*, a sort of propitiatory rite for the favours of Ceres. The event is still steeped in authentic popular feeling and shows the town's profoundly earthy character, which motorisation, radio and television have done little to change. Twenty-two hundred years after the demise of Greek culture in Sicily, it faithfully reflects the annual festival of Ceres recorded by Ovid (*Metamorphoses*, X, 431–435). 'It was the time when married women were celebrating that annual festival of Ceres at which with snowy bodies closely robed they bring garlands of wheaten ears as the first offerings of their fruits, and for nine nights they count love and the touch of man among things forbidden.'

Located, like the Petralìe, on the old road from Catania to Palermo, Gangi preserves its original medieval aspect and a deeply 'Sicilian' lifestyle that elsewhere vanished decades ago. The buildings cover the hillside like a mantle, forming a compact, minute fabric whose only real open space is the tiny central Piazza del Popolo. Here rises the massive **Torre dei Ventimiglia**, originally the residence of the town's lords and now the campanile of the **Chiesa Madre**. The church, built in the 18th century by enlarging a 14th-century oratory, is locally famous for its *Last Judgement* by Lo Zoppo (in the sanctuary); the silver altar frontal likewise repays attention. The narrow Via Vitale, Gangi's main street, has 'Roman' shops (as they are called), with shuttered arches, and a small Museo Civico, usually closed. At the top of the town is the **Castle**, with a Renaissance chapel attributed to the Gagini. Below Via Vitale, reached by the steps of Via Matrice, the church of the **Santissimo Salvatore** (1612) holds another of the numerous wood crucifixes by Fra' Umile da Petralìa. Descending further, you come upon the church of **Santa Maria degli Angeli** with its Cappuccini convent, where there is a collection of 16th- and 17th-century paintings and 17th-century decorated ceramics.

One of the massive towers of Cefalù cathedral

Sperlinga

Sperlinga's fabulous **Castle** was the last stronghold of the French in the War of the Vespers, as is recalled by the saying, *ciò che alla Sicilia piacque, sola Sperlinga negò* ('what pleased Sicily only Sperlinga denied'). It was built by Roger de Hauteville, fortified by Frederick II, and occupied by the Ventimiglia until the 16th century, when it became the residence of Giovanni Forti Natoli, founder of the town. Built on several levels over and in the sheer cliff, it is a labyrinth of rooms, passages, courtyards and corridors. Two grottoes near the entrance hold a small display of local farm and household implements, and a room within contains intriguing old photographs of Sperlinga, some taken by American photographer Robert Capa during the 1943 occupation. The charming small town spreads out at the foot of the castle; in the sheer rock face are grottoes (signposted) that were inhabited until just a few years ago.

The Atelier sul Mare at Castel di Tusa. Sogni tra Segni, *Renato Curcio, Agostino Ferrari and Gianni Ruggri*

Nicosia

Possibly standing on the site of the Siculan *Herbita* (Greek *Erbita*), **Nicosia** was the most important of the fortress-towns that lined the medieval highway from Catania to Palermo. It was occupied by the Byzantines in the 7th and 8th centuries and by the Arabs in the 9th century. The Muslim city was destroyed by the Normans and repopulated with colonies of Lombards and Piedmontese, of whose presence traces survive in the local dialect. The town's severe military aspect was refined somewhat after the 14th century by the landed aristocracy, who built handsome townhouses along its medieval streets, and by the monastic orders, who constructed convents. Today Nicosia abounds with churches and palaces, though all are in poor repair and few are open to the public. Damaged by landslide in 1757, earthquake in 1968 and flood in 1972, it is a big, chaotic place, and a visit requires a great deal of determination.

The old town, with its steep narrow streets and staircases, spreads over the slopes of four hills at the foot of the ruined Norman castle. At its centre is Piazza Garibaldi, flanked by the 15th-century portico of the **Cathedral** of San Nicola. The cathedral façade retains an elaborately carved Gothic portal and a small rose window of the 14th century. The massive campanile dates from the late 13th century. The interior, rebuilt in the 19th century, preserves several fine artworks, notably a marble pulpit and baptismal font attributed to Gian Domenico and Antonello Gagini, respectively; a venerated wooden *Crucifix* by Fra' Umile da Petralìa (carried in procession on Good Friday); and 17th-century carved stalls by Stefano and Giovanni Battista Volsi, with a relief showing Nicosia as it appeared at the time they were made.

The south door of the cathedral faces the handsome 18th-century **Bishop's Palace**. The streets east of the cathedral climb to **Santa Maria Maggiore**, with a beautiful portal carved with naturalistic and mythological subjects and, within, works removed from buildings destroyed in the 1757 landslide – notably a majestic marble ancona by Antonello Gagini (1512) and a 16th-century wooden throne with an effigy of Emperor Charles V, who stopped at Nicosia in 1535.

A breathtakingly beautiful road (Highway 117) climbs from Nicosia over the Passo del Contrasto (1107m) to Mistretta and the sea.

Castelbuono

The former seat of the Ventimiglia, **Castelbuono** still shows signs of its past importance. The 16th-century Via Sant'Anna joins two symbols of civil and religious power – on the south, the elegant 14th-century church of the **Matrice Vecchia**, with its late 15th-century marble ciborium and 16th-century polyptych; on the north, the imposing medieval **Castle**, built by the Ventimiglia in 1316. The interior has a small courtyard and a 17th-century chapel decorated with stuccoes by the Serpotta school. Behind the castle is a terrace overlooking the village of Geraci Siculo and the Madonie; a small **museum** by the Matrice Vecchia contains prehistoric archaeological material, examples of glasswork from the 16th–18th centuries, and displays illustrating the local industry of extracting manna from manna ash trees.

Practical Information

Getting There

BY AIR

Destinations on the east coast of Sicily, as well as the Æolian Islands, are most conveniently reached from **Catania Fontanarossa Airport**, which lies c 5km (3 miles) south of the city. Highway S114 and Autostrada A18/E90 connect the airport to central Catania in about 10min. There are direct flights from Bari, Bologna, Cagliari, Florence, Lampedusa, Milan, Naples, Rome, Turin, Verona and Venice; most international flights connect through Rome. For information or reservations free-phone *Alitalia* tel. 1478 65643, *Meridiana* tel. 530 006, or *Alpi Eagles* tel. 167 555 777.

If you are headed for Cefalù and the north coast west of Milazzo, you're better off flying to **Palermo Punta Raisi Airport**. There are direct flights from Bari, Bologna, Florence, Lampedusa, Milan, Naples, Pantelleria and Rome; most international flights again connect through Rome. *Meridiana* has a different free-phone number for Palermo: 323 494.

BY RAIL

Intercity trains run from **Messina to Catania** several times daily, covering the 95km (59 miles) in c 1hr 30min. They stop at Taormina-Giardini Naxos (40min), Giarre-Riposto and Acireale (1hr 10min). There is a **local service** between **Catania** and **Palermo** (243km/150 miles) taking c. 3hr 20min and stopping at Enna and Caltanisetta. Intercity trains run from **Messina to Palermo** several times daily, covering the 232km (144 miles) in c. 3hr 20min. They stop at Milazzo (40min), Sant'Agata di Militello, Cefalù (2hr 20min) and Termini Imerese.

BY ROAD

The motorway from **Messina to Catania**, Autostrada A18/E45, is one of Italy's most modern. It often runs high above the coast on tall viaducts. The journey of approximately 100km (60 miles) takes c 1hr. The motorway from **Messina to Cefalù**, A20/E90, is complete only as far as Torre del Lauro, after which you proceed by Highway S113. The journey of approximately 160km (100 miles) takes 2hr.

Here are some of the fastest routes from point to point in northeastern Sicily: **Messina–Taormina**, 50km (31 miles) in 30min by A18/E45 and local roads; **Taormina–Catania**, 50km (31 miles) in 30min by A18/E45 and local roads; **Catania–Enna**, 84km (52 miles) in 50min by S114, S417, A19 and local roads; **Catania–Piazza Armerina**, 100km (60 miles) in 1hr 20min by S417, A19, S192, S117b and local roads; **Catania–Gangi** 150km (93 miles) in 2hr by A19, S290, S120 and local roads; **Gangi–Cefalù** 56km (35 miles) in 1hr 20min by S120, S286, S113 and A20/E90; **Cefalù–Palermo**, 67km (42 miles) in 40min by S113, A20/E90 and A19/E90.

The northeastern arc of the circuit of Sicily looks like this: **Catania–Taormina**, 50km (31 miles) in 30min; **Taormina–Milazzo**, 83km (51 miles) in 1hr; **Milazzo–Cefalù**, 137km (85 miles) in 1hr 50min. **Cefalù–Palermo**, 67km (42 miles) in 40min.

BY SEA

The most usual way to reach this part of Sicily is to take a ferry to **Messina** from **Reggio Calabria** (daily, 45min) or **Villa San Giovanni** (20–35min). Service is provided by the *Ferrovie dello Stato*, Piazzale Don Blasco, Messina (tel. 090 675 201 ext. 552); and by *Società Caronte Shipping*, Viale della Libertà, Messina (tel. 090 44982). Hydrofoils connecting **Messina** with **Reggio Calabria** (daily, 15min) are run by *Aliscafi SNAV*, Via San Raineri, 22, Messina (tel. 090 7775, fax 090 717 358).

Most ferries and hydrofoils to the **Æolian Islands** leave from **Milazzo** (daily, taking 1hr 30min–4hr and 40min–2hr 45min, respectively); they are operated by *Siremar*, Agenzia Alliatour, Via dei Mille, Milazzo (tel. 090 928 3242, fax 090 928 3243) and *Aliscafi SNAV*, Agenzia Delfo Viaggi, Via Rizzo 9/10, Milazzo (tel. 090 928 7728, fax 090 928 1798); SNAV is represented on Lipari by *Eoltravel*, Via Vittorio Emanuele 116 (tel. 090 981 1122, fax 090 988 0311). The Æolian Islands can also be reached from **Messina** by hydrofoil (daily, 1hr 20min), contact *Aliscafi SNAV*, Via San Raineri, 22, Messina (tel. 090 7775, fax 090 717 358); or from **Naples** by *Siremar* ferry (Mon and Thu 15 Sep–15 Jun and Mon, Wed, Thu, Fri, Sat and Sun 15 Jun–15 Sep; 1hr); information on Lipari from *Eolian Tours*, Via Amendola (tel 090 981 1312, fax 090 988 0170). *SNAV* also provides hydrofoil services between the islands and **Cefalù** (Jun–Sep, Tue, Fri and Sat, 1hr 30min), **Palermo** (Jun–Sep, daily, 1hr 50min) and **Naples** (Jun–Sep daily, 4hr).

Tourist Information

CATANIA Largo Paisiello 5 (tel. 095 730 6233, fax 095 316 407; Railway Station (tel. 095 531 802); Airport (tel. 095 730 6266).

CEFALÙ Corso Ruggero 77 (tel. 0921 21458, fax 0921 22386).

LIPARI Via Vittorio Emanuele 202 (tel. 090 988 0095, fax 090 981 1190).

MESSINA Via Calabria 301 bis (tel. 090 674 236, fax 090 601 005).

MILAZZO Piazza Caio Duilio (tel. 090 922 2865, fax 090 922 2790).

MT ÆTNA Linguaglossa (tel 095 643 094).

SALINA Santa Marina (Jun–Sep, tel. 090 984 3190).

TAORMINA Palazzo Corvaja, Largo Santa Caterina (tel. 0942 23243, fax 0942 24941).

VULCANO Porto Levante (Jul–Sep, tel. 090 985 2028).

Hotels

ACI TREZZA
I Malavoglia, Via Provinciale 3 (tel. 095 276 711, fax 095 276 873). Near the beach, modern and comfortable; moderate.

ACIREALE
Grand Hotel Baia Verde, Via A. Musco 8/10, Cannizzaro (tel. 095 491 522, fax 095 494 464). Mediterranean-style building on a promontory with splendid views over the Riviera dei Ciclopi and two good restaurants; moderate.
Orizzonte Acireale, Highway S114 (tel/fax 095 886 006). Simple, rustic atmosphere and good views from the terrace; moderate.
Santa Tecla Palace, Località Santa Tecla (tel. 095 604 933, fax 095 607 705). A modern place in shady surroundings with sea views; moderate.
Sheraton Catania, Via Antonello da Messina 45, Cannizzaro (tel. 095 271 557, fax 095 271 380). Modern and comfortable, with antique furnishings and a good though pricey restaurant; expensive.

CAPO D'ORLANDO (MILAZZO)
La Meridiana, Località Piana (tel/fax 0941 957 713). New and comfortable, 500m from the sea; moderate.
Il Mulino, Via Andrea Doria 46 (tel. 0941 902 431, fax 0941 911 614). Near the sea and the town centre; moderate.

CATANIA
Excelsior, Piazza Verga 39 (tel. 095 537 071, fax 095 537 015). Centrally located, with functional public areas and sober rooms; expensive.

CEFALÙ
Carlton Riviera, Capo Plaia (tel. 0921 20004, fax 0921 20264, seasonal). Located 7km (4 miles) west of town. Modern architecture and décor,

balconies with sea views, garden and pool; moderate.
Grand Hotel Atelier sul Mare, Castel di Tusa (tel. 0921 34295, fax 0921 34283, seasonal). A truly extraordinary hotel with rooms designed and furnished by internationally known contemporary artists, 23km (14 miles) east of Cefalù; moderate.
Kalura, via Cavallaro 13, Caldura (tel. 0921 22501, fax 0921 23122). Tastefully decorated Mediterranean-style building in a beautiful location on the sea; moderate.
Santa Lucia e le Sabbie d'Oro, Contrada Santa Lucia (tel. 0921) 21565, fax 0921 22213). A modern establishment, with panoramic balconies and light-filled rooms; moderate.
Jolly Trinacria, Piazza Trento 13 (tel. 095 316 933, fax 095 316 832). Modern and comfortable, if not particularly memorable; expensive.

GIARDINI NAXOS
Arathena Rocks, Via Calcide Eubea 55 (tel. 0942 51348, fax 0942 51690, seasonal). An oasis of tranquillity, with trees and gardens descending to a private beach; half pension only; moderate.
Hellenia Yachting, Via Jannuzzo 41 (tel. 0942 51737, fax 0942 54310). Modern, tastefully furnished and comfortable; moderate.
Sant'Alfio Garden, Via Recanati (tel. 0942 51383, fax 0942 53934). Set in a large park, with direct access to the beach; moderate.

LIPARI
Gattopardo Park, Via Diana (tel. 090 981 1035, fax 090 988 0207, seasonal). Renovated 19th-century villa surrounded by garden terraces with incomparable views; moderate.
Giardino sul Mare, Via Maddalena 65 (tel. 090 981 1004, fax 090 988 0150, seasonal). Views of sea and coast, pool on garden terrace; moderate.
Meligunis, Via Marte (tel. 090 981 2426, fax 090 988 0149, seasonal). Tastefully renovated 18th-century villa in the city centre near the Marina Piccola; moderate.

MAZZARÒ (CATANIA)
Lido Méditeranée, Via Nazionale (tel. 0942 24422, fax 0942 24774, seasonal). Modern, Mediterranean-style building on the beach, with classical and bamboo furnishings; expensive.
Mazzarò Sea Palace, Via Nazionale 147 (tel. 0942 24004, fax 0942 626 237, seasonal). Situated on a little bay and offering modern, light-filled rooms, calm and comfort; expensive.

MESSINA
Europa Palace, Località Pistunina (tel. 090 621 601, fax 090 621 768). 6km (3¾ miles) from the city centre on Highway S114, with comfortable rooms and sea views; expensive.

Jolly dello Stretto, Corso Garibaldi 126 (tel. 090 363 860, fax 090 590 2526). Modern and functional, with good views of the strait; expensive.
Paradis, Via Consolare Pompea 441 (tel. 090 310 682, fax 090 981 047). Near the ferry port; inexpensive.
Royal Palace, Via Tommaso Cannizaro 224 (tel. 090 6503, fax 090 292 1075). Tasteful and comfortable; expensive.

PANAREA
Cincotta (tel. 090 983 014, fax 090 983 211, seasonal). View of sea and islands; moderate.
La Piazza (tel. 090 983 176, fax 090 983 003, seasonal). View of sea and islands; moderate.
Lisca Bianca (tel. 090 983 004, fax 090 983 291, seasonal). By the landing stage. Moderate.

SALINA
Signum, Malfa (tel. 090 984 4222, fax 090 984 4102, seasonal). Æolian-style architecture and décor, with views of the sea and coast; moderate.

STROMBOLI
La Sirenetta, Via Marina 33, Ficogrande (tel. 090 986 025, fax 090 986 124, seasonal). On the beach, surrounded by lush gardens and enjoying good views of the sea and volcano; moderate.

TAORMINA
Bristol Park, Via Bagnoli Croci 92 (tel. 0942 23006, fax 0942 24519, seasonal). Overlooking the public gardens near the Greek Theatre, with views of sea, coast and Ætna; expensive.
Campanella, Via Circonvallazione 3 (tel. 0942 23381). A small villa immersed in greenery; inexpensive.
Condor, Via Dietro Cappuccini 25 (tel. 0942 23124, fax 0942 625726, seasonal). A family-run establishment with just 12 rooms; inexpensive.
Continental, Via Dionysius Primo 2/a (tel. 0942 23805). Constructed in 'steps', with a panoramic terrace overlooking the sea and coast; moderate.
Excelsior Palace, Via Toselli 8 (tel. 0942 23975, fax 0942 23978). Built in the early 1900s in a Moorish-revival style, with views of sea, coast and Ætna; small park and heated pool on panoramic terrace; expensive.
Grand Hotel Miramare, Via Guardiola Vecchia 27 (tel. 0942 23401, fax 0942 626 223). A renovated patrician palace with fine views of sea and coast; expensive.
Jolly Diodoro, Via Bagnoli Croci 75 (tel. 0942 23312, fax 0942 23391). Known for its panoramic terrace, enjoying views of the sea, coast and Ætna; expensive.
Monte Tauro, Via Madonna delle Grazie 3 (tel. 0942 24402, fax 0942 24403). A modern building constructed in 'steps' on the hillside, giving all rooms views of sea and coast; expensive.

San Domenico Palace, Piazza San Domenico 5 (tel. 0942 23701, fax 0942 625 506). A former Dominican convent with beautiful gardens and views of the sea, coast and Ætna, and one of Taormina's finest restaurants; luxury.
Vello d'Oro, Via Fazzello 2 (tel. 0942 23788, fax 0942 626 117, seasonal). White walls and red-tiled roofs with a vaguely Moorish air; terrace with view of sea and coast; moderate.
Villa Belvedere, Via Bagnoli Croci 79 (tel. 0942 23791, fax 0942 625 830, seasonal). Surrounded by olive and palm trees, enjoying a view that justifies the name; moderate.
Villa Ducale, Via Leonardo da Vinci 60 (tel. 0942 28153, fax 0942) 28154, seasonal). An elegant patrician home tastefully remodelled, with cool gardens, antique furnishings, and excellent views of the sea, coast and Ætna; moderate.
Villa Fiorita, Via Pirandello 39 (tel. 0942 24122, fax 0942 625 967). A pleasant blend of old and new, with views of the sea and coast; moderate.
Villa Paradiso, Via Roma 2 (tel. 0942 23922, fax 0942 625 800, seasonal). Quiet atmosphere, personalised rooms, antique furniture, and lush gardens, with views of sea, coast and Ætna; moderate.
Villa Sirina, Contrada Sirina (tel. 0942 51776, fax 0942 51671, seasonal). Small and friendly, with garden and pool; moderate.

TINDARI
Park Philip, Via Capitano Zuccarello, Marina di Pattì (tel. 0941 361 332, fax 0941 361 184). Convenient and comfortable, on the sea; inexpensive.

VULCANO
Conti, Porto Ponente (tel. 090 985 2012, seasonal). Family-run and friendly, on the beach; inexpensive.
Eolian, Porto Ponente (tel. 090 985 2151, fax 090 985 2153, seasonal). Æolian-style building, on the beach; moderate.

Restaurants

ACI CASTELLO
Holiday's Club, Via dei Malavoglia 10 (tel. 095 277 575; closed Mon, Nov; open evenings only). Sicilian cuisine, especially fish; tasteful ambience, pool-side garden seating in summer; moderate.
Cambusa del Capitano, Via Marina 65 (tel. 095 276 298; closed Wed and three weeks in Dec). Seafood served in an informal atmosphere; inexpensive.
Villa delle Rose, Via XXI Aprile 79 (tel. 095 271024). Large and sometimes loud; inexpensive.

ACIREALE
La Brocca d'u Cinc'oru, Corso Savoia 49/a (tel. 095 607 198; closed Sun

evening and Mon). Good local dishes, including *timballi della casa, maccheroni e gnocchi con ragù al falsomagro, pesce secondo il pescato* and home-made *gelati*; moderate.

Panoramico (tel. 095 885 291; closed Mon, early Aug and early Nov). Sicilian cuisine prepared and served with care; views of Ætna and the coast.

Selene, Via Mollica 24/26, Cannizzaro (tel. 095 494 444, fax 095 492 209; closed Tue and three weeks in Aug). Seafood and traditional Sicilian dishes (*linguine tutto mare al cartoccio, pesce all'acqua di mare, cassata siciliana*), with summer seating on seaside terrace; moderate.

CAPO D'ORLANDO
Bontempo, Fiumara di Naso (tel. 0941 961 188, fax 0941 961 189; closed Mon). Large but genuine restaurant, 10km (6 miles) out; moderate.

CATANIA
Costa Azzurra, Via De Cristofaro 4, Località Ognina (tel/fax 095 494 920; closed Mon). Serving good traditional cooking and known for the views from glass-enclosed dining room and summer terrace; moderate.

La Siciliana, Viale Marco Polo 52/a (tel. 095 376 400, fax 095 722 1300; closed Sun and hol evenings, Mon and two weeks in Aug). Sicilian cuisine, notably *neonati di pesce gratinati, pasta alla Norma and sarde a beccafico*, in a renovated villa with summer seating in garden; moderate.

Lampara, Via Pasubio 49 (tel. 095)383 237; closed Wed and Aug). Local dishes, pleasant ambience; inexpensive.

Pagano, Via De Roberto 37 (tel. 095 537 045; closed Sat and Aug). A family-run establishment popular among locals; inexpensive.

Poggio Ducale (with rooms), Via Paolo Gaifami 5 (tel. 095 330 016, fax 095 580 103; closed Sun evening, Mon morning, and two weeks in Aug). Creative interpretations of traditional recipes; the *melanzana Gattopardo, risotto al timo, tortelli di aragosta in salsa al Pernod* and *spigola ai profumi dello Jonio* are especially good; moderate.

CEFALÙ.
La Brace, Via 25 Novembre 10 (tel. 0921 23570; closed Mon and Dec–Jan; small and intimate; inexpensive.

Ostaria del Duomo, Via Seminario 5 (tel. 0921 21838; closed Mon – except Jun–Sep – and Dec–Jan). Traditional Sicilian cooking and ambience, with outdoor seating in the cathedral square in summer; inexpensive.

Villa del Vescovo, Contrada Santa Lucia (tel. 0921 921 803; closed Mon). 3km (13/4 miles) west on Highway S113. Good fish and home-made pasta, in an 18th-century villa with views of Cefalù and the coast; moderate.

GIARDINI NAXOS
La Cambusa, Lungomare Schisò 3 (tel. 0942 51437; closed Jan–Feb and

Tue – except Jul–Sep). Good seafood in a maritime atmosphere, with views of the sea and Taormina; inexpensive.
Sea Sound, Via Jannuzzo 37/a (tel. 0942 54330; closed Nov–Feb). A simple, family-managed restaurant; inexpensive.

LIPARI
E Pulera, Via Diana (tel/fax 090 981 1158; seasonal, evening only). Summer seating in a garden, among the columns from which the restaurant takes its name; moderate.
Filippino, Piazza Municipio (tel. 090 981 1002, fax 090 981 2878; closed mid-Nov–mid-Dec and Mon – except Jun–Sep). Known for its *ravioloni di cernia, tagliolini all'eoliana, totani alla Filippino, pesce spada affumicato in salsa di peperoni, mousse di gelsomino, and semifreddo alle mandorle;* moderate.

MAZZARÒ
Il Delfino-da Angelo, Via Nazionale (tel. 0942 23004; closed Oct–Mar). Classical Messinese cuisine on the shore of a small bay; outside seating in summer; inexpensive.
Il Pescatore, Via Nazionale 107 (tel. 0942 23460; closed Mon and Nov–Jan). Surrounded by gardens, on a promontory with views of sea, coast and Isolabella.

MESSINA
Agostino, Via Maddalena 70 (tel. 090 718 396; closed Mon and Aug). Small, cosy atmosphere and good basic Sicilian food; moderate.
Giardino d'Inverno, Via Lascaris (tel/fax 090 362 413; closed Mon and Aug). Original variations on traditional Sicilian recipes; moderate.
Piero, Via Ghibellina 121 (tel. 090 718 365; closed Sun and Aug). A simple, unpretentious trattoria; inexpensive.
Pippo Nunnari, Via Ugo Bassi 157 (tel. 090 293 8584; closed Mon and Aug). Classic Sicilian cuisine – try the *nunnarelle, braciole alla messinese, involtini di pesce spada alla matalotta and cassata* – and antique furnishings; moderate.
Sporting da Alberto, Via Nazionale, Località Mortelle (tel. 090 321 390, fax 090 321 009; closed Mon and Jan). Creative interpretations of traditional recipes, such as *codine di gamberi con capperi, panzerotti con polpa di granchio e scampi, mupo dello stretto alle erbe fini e cicoria, crespelle di neonata and mousse di agrumi con salsa melograno;* expensive.

MILAZZO
Il Covo del Pirata, Via Marina Garibaldi (tel. 090 928 4437; closed Wed except Aug). Sicilian fare, especially fish; moderate.
Villa Esperanza, Via Baronia 191 (tel/fax 090 922 2916; closed Mon and Nov). Excellent cuisine, summer seating on panoramic terrace; try the

seasonal specialities, *linguine con vongole al pesto, tagliata di pesce spada, filetti di dentice ai profumi mediterranei, cannolo aperto, tortino di mandorle con salsa di arance caramellate*; expensive.

MT ÆTNA

Grotta del Gallo, Via Madonna delle Grazie 40, Nicolosi (tel. 095 911 301, fax 095 914 719; closed Mon in low season). Traditional Sicilian cooking, in a villa with garden between Ætna and the sea; moderate.

Trattoria Veneziano, Via Romano 8, Randazzo (tel. 095 799 1353; closed Sun evening, Mon, 25–31 Dec and three weeks in Jul). Classic Sicilian cuisine; inexpensive.

SALINA

Portobello, Santa Marina (tel 090 984 3125; closed Nov and Wed – except Jun–Sep). By the sea, with garden seating in summer; inexpensive.

TAORMINA

Al Castello da Ciccio, Via Madonna della Rocca (tel. 0942 28158; closed Jan, Sun in Jul–Aug and Wed Sep–Jun). Outside seating in summer, with views of Giardini-Naxos, the sea and Ætna; expensive.

A' Zammàra, Via Fratelli Bandiera 15 (tel. 0942 24408; closed Wed Oct–Jun and mid-Jan–mid-Feb; the name is a dialect term for *agave*; small restaurant entered through an orange orchard, offering simple, genuine cuisine; inexpensive.

Il Ciclope, Corso Umberto (tel. 0942 23263; closed Wed and Jan–Feb). A pleasant, unpretentious place in the city centre, with summer seating outside; inexpensive.

La Giara, Vico la Floresta 1 (tel. 0942 23360, fax 0942 23233; closed mornings and Mon – except Jun–Sep). Creative interpretations of traditional Sicilian dishes, notably *pesce spada con parfait di limone, costoletta di cernia al sesamo, semifreddo di mandorle* and *soufflé di ricotta con salsa all'arancia;* expensive.

La Griglia, Corso Umberto 54 (tel. 0942 23980, fax 0942 626 047; closed Tue and late Nov–late Dec). Messinese cuisine, especially fish; moderate.

TINDARI

Cani Cani (with rooms), Via Nazionale, Località Saliceto, Marina di Pattì (tel. 0941 361 022; closed Tue and winter). Traditional Sicilian cuisine, notably *parmigiana e caponata di melanzane, braciole di pesce spada arrosto e alla ghiotta, cassata* and *cannoli,* and broad sea views; inexpensive.

Museums and Monuments

ACI CASTELLO
Museo Civico: Tue–Sat 9.00–13.00 and 15.00–17.00.

ACIREALE
Biblioteca e Pinacoteca Zelantea: Mon–Sat 10.00–13.00.

BRONTE
Castello Nelson: Maniace, gardens only, 9–dusk.

CATANIA
Anfiteatro Romano: Mon–Sat 9.00–13.00, closed hols.
Casa Museo Giovanni Verga: Mon–Sat 9.00–13.00.
Museo Belliniano: Mon–Sat 9.00––3.30, Sun–hols 9.00–12.30.
Museo Civico di Castello Ursino: Mon–Sat 8.30–13.00;
Sun–hols 9.00–12.30.
Orto Botanico: Mon–Sat 9.00–13.00.
Teatro Romano: daily 9.00–dusk.

CEFALÙ
Museo Mandralisca, daily 9.00–12.30, 15.30–19.00.

GIARDINI NAXOS
Museo Archeologico Naxos: daily 9.00–14.00.

LIPARI
Museo Archeologico Eoliano: Mon–Sat 9.00–14.00, Sun 9.00–13.00.

MESSINA
Museo Regionale: summer Mon–Sat 9.00–13.30, 16.00–18.30, Sun and hols 9.00–13.30; winter Mon–Sat 9.00–13.30, 15.00–17.30, Sun and hols 9.00–13.00.

RANDAZZO
Museo Civico di Scienze Naturali: Tue–Sun 9.00–12.00, 16.00–18.00.

TAORMINA
Gole dell'Alcantara: daily 7.30–20.30.
Palazzo Corvaja: daily 9.00–13.00.
Palazzo dei Duchi di Santo Stefano: Mon–Sat 8.30–13.00, 15.00–17.00, Sun 8.30–12.30.
Teatro Greco Romano: summer 9.00–19.00, winter 9.00–16.00.

TINDARI
Zona Archeologica: daily 9.00–dusk.

GLOSSARY

ADYTUM, inner sanctuary of a temple, open only to priests

AEDICULA, a small edifice or room

AEDICULUM, a temple lacking a peristyle, or columned promenade, around the pronaos and cella

AENEOLITHIC, a transitional period between the Neolithic and Bronze ages

AMBO (pl. Ambones), pulpit in a Christian basilica, two pulpits on opposite sides of a church from which the gospel and epistle were read

ANCONA, a painted altarpiece

ANTEFIX, ornament placed at the lower corner of the tiled roof of a temple to conceal the space between the tiles and the cornice

ARCH, a typically curved structural member spanning an opening and serving as a support for the wall above. Common forms of arch include the round, the pointed (also called the lancet or ogival), the trefoil (three-part) and the quatrifoil (four-part)

ART NOUVEAU, a style of artistic expression prevalent in the late 19th and early 20th centuries, originally characterised especially by sinuous lines and plant forms

BAROQUE STYLE, a style of artistic expression prevalent in the 17th century, calculated to overwhelm the emotions of the spectator through the use of dramatic form, colour and movement

BASILICA, originally a Roman building used for public administration; in Christian architecture, an aisled church with an apse and no transepts

BAS-RELIEF, a sculptural relief in which the projection from the surrounding surface is slight

BOULEUTERION, a public meeting place in ancient Greek cities, often with steps arranged in a semi-circle as in a theatre

BRONZE AGE, the period of human culture characterised by use of bronze tools: in Sicily c 1700–800 BC

BUCCHERO, Etruscan black terracotta ware

CAMPANILE, a bell-tower, often detached from the building to which it belongs

CANTORIA, a choir loft, often richly decorated

CAPITAL, the top of a column

CATALAN GOTHIC STYLE, the Gothic architectural style of Catalonia (the region of northeastern Spain bordering on France and the Mediterranean), characterised by low, flat arches

CAVEA, the part of a theatre or amphitheatre occupied by the rows of seats

CELLA, sanctuary of a temple, usually in the centre of the building

CHIARAMONTE STYLE, from Palazzo Chiaramonte in Palermo,

a widespread Sicilian Gothic style that derived ornamental features from the Normans (interlacing arches, polychrome geometric stonework) with arched mullioned windows

CIBORIUM, a casket or tablernacle containing the Host

CIPPOLINO (or cipolin), onion-marble; a greyish marble with streaks of white or green

CLASSICAL STYLE, the style embodied in the literature, art or architecture of ancient Greece and Rome

CORINTHIAN, belonging to or resembling the Corinthian order of Greek architecture, distinguished especially by elaborate, bell-shaped capitals adorned with acanthuses

CORNICE, a molded and projecting horizontal member in architecture

CROSS, in Christian religious art, an emblem recalling the Crucifixion and invoking the blessing of Christ; common forms include the Greek cross, in which the four linear members are equal in length, and the Latin cross, in which one of the members is longer than the others

DIAZOMA, a corridor between the rows of seats in a theatre

EKKLESIASTERION, a public meeting place in an ancient Greek city (see bouleuterion)

EXEDRA, a semicircular recess in architecture

FLOREAL STYLE, a variant of Art Nouveau making profuse use of plant and flower motifs

FRESCO, a mural painting executed on moist plaster with pigments suspended in a water medium

FRIEZE, a horizontal member in architecture, often sculpted or ornamented

GOTHIC STYLE, a style of artistic expression developed in Europe from the 12th century to the 16th century, marked in architecture especially by the converging of weights and strains at isolated points and by an emphasis on verticality, and in painting and sculpture by graceful, elongated forms

HELLENISTIC, the period of Greek history, culture and art falling after the death of Alexander the Great (323 BC) and before the Roman conquest of Egypt (30 BC)

HEXASTYLE, having six columns

ICE AGE, the Pleistocene glacial epoch

ICON, an image; especially a conventional religious image painted on a small wooden panel and venerated by Eastern Christians

INTARSIA, inlay of wood, marble or metal

IONIC, belonging to or resembling the Ionic order of Greek architecture, distinguished especially by capitals in the form of spiral volutes

KORE, Greek, girl

KOUROS, Greek, boy

LIBERTY STYLE, an Italian variant of the Art Nouveau style, more austere in its decorative forms, which took its name from the Liberty fabric shop in London

LOGGIA, a covered gallery, usually preceding a larger building

LUNETTE, a semicircular space in a vault or ceiling, often decorated with a painting or relief

MEGARON, a room, home or palace : also a temple Sanctuary

METOPE, a decorative panel on the frieze of a Doric temple

MULLION, a slender vertical pier between lights of a window or door

NARTHEX, vestibule of a Christian basilica

NEOCLASSICAL STYLE, the revival of the Classical style, especially in architecture, which swept Europe in the 18th and 19th centuries

NEOLITHIC, the latest period of the Stone Age (in Sicily c 5000 – 1700 BC), characterised by polished stone implements

NYMPHAEUM, a sort of summer-house in the gardens of baths, palaces, etc; originally a temple of the Nymphs, decorated with statues of those goddesses and often containing a fountain

OGIVAL, pointed

OPISTHODOMOS, the enclosed rear part of a temple

PANTOCRATOR, the Almighty

PEDIMENT, the gable above the portico of a Classical building, or a similar form used as a decoration

PENDENTIVE, one of the sections of vaulting that spring from the corners of a structure having a rectangular ground plan

PERIPTERAL, a building surrounded by a single row of columns on all four sides

PERISTYLE, the area surrounded by a columned portico

PIETÀ, a representation of the Virgin Mary mourning over the dead body of Christ

PINAKE, a Greek sacred image, usually moulded in relief, in clay

PISCINA, Roman tank; a basin for an officiating priest to wash his hands before Mass

PLATEA, the area of a theatre facing the stage and holding the spectators

PLATERESQUE, an architectural style current in Spain in the 15th and 16th centuries and from there brought to Sicily, characterised by fanciful stonework and elaborately decorated windows and doors

PLUTEUS, a low wall that encloses the space between column bases in a row of columns, or a decorative structure resembling such a wall

POLYPTYCH, a painting or tablet in more than three sections

PREDELLA, a small painting attached to a large altarpiece

PRONAOS, porch in front of the cella of a temple

PROPYLON, entrance gate to a temenos, in plural form (propylaea) when there is more than one door

PROSTYLE, edifice with free-standing columns, as in a portico

RATIONALIST STYLE, an early Modern architectural style in which form follows function

RELIQUARY, a container for religious relics

RENAISSANCE, the transitional movement in Europe between medieval and modern times, beginning in the 14th century in Italy, lasting into the 16th century, and marked in the arts especially by a revival of Classical influence

ROMANESQUE STYLE, a style of architecture developed in western Europe between the 10th and 12th centuries and distinguished by the use of the round arch and vault

RONDEL, a circular pattern or object used in architectural design

RUSTICATION, stone blocks whose edges have been bevelled or blunted to make the joints conspicuous

SINOPIA, the sketch-like under-painting of a fresco

SCENA (Greek, skene), the stage of an ancient theatre

SPLAY, a slope or bevel especially of the sides of a door or a window

SQUINCH, a support (such as an arch) carried across a corner of a room

STELE (pl. Stelae), upright stone bearing a monumental inscription

STOA, ancient Greek portico, usually walled at the back

STYLOBATE, basement of a temple or other building

TABERNACLE, a receptacle for consecrated elements of the eucharist; also, a small shelter for a religious image

TARSIATED, decorated with intarsia (see above)

TELAMON, male figure used as a supporting column

TEMENOS, a sacred enclosure

TRABEATION, a design of horizontal lines or lintels in architecture

TRANSENNA, an open grille or screen, usually of marble, in an early Christian church separating nave and chancel

TRIBUNE, dais or platform

INDEX

Aci Trezza 185
Acireale 186
Acquacalda 203
Adrano 187
Æolian Islands 199
Agrigento 99
Alicudi 206

Bagheria 67

Caccamo 211
Caltagirone 164
Caltanissetta 166
Cannetto 202
Castelbuono 216
Catania 173
  Arco di San Benedetto 180
  Cathedral 178
  Elephant Fountain 178
  Fish Market 174
  Museo Belliniano 180
  Museo Civico 179
  Orto Botanico 181
  Palazzo Biscari 179
  Piazza del Duomo 178
  Roman Theatre 180
  San Giuliano 180
  San Nicolò 180
  Sant'Agata 179
  Villa Bellini 181
Cava Grande del Cassibile
  145
Cefalù 207
Collesano 211
Conca d'Oro 58

Enna 152, 154
Eraclea Minoa 98
Erice 71

Faraglioni dei Ciclopi 186
Favignana 84, 86
Ferla 149
Filicudi 206

Gadir 88
Gangi 213
Grotta Azzurra 70

Isole Egadi 84
Isole Pelagie 111

Khamma 88

Lampedusa 111
Lampione 112
Levanzo 84, 86
Linguaglossa 186
Linosa 112
Lipari 199

Madonie Mountains 210
Marettimo 84, 86
Marsala 91
Marzamemi 149
Megara Hyblæa 151
Messina 193
Milazzo 197
Modica 126
Mondello 61
Monreale 64
Monte Pellegrino 60
Morgantina 159
Motya 89
Mt Ætna 173, 182

Nebrodi Mountains 210
Nicosia 216
Noto 146

Oasi Naturale di Vendìcari 148
Ortygia 139

Petralìe, The 212
Palazzo Ugo 41
Palazzolo Acreide 149
Palermo 34
  Archbishop's Palace 43
  Cappella Palatina 37
  Cappella di San Cataldo 55
  Casa Professa 53
  Cathedral 42
  Chiesa del Gesù 53
  Civica Galleria d'Arte
    Moderna e Contemporanea 69
  Convento sei Cappuccini 64
  Favorita, La 59
  Flea Market 44
  Fontana Pretoria 56
  Galleria Regionale della Sicilia
    51
  Giardino Garibaldi 48
  Magione, La 52
  Martorana, La 55
  Museo Archeologico Regionale
    44
  Museo Etnografico Siciliano Pitrè
    59
  Museo Internazionale delle
    Marionette 50
  Oratorio del Rosario di San
    Domenico 46
  Oratorio di San Lorenzo 48
  Oratory of Santa Zita 46
  Orto Botanico 52
  Palazzina Cinese 59
  Palazzo Abatelli 50
  Palazzo Ajutamicristo 52
  Palazzo delle Aquile 56
  Palazzo Belmonte-Riso 42
  Palazzo Chiaramonte 48
  Palazzo Mirto 48
  Palazzo Reale 37
  Palazzo Sclafani 41

Palermo cont.
  Palazzo Speciale 41
  Palazzo Villafranca 41
  Pietà, La 51
  Quattro Canti di Città 57
  San Domenico 46
  San Francesco d'Assisi 47
  San Giorgio dei Genovesi 47
  San Giovanni degli Eramiti 41
  San Giuseppe dei Teatini 57
  Sant'Agostino 44
  Santa Caterina 56
  Santa Croce-Sant'Elia 53
  Santa Maria della Catena 50
  Santa Maria dello Spasimo 52
  Santuario di Santa Rosalia 60
  Villa Giulia 51
  Vucciria Market 47
  Zisa, La 61
Panarea 204
Pantalica 149
Pantelleria 87
Parco Regionale dell'Etna 184
Paternò 188
Peloritan Peninsula 192
Piazza Armerina 161
Pineta di Linguaglossa 187
Piscina Naturale 71
Porta Trapani 72

Quattrocchi 203

Ragusa 121
Randazzo 187
Riviera dei Ciclopi 184

Salina 205
Scauri 88
Sciacca 97
Segesta 76
Selinunte 92
Solunto 69
Sperlinga 214
Stromboli 204

Syracuse 130
  Castello Eurialo 131
  Castello Maniace 141
  Cathedral 140
  Fonte Aretusa 141
  Foro Siracusano 139
  Galleria Regionale di Arte
    Medievale e Moderna 144
  Greek Theatre 133
  Museo Archeologico Regionale
    Paolo Orsi 137
  Museo del Papiro 138
  Palazzo Bellomo 144
  Passeggio Adorno 140
  Piazza Archimede 144
  Piazza del Duomo 140
  Roman Amphitheatre 136
  San Giovanni 138

Syracuse cont
  Santa Lucia 138
  Santuario di Apollo
    Temenite 135
  Tempio di Apollo 140
  Via dei Sepolchri 135

Taormina 188
Terme di San Calogero 203
Tindari 198
Tracino 88
Trapani 79

Ustica 69

Villa Palagonia 68
Vulcano 204